INTELLECTUAL PROPERTY AND THE HUMAN RIGHTS OF COMPANIES IN EUROPE

The aim of this book is to investigate the history and rationale for the paradoxical extension of human rights to companies in the European Convention on Human Rights (ECHR) and to analyse the Court's jurisprudence on protection of companies' intellectual property in this light. The study shows how, before the adoption of the ECHR, the concepts of legal personality and possessions functioned as legal fictions in European civil and common law to facilitate ownership and sale of tangible and intangible property, shares, debts, securities and intellectual property. The Court's construction of the ambiguous text of Article 1 of the First Protocol and its application to corporate intellectual property rights is reviewed in this light and shown to have been initially anchored in the legal fictions of national laws and later expanded and reinforced by European Union law.

Aurora Plomer is Professor Emeritus of Intellectual Property and Human Rights at the University of Bristol. She has published numerous books and articles in peer-reviewed international journals on the interface between intellectual property, human rights and innovation. The research for this monograph was funded by a Major Research Fellowship from the Leverhulme Trust (MRF 2019-112).

Intellectual Property and the Human Rights of Companies in Europe

AURORA PLOMER
University of Bristol

CAMBRIDGE
UNIVERSITY PRESS

CAMBRIDGE
UNIVERSITY PRESS

Shaftesbury Road, Cambridge CB2 8EA, United Kingdom

One Liberty Plaza, 20th Floor, New York, NY 10006, USA

477 Williamstown Road, Port Melbourne, VIC 3207, Australia

314–321, 3rd Floor, Plot 3, Splendor Forum, Jasola District Centre, New Delhi – 110025, India

103 Penang Road, #05-06/07, Visioncrest Commercial, Singapore 238467

Cambridge University Press is part of Cambridge University Press & Assessment, a department of the University of Cambridge.

We share the University's mission to contribute to society through the pursuit of education, learning and research at the highest international levels of excellence.

www.cambridge.org
Information on this title: www.cambridge.org/9781108841771

DOI: 10.1017/9781108894883

When citing this work, please include a reference to the DOI 10.1017/9781108894883

First published 2025

A catalogue record for this publication is available from the British Library

Library of Congress Cataloging-in-Publication Data
NAMES: Plomer, Aurora, author.
TITLE: Intellectual property and the human rights of companies in Europe / Aurora Plomer, University of Bristol.
DESCRIPTION: Cambridge, United Kingdom ; New York, NY : Cambridge University Press, 2025. | Includes bibliographical references and index.
IDENTIFIERS: LCCN 2024057720 (print) | LCCN 2024057721 (ebook) | ISBN 9781108841771 (hardback) | ISBN 9781108795302 (paperback) | ISBN 9781108894883 (epub)
SUBJECTS: LCSH: Social responsibility of business–Law and legislation–Europe. | Intellectual property–Europe. | Corporate governance–Law and legislation–Europe. | Tort liability of corporations–Europe. | Human rights–Europe. | Liability for human rights violations–Europe. | Convention for the Protection of Human Rights and Fundamental Freedoms (1950 November 5) | European Court of Human Rights.
CLASSIFICATION: LCC KJC2467 .P56 2025 (print) | LCC KJC2467 (ebook) | DDC 346.2404/8–DC23/eng/20241203
LC record available at https://lccn.loc.gov/2024057720
LC ebook record available at https://lccn.loc.gov/2024057721

ISBN 978-1-108-84177-1 Hardback

Contents

Acknowledgements

The idea for this book has been a long time in the making. I have a long-standing interest in human rights. So, when I started teaching intellectual property, I was puzzled by the extension of human rights to companies in the First Protocol of the European Convention on Human Rights and by the European Court of Human Right's protection of companies' intellectual property as a fundamental human right. Tuomas Mylly's invitation to collaborate on his groundbreaking project 'Constitutional Hedges of Intellectual Property' and his encouragement were the ideal prompt for me to pursue the puzzle. A Major Research Fellowship from the Leverhulme Trust (MRF – 2019–112) enabled me to take time off from my teaching and administrative duties at the University of Bristol and turn my attention fully to the research. Without the Trust's support, this research would not have been possible. I am hugely indebted.

Much of the research took place during the Covid lockdowns, limiting my ability to interact with other scholars in person and delaying visits to the London School of Economics, the Centre for International Intellectual Property Studies in Strasbourg and the Council of Europe. Nevertheless, I benefitted from discussions with numerous scholars, including Christophe Geiger, Gustavo Ghidini, Sarah Green, Stephen Greer, Jonathan Griffiths, Paddy Ireland, Elena Izyumenko, Yin Harn Lee, Katie MccKay, Spyros Maniatis, Luke McDonagh, Alexander Peukert, Tony Prosser, Julian Rivers and Hanns Ullrich. Genevieve Woods, head librarian at the European Court of Human Rights, provided exceptional help and support at helping me navigate the Council of Europe's archives. I am also particularly grateful to have received detailed comments on working drafts from the Rt Hon Lord Justice Arnold, Ian Cram, Sir Robin Jacob, Phillip Johnson and Jan Klabbers. I completed the writing of the book during a stimulating visit to the British Institute of

International and Comparative law as a research fellow in 2023–2024. When production of the book got underway, Balamuthukumaran Pasupathy facilitated the process with his helpful, timely and efficient handling of queries. Needless to say, the errors and views expressed here are all mine.

This book is dedicated to my children, Seumas and Fiona.

Table of Cited Cases

EUROPEAN COMMISSION OF HUMAN RIGHTS

Case No. 511/59, *Gudmundsson* v. *Iceland*, decision 20 December 1960

Case No. 712/60, *Retimag S.A.* v. *Federal Republic of Germany*, decision 16 December 1961

Case No. 1008/61, X v. *Austria*, decision 5 March 1962

Case No. 1017/61, X v. *The Netherlands*, decision 18 September 1961

Case No. 4130/69, X v. *The Netherlands*, decision 20 July 1971

Case No. 5178/71, *De Geillustreerde Pers N.V.* v. *the Netherlands*, decision 6 July 1976

Case No. 6572/74, X v. *Federal Republic of Germany*, decision 4 March 1976

Case No. 7427/76, W., X., Y. *and* Z. v. *Austria*, decision 27 September 1976

Case No. 7456/76, *Wiggins* v. *the United Kingdom*, decision 8 February 1978

Case No. 12048/86, *University of Illinois Foundation* v. *the Netherlands*, decision 2 May 1988

Case No. 12633/87, *Smith Kline and French Laboratories Ltd* v. *the Netherlands*, decision 4 October 1990

Case No. 13585/88, *Observer and Guardian* v. *the United Kingdom*, decision 26 November 1991

Case No. 18139/91, *Tolstoy Miloslavsky* v. *the United Kingdom*, decision 13 July 1995

Case No. 23452/94, *Osman* v. *the United Kingdom* (Grand Chamber), decision 28 October 1998

Case No. 28957/95, *Christine Goodwin* v. *the United Kingdom* (Grand Chamber), decision 7 July 2002

Case No. 29392/95, *Z and Others* v. *the United Kingdom* (Grand Chamber), decision 4 April 2001

Case No. 30262/96, *Société Nationale de Programmes FRANCE 2* v. *France*, decision 15 January 1997

Case No. 38817/97, *Lenzing AG* v. *the United Kingdom*, decision 22 May 1997

EUROPEAN COURT OF HUMAN RIGHTS

Application no. 562/05, *SIA AKKA/LAA* v. *Latvia*, decision 12 July 2016

Application no. 885/12, *Safarov* v. *Azerbaijan*, decision 1 September 2022

Application no. 931/13, *Satakunnan Markkinaporssi Oy and Satamedia Oy* v. *Finland* (Grand Chamber), decision 27 June 2017

Application no. 2694/08, *Reynolds* v. *the United Kingdom*, decision 13 March 2012

Application nos. 3002/03 and 23676/03, *Times Newspapers Ltd.* v. *the United Kingdom*, decision 10 March 2009

Application no. 5029/71, *Klass and others* v. *Germany*, decision 6 September 1978

Application no. 5493/72, *Handyside* v. *the United Kingdom*, decision 7 December 1976

Application no. 6169/13, *Mindek* v. *Croatia*, decision 30 August 2016

Application no. 6538/74, *The Sunday Times* v. *the United Kingdom*, decision 26 April 1979

Application no. 6833/74, *Marckx* v. *Belgium*, decision 13 June 1979

Application nos. 7151 and 7152/75, *Sporrong and Lonnroth* v. *Sweden*, decision 23 September 1982

Application no. 8695/79, *Inze* v. *Austria*, decision 28 October 1987

Application no. 8919/80, *van der Mussele* v. *Belgium*, decision 23 November 1983

Application no. 9074/07, *Mullai and Others* v. *Albania*, decision 23 March 2010

Application no. 9405/81, *Lithgow and Others* v. *the United Kingdom*, decision 8 July 1986

Application no. 10572/83, *Markt Intern Verlag GmbH and Klaus Beermann* v. *Germany*, decision 20 November 1989

Application no. 10890/84, *Groppera Radio and Others* v. *Switzerland*, 10 March 1990

Application no. 12726/87, *Autronic AG* v. *Switzerland*, decision 22 May 1990

Application no. 12742/87, *Pine Valley Developments Ltd. and Others* v. *Ireland*, decision 29 November 1991
Application no. 13778/88, *Thorgeir Thorgeirson* v. *Iceland*, decision 26 June 1992
Application nos. 13914/88, 15041/89, 15717/89, 15779/89 and 17207/90, *Informationsverein Lentia* v. *Austria*, decision 24 November 1993
Application no. 15375/89, *Gasus Dossier und Fordertechnick GmbH* v. *the Netherlands*, decision 23 February 1995
Application no. 15890/89, *Jersild* v. *Danemark*, decision 23 September 1994
Application no. 16023/07, *Gutiérrez Suárez* v. *Spain*, decision 1 June 2010
Application no. 17849/91, *Pressos Compania Naviera SA and Others* v. *Belgium*, decision 20 November 1995
Application no. 19247/03, *Balan* v. *Moldova*, decision 29 January 2008
Application no. 19589/92, *British-American Tobacco Company Ltd* v. *the Netherlands* (Grand Chamber), decision 20 November 1995
Application no. 19965/06, *Kamoy Radyo Televizyon Yayincilik Ve Organizasyon A.S.* v. *Turkey*, decision 16 April 2019
Application nos. 21279/02 and 36448/02, *Lindon, Otchakovsky-Laurens and July* v. *France* (Grand Chamber), decision 22 October 2007
Application no. 21980/93, *Bladet Tromsø and Stensaas* v. *Norway* (Grand Chamber), decision 22 May 1999
Application no. 22279/04, *Plechanow* v. *Poland*, decision 7 July 2009
Application no. 23662/08, *Tokel* v. *Turkey*, decision 9 February 2021
Application nos. 25088/94, 28331/95 and 28443/95, *Chassagnou and Others* v. *France* (Grand Chamber), decision 29 April 1999
Application no. 25181/94, *Hertel* v. *Switzerland*, decision 25 July 1998
Application no. 28743/03, *Melnychuc* v. *Ukraine*, admissibility decision 5 July 2005
Application no. 33949/05, *Potomska and Potomski* v. *Poland*, decision 29 March 2011
Application no. 35382/97, *Comingersoll SA* v. *Portugal*, decision 6 May 2000
Application no. 36769/08, *Ashby Donald and Others* v. *France*, decision 10 January 2013
Application No. 38433/09, *Centro Europa 7 S.R.L. and Di Stefano* v. *Italy* (Grand Chamber), decision 7 June 2012
Application no. 39401/04, *MGN Ltd* v. *the United Kingdom*, decision 18 January 2011
Application no. 39544/05, *Zagrebačka banka d.d.* v. *Croatia*, decision 12 December 2013

Application no. 39794/98, *Gratzinger and Gratzingerova* v. *the Czech Republic* (Grand Chamber), admissibility decision 10 July 2002
Application no. 40397/12, *Neij and Sunde Kolmisoppi* v. *Sweden* ('The Pirate Bay case'), decision 19 February 2013
Application no. 40660/08 and 60641/08, *Von Hannover* v. *Germany (no. 2)*, decision 7 February 2012
Application no. 42527/98, *Prince Hans-Adam II of Liechtenstein* v. *Germany* (Grand Chamber), decision 12 July 2001
Application no. 44912/98, *Kopecky* v. *Slovakia* (Grand Chamber), decision 28 September 2004
Application no. 48679/99, *Aepi S.A.* v. *Greece*, decision 11 April 2002
Application no. 48939/99, *Öneryıldız* v. *Turkey* (Grand Chamber), decision 30 November 2004
Application no. 58472/00, *Dima* v. *Romania*, admissibility decision 26 May 2005
Application no. 64569/09, *Delfi AS* v. *Estonia* (Grand Chamber), decision 16 June 2015
Application no. 66801/01, *Vorsina and Vogralik* v. *Russia*, decision 5 February 2004
Application no. 73049/01, *Anheuser-Busch* v. *Portugal* (Grand Chamber), decision 11 January 2007

UNITED KINGDOM

Colonial Bank v. *Whinney*, 30 Ch. D. 284 (CA) (1885)
OBG Ltd v. *Allan* [2007] UKHL 21

UNITED STATES

Seymour v. *Osborne*, 78 US 516 (1870)

THE NETHERLANDS

Anne Frank Fonds v. *Het Parool*, Court of Appeal Amsterdam 8 July 1999, [1999] Informatierecht/AMI 116
Dior v. *Evora*, Dutch Supreme Court (Hoge Raad) 20 October 1995, [1996] Informatierecht/AMI 51

Abbreviations

A1P1	Article 1 of the First Protocol
AB	Anheuser-Busch
AI	artificial intelligence
AO	appellation of origin
BAT	British-American Tobacco
BB	Budejovicky Budvar
CJEU	Court of Justice of the European Union
ECHR	European Convention on Human Rights
ECtHR	European Court of Human Rights
EEC	European Economic Community
EM	European Movement
EPC	European Patent Convention
EPO	European Patent Organization
EU	European Union
GC	Grand Chamber
IBR	An International Bill of the Rights of Man
ICCPR	International Covenant on Civil and Political Rights
ICESCR	International Covenant on Economic, Social and Cultural Rights
ICJ	International Court of Justice
ILO	International Labour Organization
IP	intellectual property
IPR	intellectual property right
MRP	Mouvement Républicain Populaire
NGO	non-governmental organization
NIIPI	National Institute of Intellectual Property
TM	trademark
TRIPS	Trade-Related Aspects of Intellectual Property Rights
UDHR	Universal Declaration of Human Rights

UEF	Union of European Federalists
UK	United Kingdom
UN	United Nations
US	United States
USSC	United States Supreme Court
VCLT	Vienna Convention on the Law of Treaties
WHO	World Health Organization
WIPO	World Intellectual Property Organization
WTO	World Trade Organization
WWII	World War II

Introduction

This book is based on a research project funded by the Leverhulme Trust on Intellectual Property and the human rights of corporations in Europe.[1] The aim of the project was to investigate the history and rationale for the paradoxical extension of human rights to companies in the European Convention on Human Rights (ECHR)[2] and to analyse the Court's jurisprudence on protection of companies' intellectual property in this light.

Whilst there is a substantial body of scholarship on the human rights obligations of companies,[3] there is extraordinarily little scholarship on the human rights of companies as victims of human rights violations in the ECHR.[4] The first systematic study defending the 'human' rights of companies in the European Convention system was published by Emberland in 2006.[5] According to Emberland, the ECHR is founded on a distinctive, sui generis

1 Leverhulme Major Research Fellowship (MRF 2019 – 112).

2 'Convention for the Protection of Human Rights and Fundamental Freedoms' opened for signature 4 November 1950, European Treaty Series no. 5.

3 See John G. Ruggie, *Just Business: Multinational Corporations and Human Rights* (London: WW Norton & Company, 2013); John G. Ruggie, 'Business and Human Rights: The Evolving International Agenda' (2007) 101(4) *American Journal of International Law* 819–840; John G. Ruggie et al., 'Ten Years After: From UN Guiding Principles to Multi-fiduciary Obligations' (2021) 6(2) *Business and Human Rights Journal* 179–197; Lise Smit et al., *Study on due Diligence Requirements through the Supply Chain* (Luxembourg: Publications Office of the European Union, 2020); Robert McCorquodale, *Business and Human Rights* (Oxford: Oxford University Press, 2024); Stefanie Khoury and David Whyte, *Corporate Human Rights Violations: Global Prospects for Legal Action* (London: Routledge, 2016).

4 The leading study is by Silvia Steininger and Jochen Von Bernstorff, 'Who Turned Multinational Corporations into Bearers of Human Rights? On the Creation of Corporate 'Human' Rights in International Law' in *Max Planck Institute for Comparative Public Law & International Law (MPIL) Research Paper No. 2018-25* (2018).

5 Marius Emberland, *The Human Rights of Companies: Exploring the Structure of ECHR Protection* (Oxford: Oxford University Press, 2006).

European conception of human rights which includes private property and free enterprise as central characteristics and integral components of the European liberal state. Ten years on, Dean Spielmann, former president of the European Court of Human Rights (ECtHR), concurs that not only do companies enjoy human or fundamental rights in the European Convention system, but argues that it is also fair and just that companies should be given the same rights as individuals.[6] Similarly, Peter Oliver states that 'it would be wrong to treat companies less favourably than natural persons'.[7] Emberland and Oliver allude to utilitarian and functionalist justifications (derived from J. S. Mill) without adverting to the conceptual tensions between utilitarianism and human rights extensively discussed by legal theorists and philosophers.[8] In particular, beyond the laconic reasoning of the ECtHR in the decided cases, little is offered by way of historical evidence or systematic, conceptual or theoretical insight into the rationale for the grant of property rights to 'legal persons' in Article 1 of the First Protocol (A1P1) ECHR.[9] In contrast, political scientists and international and intellectual property lawyers have voiced concern about the appropriation of human rights by private economic actors, accelerated by the World Trade Organization's (WTO) adoption of the Trade-Related Aspects of Intellectual Property Rights (TRIPS) agreement.[10] Critics point out that 'TRIPS was never enough'[11] for transnational pharmaceutical and tobacco corporations which have shifted legal regimes to secure heightened legal protection for their intellectual property in bilateral Free Trade Agreements and aggressively sued states around the world.[12] From this

6 Dean Spielmann, 'Companies in the Strasbourg Courtroom' (2016) 5(3) *Cambridge International Law Journal* 405.

7 Peter Oliver, 'Companies and Their Fundamental Rights: A Comparative Perspective' (2015) 64(3) *International and Comparative Law Quarterly* 662.

8 For instance, John Rawls, *A Theory of Justice*, rev. ed. (Oxford: Oxford University Press, 1999) and Ronald Dworkin, *Taking Rights Seriously* (London: Duckworth, 1977) and, more generally, Peter Drahos, *A Philosophy of Intellectual Property* (London: Routledge, 2016).

9 Protocol to the Convention for the Protection of Human Rights and Fundamental Freedoms (ETS No. 9), 213 U.N.T.S. 262, entered into force 18 May 1954.

10 Agreement on Trade-Related Aspects of Intellectual Property Rights, Apr. 15, 1994, Marrakesh Agreement Establishing the World Trade Organization, Annex 1C, 1869 U.N.T.S. 299, 33 I.L.M. 1197 (1994).

11 Susan K. Sell, *Private Power, Public Law: The Globalization of Intellectual Property Rights* (Cambridge: Cambridge University Press, 2003).

12 Laurence R. Helfer, 'Regime Shifting: The TRIPs Agreement and New Dynamics of International Intellectual Property Lawmaking' (2004) 29(1) *Yale Journal of International Law*; Eyal Benvenisti and George W. Downs, *Between Fragmentation and Democracy: The Role of National and International Courts* (Cambridge: Cambridge University Press, 2017); Stephanie Hartmann, 'When Two International Regimes Collide: An Analysis of the Tobacco Plain Packaging Disputes and Why Overlapping Jurisdiction of the WTO and Investment Tribunals

perspective, the exceptionalist conceptualization of companies as legitimate victims of violations of human rights in the European Convention system, far from justified, appears to confirm that a capture and appropriation of public international law by powerful private actors is underway, facilitated by economic institutions and new forms of global constitutionalism.[13] Which of these approaches is right? Specifically, what was the history and rationale for the extension of human rights to legal persons' enjoyment of their possessions in A1P1 and how has A1P1 been applied by the Court to intellectual property rights (IPRs)? To answer these questions, the methodology adopted in this study involves a combination of historical, theoretical, and comparative legal analysis.

The book begins with an examination of the conceptual and normative foundations of international human rights to elucidate whether there is a distinctive European human rights ethos which, by contrast to international human rights, necessitates extension of property rights to companies. Contrary to the ECHR exceptionalist thesis, the first chapter argues that the normative foundations of the ECHR mirror the moral foundations of international human rights in the Universal Declaration of Human Rights (UDHR).[14] The chapter recalls the historical context which prompted calls for the entrenchment of human rights in international law and examines the theoretical foundations of international human rights, highlighting the centrality of the individual human person as the subject of human rights. The analysis is based on Lauterpacht's *International Bill of Rights* (1945),[15] the first and only text setting out a complete scheme for the international protection of human rights at the time and the main intellectual influence on the drafting for the UDHR on which the European Convention was

Does Not Result in Convergence of Norms' (2017) 21(2) *UCLA Journal of International Law and Foreign Affairs* 204–245; Peter K. Yu, 'The Investment-Related Aspects of Intellectual Property Rights' (2016) 66 *American University Law Review* 829; Graeme B. Dinwoodie, *A Neofederalist Vision of TRIPS: The Resilience of the International Intellectual Property Regime* (Oxford: Oxford University Press, 2012); Christophe Geiger (ed.), *Research Handbook on Intellectual Property and Investment Law* (Cheltenham: Edward Elgar, 2020).

13 Stephen Gill and A. Claire Cutler (eds.), *New Constitutionalism and World Order* (Cambridge: Cambridge University Press, 2014); Quinn Slobodian, *Globalists: The End of Empire and the Birth of Neoliberalism* (Cambridge, MA: Harvard University Press, 2018); Jonathan Griffiths and Tuomas Mylly (eds.), *Global Intellectual Property Protection and New Constitutionalism: Hedging Exclusive Rights*, 1st ed. (Oxford: Oxford University Press, 2021).

14 Universal Declaration of Human Rights (adopted 10 December 1948 UNGA Res 217 A(III) (UDHR) Article 5.

15 Hersch Lauterpacht and Philippe Sands, *An International Bill of the Rights of Man* (Oxford: Oxford University Press, 2013).

expressly based.[16] The chapter explains how the list of civil, political, social and economic fundamental human rights is derived from the idea of respect for individual human freedom as distinct from economic market freedoms. The final part of the chapter examines how a human right to private property may be grounded on protection of home and personal possessions to facilitate development of the human personality and enable the individual human person to live a life with dignity. Not unexpectedly, the theories discussed in this chapter did not form part of the discourse of representatives and lawyers at the Council of Europe involved in the drafting of the ECHR. However, as shown in the next chapter, advocates of the inclusion of the right to property in the ECHR repeatedly mentioned the importance of protecting home and personal possessions as a natural or even sacred right. The theoretical justifications thus offer a deeper understanding of the subject and object of human rights in the ECHR.

The inclusion of property rights in the ECHR proved highly controversial and was delayed until the adoption of the First Protocol. Chapter 2 retraces the drafting history of the text of A1P1 declaring that 'every natural and legal person is entitled to the peaceful enjoyment of his possessions'. The meaning of the text is anything but straightforward. There is no mention of companies, but in common and civil law jurisdictions there is no doubt that companies are 'legal persons' or 'personnes morales' in French. Neither is the term 'property' used; instead, the French version uses the term 'biens' whilst the English version uses the word 'possessions'. Yet, it is well established in the jurisprudence of the ECtHR that A1P1 protects property rights and that companies have standing to launch claims as victims of violations of their right to property. Why was this not made unambiguously clear by the drafters? And why would a human rights treaty include companies as victims of violations of human rights? The chapter uncovers an important connection hitherto unnoticed by scholars in the evolution of the ECHR text on A1P1. The provisions on individual rights of petition to the Court in the original template produced by the European Movement (EM) envisaged that 'corporate bodies' would enjoy rights of petition to the Court. Corporate bodies were removed from the text by the Council of Ministers, but corporations made their reappearance as 'legal persons' in the final iteration of the Article on property rights (A1P1). The elusive terminology was introduced by the lawyers who had drafted the original template for the EM, whose aim was a federalist

[16] As detailed by Brian Simpson in his seminal study of the genesis of the ECHR: A. W. Brian Simpson, *Human Rights and the End of Empire: Britain and the Genesis of the European Convention* (Oxford: Oxford University Press, 2004).

Europe based on market freedoms and economic integration. The drafting history shows that the Assembly representatives were unclear about the precise meaning and implications of the formula, but their assent was secured on the understanding that the wording would entrench the natural or 'sacred' right of each human person to protection of their home and personal possessions. Those who had originally opposed the inclusion of property rights in the Convention relented carried along by a shared sense of urgency across the political spectrum that the moment had to be seized or the opportunity to adopt a European Convention on Human Rights would be lost. The ambiguous text of A1P1 was a triumph for the lawyers who had seized the political momentum to convince delegates to vote with their hearts (recalling the mass confiscations of millions of people's homes and belongings by the Nazis) when the cold legal reality was that they were voting for a text which secured supranational protection of companies' assets and capital, tangible and intangible property, including debts, securities and intellectual property. The ECHR was revolutionary not only because it included individual rights of petition to an international court, but also because these rights were implicitly extended to companies (as subjects of human rights) whose 'possessions' would be protected in the forthcoming Protocol on pretence that a home and minimum of personal belongings were required for each individual human person to live a life with dignity.

Chapter 3 investigates the connection between the original template for the ECHR (which envisaged that corporations would enjoy a right of petition) and the final text of A1P1. The deletion of corporate bodies by the Committee of Ministers in the Article on individual rights of petition was criticized in the Assembly as a regressive step on the grounds that the trend in international law had been to emphasize the rights and duties of individuals. The analysis shows that this claim was misleading. The concept of legal personality in international law was indeed undergoing significant changes in the aftermath of WWII. There was a nascent debate on whether international organizations such as the United Nations (UN) could acquire legal personality and file complaints on behalf of victims of injury at the International Court of Justice (ICJ), but there was no question of the individual having standing to enforce these rights in an international court. In contrast corporate bodies had historically enjoyed legal personality in civil and common law systems in Europe. The 'legal person' was not a person as ordinarily understood but a legal fiction originating in Roman law and created to facilitate ownership and transfer of property by groups of individuals. In European national laws, legal personality was extended, inter alia, to companies, in the wake of the industrial revolution, to enable ownership sale and transfer of tangible and intangible property.

At the same time, deep theoretical and political divisions emerged on the nature of the corporation and the aims of corporatism and free markets. The chapter documents how these divisions were still alive at the end of WWII and formed the background to the political compromise which resulted in the addition of legal persons to the Article on property rights in the ECHR. In short, the term 'legal person' literally meant different things to different politicians on opposite ends of the political spectrum in Europe. Only in the fictional language of national laws did 'legal persons' have rights, notably the right to own, use and dispose of property. There were no such persons as subjects of law in international human rights, only real individual human persons. Thus, the inclusion of companies as subjects of human rights in the ECHR in the form of 'legal persons' was not necessitated by a distinctive European conception of human rights based on market freedoms. It was a semantic compromise to accommodate competing political ideals on the nature and function of corporations in a united Europe. The next chapter shows how the term 'possessions' had an equally fictional character in domestic European laws.

Chapter 4 argues that by contrast to the meaning of the term in natural language, 'possessions' in law has a much wider technical meaning. Much like fictitious 'legal persons', 'intangible possessions' were created as legal fictions in civil and common law jurisdictions in Europe to accommodate shares, debts, securities and intellectual property as novel types of fictitious commodities. The analysis retraces the roots of such legal fictions in European property law in Roman law's dual categories of rights in rem, over tangible, corporeal 'things', and rights in personam or over intangible, incorporeal 'things', and shows how these concepts were stretched to accommodate the economic and technological changes unleashed by the industrial revolution. The chapter details how 'intellectual' property was added to the legal category of intangible fictitious possessions in civil and common law jurisdictions in Europe in the nineteenth century. By the time the Convention was adopted, the term 'possessions' had been firmly established in European national laws to include all types of intangible property, well beyond the types of personal possessions that advocates of property rights at the Council of Europe had argued were morally required to facilitate development of the human personality. Overall, the analysis reveals a profound disconnect between the wide legal meaning and reach of the term 'possessions' ('biens') in A1P1 and the moral discourse on property rights at the Council of Europe. The obfuscation between the ordinary meaning of 'possessions' and the technical legal meaning, combined with the assignment of fundamental rights to legal persons in

A1P1, completed a virtuous fictitious legal circle. This facilitated judicial protection of the intangible assets, profits and intellectual property of transnational companies in Western capitalist market economies under the purview of a supranational Court ostensibly created to secure protection of the fundamental *human* rights of each individual human person. The text of A1P1 thus conceals an underlying tension between the moral discourse of property rights advocates at the Council of Europe and the subject and legal reach of the interests protected. The potential tensions and contradictions inevitably surface when looking for a coherent ethos and principled basis for the text. It was left to the now-defunct Commission and the Court to navigate through the ambiguities and tensions embodied in the text to distil the essence of the right to property. Chapter 5 provides a systematic review of the case law of the Commission and Court's application of A1P1 to companies IPRs and Chapter 6 examines the Court's external balancing of IPRs with other Convention rights.

The first wave of companies' claims relating to IPRs was not tested until the early 1980s. Chapter 5 shows that, by then, the Commission and Court had developed a set of rules and principles grounding the extension and expansion of A1P1 to IPRs. In the early cases filed by companies in the 1960s and 1970s, the Commission and Court had deferred to national laws legal fictions in the construction of 'legal persons' and 'possessions'. Initial doubts expressed by some judges on the scope of application of the term 'possessions' to intangibles were resolved in the Court's landmark majority decision in *Sporrong v. Sweden* (1982) entrenching protection of private companies' profits under A1P1 based on the Court's 'autonomous' reading of the term 'possessions'. Thus, when the first claims relating to companies' IPRs reached the Commission in the early 1980s, it had no difficulty in hearing complaints from a multinational pharmaceutical corporation which alleged to be a victim of a State's violations of its right to enjoyment of possessions. The turning point came with the Grand Chamber's (GC) landmark judgment of *Anheuser-Busch v. Portugal* (2007). The detailed analysis of the judgment suggests a tacit alignment of the scope of protection of IPRs under the Convention with the European Union's (EU) regulatory framework on IPRs, grounding a further extension of A1P1. In the last decade, in a series of cases relating to patents, copyright and trademarks, the Court has adopted a 'rule of law' approach to the construction of A1P1, eschewing a substantive application of the internal balancing test of private and public interests. The review of the case law concludes that the future points to an inevitable tilt of the Court's construction of companies IPRs towards the EU legal order, consolidating and deepening supranational legal protection of companies' IPRs in Europe with little trace left of the original moral intent of securing protection of the fundamental right of each individual human person to protection of a minimum of home and personal possessions to live a life with dignity.

Chapter 6 completes the analysis of the Court's jurisprudence on IPRs with a review of the Court's approach to the external balancing of IPRs with other Convention rights, notably freedom of expression in Article 10 ECHR. The review takes as its starting point the optimistic expectations, of European IP scholars at the turn of the century who had welcomed the turn to human rights as counterweights to the seemingly unstoppable expansion of IPRs. The analysis of the Court's case law details why the expectations were not met. The Court's case law on Article 10 ECHR, it is suggested, is underpinned by incongruent rationales: a moral rationale, whereby autonomy is deemed necessary for each individual person's development and participation in democratic society, and an economic rationale grounded on the commercial interests of corporations in free markets. A number of key decisions from the Court in the 1990s are shown to blur the two rationales, conflating freedom of expression with unfair competition and granting Member States a wide margin of appreciation and discretion to adopt a light-touch approach to the regulation of commercial speech deemed by the Court to lack a public interest or political dimension. The discussion further shows how the Court's approach to protection of commercial speech, combined with the elevation of IPRs to fundamental rights in A1P1, has resulted in the strengthening of IP owners' rights in the external balancing exercise between Article 10 ECHR and protection of IPRs in A1P1. For Emberland, the Court's liberal free market interpretive lens, whilst at odds with the moral rationale for Convention rights, is nevertheless justified on the grounds that the Court has adopted a teleological approach centred on protection of the core values of a functional liberal market economy, democracy, equality and the rule of law. However, the Court's entrenchment of corporate commercial interests in pursuit of a liberal, free-market, economic conception of democracy risks encroachment of the human rights and freedoms of individual human beings. Supranational, legal protection of commercial expression and corporate ownership of IP can allow monopolistic behaviour to thrive unchecked at the expense of individual human persons whose human rights the Convention was originally intended to protect. Unlike ordinary citizens, global corporations have the financial and legal capability to leverage a wealth of resources to secure protection of their intellectual property in national courts, international Courts, investment tribunals and at WTO. The liberal economic interpretation of Convention rights grounded in market freedoms can ultimately result in an emasculation of the personal freedoms that the Convention founders were seeking to entrench as necessary to enable the full development of the human personality. For these reasons, protection of companies IPRs in the ECHR has become the ground on which the inherent tensions and contradictions in A1P1 are playing out. The concluding chapter explores three scenarios on the future direction of protection of IPRs at the ECHR.

1

The Foundations of Human Rights and Property Rights

INTRODUCTION

The European Convention on Human Rights (ECHR) was opened for signature in Rome on 4 November 1950.[1] On 8 March 1951, the UK was the first State to ratify the ECHR. Ratifications by Norway, Sweden and Germany followed in 1952, but it took another year for the required ten ratifications for the Convention to enter into force on 3 October 1953.[2] Property rights were left out of the list of protected rights in the ECHR, and their inclusion was delayed until the adoption of Article 1 of the First Protocol (A1P1) in 1952.[3] This chapter sets out the historical context for the adoption of the ECHR and the normative foundations of European human rights. In contrast to the exceptionalist thesis that the ECHR sought to give expression to a sui generis European conception of human rights founded on liberal market freedoms, this chapter argues that the normative foundations of the

[1] Council of Europe, *European Convention for the Protection of Human Rights and Fundamental Freedoms*, 4 November 1950, ETS 5. The original signatories were Belgium, Denmark, France, Germany, Iceland, Ireland, Italy, Luxembourg, Netherlands, Norway, Turkey and the UK.

[2] Denmark, Iceland, Ireland, Italy and Luxembourg ratified in 1953. Pierre-Henri Teitgen recounts that, to his shame, France, which had played a leading role in the adoption of the Convention and was one of the original signatories, did not ratify the Convention until 3 May 1974. Originally, this was due to socialist opposition to the A1P1, then France's role in the Algerian war and finally General De Gaulle's unwillingness to accept control of domestic policies by a 'foreign' supranational court. Pierre-Henri Teitgen, *Faites entrer le témoin suivant: 1940–1958: de la Résistance à la Ve République* (Rennes: Ouest France, 1988), p. 483.

[3] Council of Europe, *Protocol to the Convention for the Protection of Human Rights and Fundamental Freedoms*, 20 March 1952, ETS No. 009.

ECHR mirror the moral foundations of international human rights in the Universal Declaration of Human Rights (UDHR).[4] Section 1.1 outlines the historical context which prompted calls for international legal protection of human rights. Section 1.2 examines the theoretical foundations of international human rights, highlighting the centrality of the individual human person as the subject of human rights. Section 1.3 explains how the list of fundamental human rights is derived from the idea of respect for human freedom as distinct from economic, market freedoms. Section 1.4 examines the theoretical justifications for the protection of property rights as fundamental human rights.

1.1 THE GENESIS OF INTERNATIONAL HUMAN RIGHTS IN THE TWENTIETH CENTURY

The scale of human, social and economic destruction unleashed by World War II (WWII) had a profound impact on the evolution of international law. Military cooperation between Western Allied powers and the Soviet Union to defeat the Nazis paved the way for the creation of the United Nations (UN) in 1945. International protection of human rights was seen by the Allied powers as necessary to secure peace and avert the resurgence of totalitarianism.[5] Human rights were given centre stage in the UN Charter. The Preamble proclaimed States' faith in 'fundamental human rights, in the dignity and worth of the human person, in the equal rights of men and women' and Article 1 further proclaimed that the aim of the UN was to promote and encourage 'respect for human rights and for fundamental freedoms for all without distinction as to race, sex, language, or religion'.

Three years later, the ideal of respect for the inherent dignity and freedom of each individual human being found expression in the adoption of the UDHR on 10 December 1948.[6] The UDHR placed the individual, rather than the State, at the centre of international law, prompting what international law scholars described as a new 'Grotian moment' whereby 'the individual is the ultimate unit of all law (...) in the double sense that the obligations of international law are ultimately addressed to him and that the development,

4 UN General Assembly, *Universal Declaration of Human Rights* (217 [III] A), Paris (1948).

5 See A. W. Brian Simpson, *Human Rights and the End of Empire: Britain and the Genesis of the European Convention* (Oxford: Oxford University Press, 2004); Elizabeth Borgwardt, *A New Deal for the World: America's Vision for Human Rights*, 1st Harvard University Press pbk. ed. (Cambridge, MA: Harvard University Press, 2007).

6 On the origins of the UDHR, see Johannes Morsink, *The Universal Declaration of Human Rights: Origins, Drafting, and Intent* (Philadelphia: University of Pennsylvania Press, 1999).

the well-being and the dignity of the individual human being are a matter of direct concern to international law'.[7]

In his seminal study on the ECHR, Brian Simpson describes Lauterpacht's book *An International Bill of Rights* published in 1945[8] as the most significant contribution on international human rights when the UN was established in 1945.[9] Lauterpacht's was the first and only text at the time setting out a complete scheme for the international protection of human rights.[10] In his moving commentary on Lauterpacht's work, Philippe Sands recounts how Lauterpacht's experience of 'xenophobia, racism, group identity and conflict'[11] had a profound influence on Lauterpacht's vision of international law. Sands describes Lemberg, the city where Lauterpacht studied law, as a city which had been catapulted into the bloody conflict between the Poles and the Ukrainians at the end of WWII. As the leader of the Organization of Zionist Academics in Galicia, Lauterpacht was acutely aware of the limits and constraints on the treatment of minorities in international law. He headed for Vienna to complete his studies under the distinguished legal philosopher Hans Kelsen, unable to take his final law exams in Lemberg 'because the University closed its doors to the Jews of Eastern Galicia'.[12] Kelsen's contribution to the drafting of Austria's new constitution, where the individual was put at the centre of the legal order, proved inspirational for the young Lauterpacht. The growing anti-Semitism and pogroms in Vienna impressed upon Lauterpacht the 'vital necessity' of protecting the rights of individuals and prompted his move to Britain in 1923.[13] He started his academic career at the London School of Economics, trained for the Bar at Gray's Inn and in 1938 was appointed Whewell Professor of International Law at the University of Cambridge, where he systematized his thoughts on international law and human rights. Lauterpacht's personal trajectory had deeply impacted his view of the shortcomings of international law and the League of Nations which he attributed to the lack of legal constraints on States and the absence of enforcement mechanisms. Lauterpacht envisaged that States would consent to interference with their sovereignty and to supranational judicial settlement

7 Hersch Lauterpacht, 'The Grotian Tradition in International Law' (1946) 23 *British Yearbook of International Law*, 1–53, 27.
8 Hersch Lauterpacht and Philippe Sands, *An International Bill of the Rights of Man* (Oxford: Oxford University Press, 2013).
9 Simpson, *Human Rights and the End of Empire*, p. 205.
10 Ibid.
11 Philippe Sands, *East West Street: On the Origins of Genocide and Crimes against Humanity* (London: Weidenfeld & Nicolson, 2016), p. 63.
12 Ibid., p. 74.
13 Ibid., p. 77.

in order to secure long-lasting peace and effective protection of fundamental human rights. Human rights provided moral and spiritual authority by laying down the foundational and unifying principles of justice and fairness on which an effective international legal order would be built. The overarching vision was of a universalist, Kantian order in which the State fulfils the destiny of mankind towards rationality and perfection.[14] For Lauterpacht, human rights and the law of nations were inherently linked because:

> It is only within the structure of a wider system in which the State has ceased to be an absolute law unto itself and an absolute purpose unto itself that the inviolate character of inherent human rights can receive adequate legal expression and that the sanctity of the individual human being as the ultimate subject of all law asserts itself in full vigour.[15]

The opportunity to develop his thinking on human rights arose when, in the summer of 1942, Lauterpacht was commissioned to write *An International Bill of the Rights of Man* (IBR) by the American Jewish Society. In his preface to the IBR, Lauterpacht acknowledges the American Jewish Committee's active interest in a Bill of Rights since the end of World War I (WWI) and how fitting it was for the Committee to take on such a project for 'no people has suffered more cruelly from a denial of elementary human rights'.[16] Lauterpacht had been acting as an advisor to the Committee on War Crimes, which was set up in June 1942, and to the British and US prosecutors at the Nuremberg trials.[17] He worked closely with David Maxwell-Fyfe, the UK prosecutor who subsequently played a critical role in the elaboration of the ECHR. In his memoirs, Maxwell-Fyfe said that he had received invaluable help from Lauterpacht in drafting the text.[18] According to Simpson, the influence of Lauterpacht's IBR would have been considerable because of Lauterpacht's lucid style and his skilful and realistic analysis of the difficulties involved in the elaboration of a system for the legal protection of fundamental human rights.[19]

14 Lauterpacht and Sands, *An International Bill of the Rights of Man*, p. 27; Martti Koskenniemi, *The Gentle Civilizer of Nations: The Rise and Fall of International Law, 1870–1960* (Cambridge: Cambridge University Press, 2002).

15 Hersch Lauterpacht, 'The Law of Nations, the Law of Nature and the Rights of Man' (1943) 29 *Transactions of the Grotius Society* 1–33, 12.

16 Lauterpacht and Sands, *An International Bill of the Rights of Man*, preface.

17 On Lauterpacht's involvement see Sands, *East West Street*, pp. 100 ff.

18 David Patrick Maxwell Fyfe, *Political Adventure: The Memoirs of the Earl of Kilmuir* (London: Weidenfeld & Nicolson, 1964), p. 176.

19 Simpson, *Human Rights and the End of Empire*, p. 206.

1.2 THE MORAL FOUNDATIONS OF INTERNATIONAL HUMAN RIGHTS

1.2.1 *The Subject of Human Rights*

The publication of Lauterpacht's IBR coincided with the adoption of the UN Charter in 1945. Human rights had formed part of the discussion on the establishment of a worldwide organization for the preservation of peace and security between the USSR, China, the United States, the UK, and France at the Dumbarton Oaks conference in May 1944.[20] In the preface to the IBR, Lauterpacht noted that the Dumbarton Oaks proposals cited respect for human rights and fundamental freedoms as one of the objects of the UN. However, Lauterpacht continued, declarations of principle devoid of any legal obligation and sanctions on infringing States could not achieve the 'enthronement of human rights' which Winston Churchill had said should mark the end of WWII, nor could they secure the effective protection of human rights and lasting world peace.[21] Thus, the crucial question was how protection of human rights could be secured effectively. The IBR sets out to answer that question, acknowledging the considerable challenges in determining the nature and scope of the rights to be secured, the political difficulties surrounding judicial empowerment in democratic societies and the reluctance of States to consent to interference with national sovereignty.

Lauterpacht's study is divided into three parts. The first part sets out the philosophical foundations of human rights on which an IBR are to be founded. The second part identifies the fundamental human rights to be protected by the Bill and their rationale. The last part details the enforcement mechanisms to secure effective protection of the rights. In the first part, Lauterpacht argues that the 'revolutionary' and innovative legal order which he is proposing is founded on the premise that the individual human being is 'the ultimate subject of all law'.[22] The revolutionary dimension is that protection of the individual human being, to be effective, must be secured through positive, international law over and above national laws and supersede all other objectives. In an intellectual tour de force spanning the history of Western political philosophy from antiquity to the twentieth century, Lauterpacht locates the rationale for the transcendence of universal human rights over positive laws in natural law. The reader is told that 'the association

[20] See Borgwardt, *A New Deal for the World* and Simpson, *Human Rights and the End of Empire*.
[21] Lauterpacht and Sands, *An International Bill of the Rights of Man*, pp. 8–9.
[22] Ibid., p. 53.

of the law of nature and of the natural rights of man goes back to antiquity'.[23] The ideal of transcendent human rights and of the 'indestructible sovereignty of man'[24] are claimed to be a running thread through the philosophy of the stoics and Plato's idealism, the Thomist Christian revival, the social contract theories of the sixteenth and seventeenth centuries, the rationalist theories of the enlightenment and the turn to positivism in the nineteenth century. The 'natural law of humanity', Lauterpacht argues, is revealed in the experience of human beings across different cultures and ages and in the writings of philosophers from different persuasions. It shows that the individual human being is naturally endowed with the ability 'to develop its capacities to all attainable perfection'.[25] The normative implication is that each individual human being has both a moral duty and a right, grounded in natural law, to develop his personality to the fullest.[26] Freedom is necessary in order to enable the fullest development of the individual human person not only as a means but 'as an end in itself'.[27] From this, it follows that the State's obligation is to secure the freedom necessary for each individual human being to realize his/her essence as a rational and social being. This obligation is ultimately secured by international law which 'exists for the purpose of . . . making man's freedom secure from the State and by rendering the State secure from external danger'.[28] Natural law thus provides both the lens through which universal human rights are identified and the foundation on which just and fair positive law(s) are to be built to secure effective protection of human rights.

Whether Lauterpacht's view that affirmation of the inherent dignity and freedom of each human person may be found as a thread running throughout the history of philosophy is debatable.[29] For our purposes, the significance of Lauterpacht's thesis is that human rights put States under a morally grounded obligation to respect human freedom and dignity by creating the conditions

23 Ibid., p. 31.
24 Ibid., p. 49.
25 Ibid.
26 Ibid.
27 Ibid.
28 Ibid., p. 50.
29 Contrast Hume's theory that reason is and ought to be the slave of the passions in David Hume, *A Treatise of Human Nature: Being an Attempt to Introduce the Experimental Method of Reasoning into Moral Subjects* (Cambridge: Cambridge University Press, 2009) or Aristotle's casuistic approach to human virtue and human good in Sarah Broadie and Christopher Rowe (eds.), *Aristotle Nicomachean Ethics: Translation, Introduction, and Commentary* (Oxford: Oxford University Press, 2002). For a contemporary philosophical defence of the idea of inherent human rights and their expression in the UDHR see Johannes Morsink, *Inherent Human Rights: Philosophical Roots of the Universal Declaration* (Philadelphia: University of Pennsylvania Press, 2009).

under which each human person can realize their inherent capacity for self-determination. Protection of human dignity and of the individual human person are therefore not incidental to the entrenchment of human rights in international law; on the contrary, they represent the essence and purpose of a *human* rights treaty as distinct from international treaties on trade or commerce. For Lauterpacht, an IBR, grounded on universal values, offered a safeguard to limit the authority and sovereignty of States in recognition that they are the 'trustees of the welfare and the final purpose of man'.[30] Evidently, since companies are not human beings, the justification for securing transnational legal protection of their interests necessarily lies outwith the conceptual and normative framework of human rights treaties. The subject of protection of international human rights is the individual human person, and this in turn also explains the rationale for the list of protected fundamental freedoms.

1.3 THE GREAT DIVIDE: FUNDAMENTAL FREEDOMS

1.3.1 *Civil and Political Freedoms*

Human freedom and human dignity provide the moral foundation for Lauterpacht's list of human rights, which includes all the civil and political freedoms historically found in a classical bill of rights. Under Part I of the IBR, entitled *Personal Freedom*, Lauterpacht argues that the State has an overriding obligation to protect individual liberty because 'personal freedom, that is, freedom from arbitrary physical restraint ... is the first claim of man in his struggle against the arbitrariness of the State'.[31] This, we are told, is reflected, inter alia, in the English Magna Carta's powerful remedy of habeas corpus against arbitrary arrest. Similarly, the prohibition of slavery and forced labour in Article 2 IBR seeks to vindicate 'the freedom of man in its primary and most fundamental aspect'[32] and treat the individual as a subject rather than an object (of law). Freedom of Religion in Article 3 IBR is based on the 'absolute autonomy of human will'[33] and 'inviolate sphere of individual conscience'.[34] Its recognition in nineteenth- and twentieth-century constitutions vindicates the 'absolute right of the individual as against the State'[35] and is closely

30 Lauterpacht, 'The Law of Nations, the Law of Nature and the Rights of Man', p. 29.
31 Ibid., chapter IX, Article I, p. 93.
32 Ibid., p. 100.
33 Ibid., p. 104.
34 Ibid., p. 105.
35 Ibid.

connected to freedom of expression in Article 4 IBR. Freedom of association in Article 5 is the 'most potent instrument of the freedom of the person'[36] because the human personality is stifled by isolation and grows in richness as it is 'woven into the structure of the diverse associations'.[37] Freedom of association, in Lauterpacht's IBR, is also linked to what Jefferson described as the right of free communication between citizens[38] and to the idea that political authority and legitimacy in a democracy ultimately rest on consent. An individual human being who has no right to vote, Lauterpacht tells us, is not governed by consent and is not free.[39] Thus, Article 10 IBR asserts the right to vote in free, secret and periodic elections. The counterpart in the ECHR is to be found in Article 3 of the First Protocol. The same human-centred rationale does not carry over to companies/legal persons.

The classical civil and political rights of the Enlightenment are grounded on a human-centred conception of freedom and the inherent dignity of each individual human person. From this perspective, companies cannot be the subjects of human rights, nor is it appropriate to secure protection of companies' economic interests through a human rights treaty. This is not to say that, in a democracy, companies should not be recognized as subjects of legal protection. It is simply to note that the normative foundations of human rights are not applicable to companies and that the appropriate legal vehicle to protect companies' interests is not a human rights treaty.

1.3.2 *Social and Economic Freedoms*

Lauterpacht's IBR was both a continuation and a departure from the classical human rights vision of the Enlightenment which had found expression in French and US constitutional entrenchments of fundamental rights. The continuing thread in the IBR lies in the inclusion of the negative civil and political rights which protected the individual from arbitrary interference from the State. The departure took two forms: on one hand, Lauterpacht's IBR includes several social and economic rights which impose 'positive' obligations on States, while, on the other hand, it deliberately excludes property rights. The reasons lie in Lauterpacht's rejection of the classical liberal view of fundamental rights. For Lauterpacht, political freedom, though of fundamental importance, is not sufficient to enable individuals

[36] Ibid., p. 113.
[37] Ibid.
[38] Ibid., p. 112.
[39] Ibid., p. 135.

to exercise true choices and is 'utterly meaningless because of the overwhelming impact of economic necessity and dependence'.[40] The classical 'negative' conception of freedom in the IBR is to be replaced by a 'positive' conception of freedom because

> in modern society, economic freedom, conceived as the mere absence of restraints imposed by the State, results in economic anarchy, in exploitation of the weak and isolated individual by economically powerful and organized forces and in the denial of substantive freedom of contract.[41]

Thus, Article 13 IBR imposes a qualified duty on States to secure 'the right to work, to education and to public assistance in case of unemployment, old age, sickness, disablement and other cases of underserved want'. Article 14 IBR requires States to cooperate with the International Labour Organization (ILO) to 'make provision for securing just and humane conditions of work'. For Lauterpacht, the inclusion of social and economic rights reflected the values of the Atlantic Charter, partly vindicated by the growing constitutional recognition and international affirmation of Roosevelt's Four Freedoms and the 'War on Want'.[42] It was further justified because of the close connection between equality in law and social and economic equality of opportunity. Individual freedoms, reduced to negative freedoms from State interference, Lauterpacht argued, were illusory and did not enable individuals to fully realize their abilities nor did they secure real, positive freedom.[43] By contrast to classical liberals, Lauterpacht thought that 'the value of political freedom is impaired by the absence of substantive economic freedom, by economic insecurity, by underserved want, and by absence of educational opportunity'.[44] Conversely, economic freedom results in exploitation of the weak and 'a denial of substantive freedom of contract'.[45] Lauterpacht argues that there is no point in speculating whether the right to work and other socio-economic rights are inherent natural rights or whether State obligations are 'implied in the fact of social solidarity and independent of any individualistic doctrine of society'.[46] These rights, he

40 Ibid., p. 156.
41 Ibid.
42 Ibid., pp. 159–160. See also Simpson, *Human Rights and the End of Empire*.
43 Ibid., p. 155.
44 Ibid., p. 156. Lauterpacht goes on to argue that 'economic freedom, conceived as the mere absence of restraints imposed by the State, results in economic anarchy, in exploitation of the weak and isolated individual by economically powerful and organized forces and in the denial of substantive freedom of contract'.
45 Ibid.
46 Ibid., p. 157.

tells us, are to be found in some modern constitutions.[47] They were also later included in the UDHR (1948).[48]

1.3.3 *The Exclusion of Property Rights*

Whilst Lauterpacht defended the inclusion of socio-economic rights in the IBR, he was strongly of the view that property rights should not be included. There are three strands to Lauterpacht's dismissal of property rights as fundamental human rights. First, he rejects as artificial the view that property rights are grounded in natural law. Second, he does not accept the classical liberal conception of property rights which theorizes human rights as 'negative' freedoms requiring States to refrain from interfering with the individual's right to exclusive use, sale, trade or disposal of their property. Third, he argues that economic policies based on market freedoms are of no benefit to individuals bereft of property or substantive opportunities, leading to individuals suffering economic exploitation and lacking substantive freedoms.

As noted by commentators at the time,[49] Lauterpacht's exclusion of property rights from the IBR was at odds with the prominence given to property rights in landmark constitutions of the eighteenth and nineteenth centuries and in the Lockean theories from which they drew their inspiration. In his sympathetic retracing of Lauterpacht's personal journey and his own, Philippe Sands suggests that the omission was likely a nod to 'the wind from the east' and the UK political climate at the time.[50] That may be so, but the omission is also consistent with Lauterpacht's deliberate decoupling of political freedoms from economic freedoms in the articulation of human rights. The distinction between the necessary political freedoms to secure human rights and economic freedoms is drawn by Lauterpacht in three ways. First, it is to be found in Lauterpacht's analysis of the legitimacy and political foundations of the State based on the consent of the governed. Second, it is evident in Lauterpacht's explicit critique of the extension of the concept of human freedom to economic/market freedoms. Finally, it is articulated in the rationale for each of the discrete substantive rights identified by Lauterpacht as fundamental human rights.

47 Ibid. Lauterpacht cites the Russian Constitution of 1936.

48 For a contemporary version of human freedom as the moral foundations of human rights see Amartya Sen, *Development as Freedom* (Oxford: Oxford University Press, 2001).

49 For instance, Quincy Wright, 'International Law and Commercial Relations' (1941) *Proceedings of the American Society of International Law* 30–40.

50 Sands, *East West Street*, p. 109.

In the landmark Constitutions and Bills of Rights of the eighteenth century, and in the works of Locke and others, rights to life, liberty and property are typically enumerated as a trinity and justified by reference to laws of nature which establish that human beings are born free and equal.[51] Lauterpacht acknowledges the monumental influence of Locke on the inclusion of inalienable rights to property in eighteenth- and nineteenth-century Bills of Rights.[52] He concedes that Locke, perhaps more than any other thinker, treated property rights with a reverence second to none[53] But in Lauterpacht's view, there had been significant social and economic developments since Locke's thesis of the right to property as sacred. In States whose economies are based on private property, the scale of State interference through taxation or regulation in pursuit of social welfare renders the inclusion of the right to property highly artificial. In other States, collective, rather than individual, private ownership has become the main mode of production. Presciently, Lauterpacht foresaw that the entrenchment of property rights as basic human rights in an international bill of rights would prove contentious as it sought to solve 'controversial and complex problems of economics in the national and international sphere'.[54] Although the right to own property was included in Article 17 UDHR (1948), it was omitted from the International Covenant on Civil and Political Rights (ICCPR) (1966)[55] and the International Covenant on Economic, Social and Cultural Rights (ICESCR) (1966)[56] which were adopted to give legal effect to the UDHR.[57]

[51] For instance, Virginia Declaration of Rights (1772) Article 1: That all men are created equally free & independent, & have certain inherent natural Rights, of which they cannot, by any Compact, deprive or divest their posterity; among which are the Enjoyment of Life & Liberty, with the Means of acquiring & possessing property, & pursuing & obtaining Happiness & Safety incorporated in Fifth Amendment of US Bill of Rights (1791) No person shall ... be deprived of life, liberty, or property, without due process of law; nor shall private property be taken for public use, without just compensation. French Declaration of the Rights of Man (1789) Article 2: The aim of every political association is the preservation of the natural and imprescriptible rights of Man. These rights are Liberty, Property, Safety and Resistance to Oppression.

[52] Lauterpacht and Sands, *An International Bill of the Rights of Man*. For instance, he praises Locke's unequivocal defence of freedom against the arbitrariness of the State: 'it is an assertion of the legal right of rebellion against the State encroaching on the natural rights of man'.

[53] Ibid., p. 11.

[54] Ibid., p. 164.

[55] UN General Assembly, 'International Covenant on Civil and Political Rights', Treaty Series, vol. 999 (December 1966), p. 171.

[56] UN General Assembly, 'International Covenant on Economic, Social, and Cultural Rights', Treaty Series, vol. 999 (December 1966), p. 171.

[57] William A. Schabas, 'The Omission of the Right to Property in the International Covenants' (1991) 4 *Hague Yearbook of International Law* 135–170.

According to Lauterpacht, the modern variants of the classical conception of property rights typically rest on a conflation of civil/political freedoms with market freedoms.[58] Examples cited by Lauterpacht include Quincy Wright, a contemporary US international lawyer. Wright argued in favour of 'a basic human right to contract and to trade, qualified, of course, by reasonable governmental control in the public interest' on the grounds that the right to buy and sell are natural human rights.[59] Similarly, H. G. Wells, who was a Fabian, stated in *The Rights of Man* that 'he shall have the right to buy or sell without any discriminatory restrictions anything which may be lawfully bought or sold, in such quantities and with such reservations as are compatible with the common welfare'.[60] For Lauterpacht, these claims are a 'misuse' of natural rights and have hindered 'vital measures of social reform intended to protect the individual against the soulless inhumanity of modern economic power'[61] and enabled the 'gross exploitation of special pleading'[62] to protect economic stability and vested economic interests.[63]

Notwithstanding their exclusion in Lauterpacht's IBR, property rights were included in the UDHR and the ECHR. Article 17 UDHR declares the right of everyone to own property alone or in association with others. The corresponding right to property in the ECHR, which was intended by the drafters to be aligned with Article 17 UDHR,[64] is expressed in A1P1 to the ECHR as the right of every natural and legal person to enjoyment of their possessions. The question then is whether it is possible to develop a plausible justification for a right to property as a basic human right which does not conflate human freedom with market freedoms.

1.4 A HUMAN RIGHT TO PRIVATE PROPERTY?

A helpful starting point is Waldron's critical examination of the right to private property.[65] Waldron distinguishes between theories which are based

58 In retrospect, the most influential free market proponents were in fact Hayek and Freedman. For an example of the link between economic and political freedoms see Milton Friedman, *Capitalism and Freedom* (Chicago: University of Chicago Press, 1962), and Friedrich A. von Hayek, *The Road to Serfdom* (London: Routledge, 2001).

59 Lauterpacht and Sands, *An International Bill of the Rights of Man* citing Wright, 'International Law and Commercial Relations'.

60 Cited by Wright in Wright, 'International Law and Commercial Relations', at note 37.

61 Lauterpacht and Sands, *An International Bill of the Rights of Man*, p. 12.

62 Ibid., p. 39.

63 For a detailed discussion, see Philip A. Hamburger, 'Natural Rights, Natural Law, and American Constitutions' (1993) *Yale Law Journal* 907–960.

64 On the intent of the drafters see Chapter 2.

65 Jeremy Waldron, *The Right to Private Property* (Oxford: Clarendon Press, 1988).

on historical entitlements and those which are based on universal attributes of all human beings. Locke's labour theory of property, based on the idea that each human being owns the fruit of his/her labour as an extension of self-ownership, is an example of the first type of theory. Waldron sides with critics, noting that, aside from the theological underpinnings, Locke's view is unconvincing. The difficulties arise from the fact that private property rights are typically taken to confer on the holder the right to freely use and dispose of the property as he/she wishes and the right to exclude all others. Locke's examples are mostly drawn from the world of material, tangible objects such as physical resources and land which are typically finite. Private appropriation of a parcel of an originally 'common' piece of land (in the Lockean state of nature) will of necessity diminish the amount left to others. Over time, private enclosure of finite resources is bound to lead to exhaustion of the original commons. Locke's argument to address this problem is that appropriation must be consistent with the overriding right of everyone to life and subsistence, which is ultimately grounded in God's divine order. A modern variant, free of the theological underpinnings in Locke's theory, has been articulated by Nozick in his celebrated defence of private property in *Anarchy, State and Utopia.*[66] For Nozick, all rights ultimately flow from each individual's natural right to property. Nozick's right to property is not based on the individual's mixing of their labour with the object/land but on historical first use/appropriation.[67] Each individual has a natural right to make free use of whatever he/she has acquired legitimately. Unlike classical libertarians like Mill or Hayek, Nozick does not accept that social welfare or utility considerations could constrain or outweigh individual property rights.[68] As argued by Waldron, the main difficulty with the Lockean natural law account of property rights or Nozick's account is that it is simply unclear why the mixing of an individual's labour with an object/land or first occupancy/historical acquisition justifies individual appropriation and exclusive use, let alone the vesting of property rights on an individual's successors.

As property rights are liable to obstruct the social and economic well-being of others, their advocates rarely claim that the rights are absolute. For

[66] Robert Nozick, *Anarchy, State, and Utopia* (New York: Basic Books, Don Mills, Ontario; General Publishing, 1974).

[67] Onora O'Neil has argued that Nozick's account is broadly related to Locke's labour theory, but Waldron disputes her reading and argues that Nozick rejects it completely: Waldron, *The Right to Private Property*, p. 256.

[68] See further Alan Ryan, *Property and Political Theory* (New York: Blackwell, 1986).

instance, Nozick concedes that the owner of the only waterhole in a desert cannot charge what he/she will for its use.[69] More generally, property rights advocates concede that property has a social function which may justify State restrictions based on social or economic considerations. These could take the form of taxes or other interventions alluded to by Lauterpacht in his dismissal of natural law justifications of property rights as artificial. However, liberal property rights advocates do not typically ground individual rights in natural law. Instead, Hume,[70] Bentham,[71] Hayek[72] and others concur that individual rights and freedoms are created by positive law. In general, they argue that there is a connection between political freedom, market freedoms and the right of each individual to acquire, use and dispose of property as he/she wishes whilst also justifying private property instrumentally on the grounds that it maximizes public wealth and that 'giving people property rights in anything of value is the best way of ensuring that resources are used as efficiently as possible'.[73] What classical liberal theories and modern twentieth-century liberal economic variants of property rights thus share is a 'negative', political conception of individual freedom. In Alan Ryan's words, the liberal conception of property rights is 'political' in the sense that the State's primary role is conceptualized as protection of individual property[74] and non-interference with the individual's freedom to use the resources which he/she owns.[75] Hayek's depiction of central, State-led planning and regulation of economic life as 'The Road to Serfdom' most vividly encapsulates the political dimension of property rights as negative freedoms.[76] This enables us to pinpoint the main source of disagreement between Lauterpacht and advocates of (private) property rights.

69 In Nozick's case this is because of 'internal constraints to the theory of property and acquisition itself' or because the right to property is grounded on the right to life. Hayek relies on the necessity of the good in question to meet basic needs. See Plant's discussion in Raymond Plant, *Equality, Markets, and the State* (London: Fabian Society, 1984), pp. 104 ff.

70 'Those rules by which properties, rights and obligations are determined have in them no marks of a natural origin but many of artifice and contrivance . . . they are changeable by human laws: and have all of them a direct and evident tendency to public good.' Hume, *A Treatise of Human Nature*, p. 794.

71 Jeremy Bentham, 'Anarchical Fallacies' in Jeremy Waldron (ed.), *Nonsense upon Stilts: Bentham, Burke and Marx on the Rights of Man* (London: Methuen, 1987).

72 von Hayek, *The Road to Serfdom*.

73 See Ryan, *Property and Political Theory*, p. 106.

74 Ibid., p. 35.

75 Ibid., p. 36.

76 von Hayek, *The Road to Serfdom*.

1.4.1 *Personality, Freedom and Property*

In his seminal analysis of 'The Right to Private Property', Jeremy Waldron argues that Isaiah Berlin's celebrated exposition of the controversy over negative and positive freedoms 'confuses matters a bit in contrasting negative conceptions of liberty with a *single* ideal of positive liberty'.[77] Berlin's analysis, Waldron argues, overlooks the variety of 'positive' conceptions of freedom which concur that something more is required than the absence of obstacles, threats of sanctions or imposition of impediments for an individual to be truly free. Waldron draws on Hegel's positive conception of freedom, stripped of the metaphysics, to show that it is possible to justify rights to private property without committing oneself to the view that 'true freedom consists in the pursuit of collective purposes or in the life or projects of the community'.[78] Waldron's argument is particularly relevant to our discussion, partly because it provides an alternative to natural law justifications of private property and partly because Hegel's personality theory is commonly invoked as a justification for intellectual property rights.[79]

Waldron's theory starts from a rejection of utilitarian, consequentialist and interests-based justifications of private property which appeal to economic efficiency, welfare or well-being. Liberal and economic variants of property rights often claim to be 'rights-based' but typically allow for individual rights to be 'trumped' when they do not coincide with the maximization of general utility.[80] Waldron suggests that a genuine rights-based justification for private property can be derived from Hegel's personality theory as a necessary prerequisite for each individual human being to be truly free.[81] True freedom for an individual entails the individual being able to assert his/her goals and express his/her abilities and his/her knowledge and skills being recognized as such by others. What is necessary, says Waldron, is that each individual involved in a project must see himself/herself as

77 Waldron, *The Right to Private Property*, p. 299.

78 Ibid., p. 313.

79 For an overview of theories of IP, see Peter Drahos, *A Philosophy of Intellectual Property* (London: Routledge, 2016).

80 Waldron also argues that first occupancy theories/possession are typically reliant on general utilitarian considerations in Waldron, *The Right to Private Property*, chapter 8.

81 Following Raz's approach, Waldron starts from the premise that a justification of private property is *rights* based if 'it takes some individual's interest (or the interest of some or all individuals severally) as a sufficient justification for holding others (usually governments) to be under a duty to create, secure, maintain, or respect an institution of private property' in Waldron, *The Right to Private Property*, p. 87.

> participating in the *willing, planning, and controlling* aspect of the enterprise; rather than merely being harnessed to somebody else' or to a group's appropriative enterprise as though he were merely natural force, like a bit of burden or like water-power.[82]

Private property is necessary because individuals 'need to "embody" their personalities in external objects' to be recognized by others as free persons. This is because an individual's self-consciousness and personality are only manifested and recognized by others through the individual's activities and 'shaping' of external objects. The 'shaping' of an object, the working of land and the carving of a chair are forms of 'active possession' which signify ownership of the object. In civil society, the individual can use, exchange or sell his/her products to others and secure mutually beneficial arrangements by means of contracts. In this way, Waldron suggests, Hegel's theory justifies a system of private property rights which assigns exclusive rights of use to the individual on the grounds that it is only through owning and controlling property that the individual can manifest/embody his/her free will and be recognized as a free subject by others.[83] Without exclusive use and control of the objects which they have 'shaped', individuals would be unable to develop their personalities and achieve full realization of their capacities as free agents.

There are some difficulties with Hegel's thesis which are highlighted by Waldron. If private property is necessary for true freedom and personal self-realization, then poverty becomes a matter of grave concern because a propertyless person can never be truly free.[84] In Waldron's view, Hegel doesn't address this point adequately. Waldron acknowledges that Hegel expressed concerns about poverty. The depth of material hardship and spiritual degradation to which the poor would descend, Hegel thought, was evident in Victorian urban England. Hegel argued that the logic of the unrestrained operation of a free market is to create structural unemployment and the 'cancer' of poverty at the heart of civil society.[85] Thus, private property would have to be transcended for the individual to achieve true freedom. The acquisition and exchange of private property, originally directed at fulfilling the individual's interests, would necessarily accelerate competition, division of labour, alienation, inequality and ultimately lead to mass unemployment in industrially advanced capitalist societies. Hegel's answer to the scourge of

82 Waldron, *The Right to Private Property*, p. 302.

83 Ibid., p. 375.

84 Ibid., p. 378.

85 For an overview of Hegel's theory, see Stephen Houlgate, *An Introduction to Hegel: Freedom, Truth, and History*, 2nd ed. (Malden, MA: Blackwell, 2005).

poverty was that the pursuit of private interests needed to be interwoven with the pursuit of the common good for each person to be free. If poverty was to be minimized and contained in a system based on private property and free enterprise, it would be necessary for the State to introduce controls not only to assure fair competition but also to regulate the distribution and amount of competition. For Waldron, this misses the point that if private property is something that all individuals need for self-realization, then, in Hegel's words, everyone must have property.[86] Private property as a right that everyone has, much in the same way as the right to freedom of expression, is not something contingently acquired but is part and parcel of respect for persons as free moral agents.[87] For Waldron, the radical implication of the view that private property is required for development of the human personality is that property is something that every human person must have. If true freedom requires private property, then the opportunity to acquire resources will not be sufficient. Actual ownership of at least a minimum of resources is required. Hence, there are important practical distributive implications that follow from the idea of private property as a right.[88]

The value of Waldron's analysis of the right to private property is that it articulates a convincing rationale for the view that private property is a right grounded in the requirements for development of the human personality and human freedom. Needless to say, none of the theories discussed in this chapter were expressly alluded to by the politicians and lawyers involved in the drafting of the ECHR. However, as will be seen in Chapter 2, advocates of the inclusion of property rights in the ECHR did talk about the importance of protecting home, land and personal possessions. In looking at the theoretical justifications for international human rights and the right to property, this chapter aimed to illuminate and provide a deeper understanding of the principled foundations of the ECHR. Chapter 2 retraces the drafting history of the right to property in the ECHR.

[86] Waldron, *The Right to Private Property*, p. 419.

[87] Ibid., p. 444.

[88] These are briefly sketched out in the last few pages of Waldron, *The Right to Private Property*.

2

First Protocol

Drafting History

INTRODUCTION

Article 1 of the First Protocol (A1P1) to the European Convention on Human Rights (ECHR) provides that every natural and legal person has a right to enjoyment of their possessions. The meaning of the text is anything but straightforward. There is no mention of companies, but in common and civil law jurisdictions there is no doubt that companies are 'legal persons' ('personnes morales'). Neither is the term 'property' used. Instead, the French version uses the term 'biens', whilst the English version uses the word 'possessions'. Nor does the English text proclaim a right to own property but mentions instead 'enjoyment' or use of possessions. Yet it is well established in the jurisprudence of the European Court of Human Rights (ECtHR) that A1P1 protects property rights and that companies have standing to launch claims as victims of violations of their right to property. Why was this not made unambiguously clear by the drafters? And why would a human rights treaty include companies as victims of violations of human rights? One view which has gathered support in the last fifteen years is that the Convention discloses a unique, sui-generis European liberal vision of human rights which necessitates protection of companies as subjects of fundamental rights. An alternative view defended in this chapter is that the inclusion of companies in the Convention represents a dissonant break with the moral ethos of international human rights and that, far from being logically necessitated, the inclusion of companies was the outcome of a contingent political compromise.

This chapter retraces the drafting history of the text of A1P1. It shows that States' delegates at the Council of Europe were unclear about the precise meaning and implications of the formula. Their assent was secured on the understanding that the aim was to entrench the 'sacred' right of each human person to protection of their home and personal belongings. The analysis reveals that the elusive terminology was introduced by lawyers overseeing the draft and that other lawyers who had misgivings about the language relented. They were swept along by a common feeling that, despite its weaknesses, the Convention represented a remarkable, revolutionary turn in international law, enabling individuals to secure enforcement of their rights in an international court. Hitherto, the existing scholarship on the origins and rationale of A1P1 had overseen the close interconnection between the wording of the Article on rights of petition and the wording of the Article on property rights. Section 2.3 shows that the original Article on rights of petition proposed by the Council of Europe's Consultative Assembly included corporate bodies, even though the basic list of substantive rights protected was meant to reflect the rights of each individual human person in the Universal Declaration of Human Rights (UDHR). Section 2.4 shows how the Article on property rights became a vehicle for the Assembly's reintroduction of corporate/legal persons in the text of the Convention after the Committee of Ministers deleted corporate bodies from the Assembly's Article on rights of petition. Overall, the chapter illuminates the enduring legacy of the vision of a liberal, economic European order shared by the lawyers in charge of drafting both Articles in the Assembly who succeeded in importing these extraneous values into the moral ethos of universal human rights.

2.1 THE AIMS OF THE CONVENTION

2.1.1 *The Statute of the Council of Europe*

The Council of Europe was created to secure peace and achieve greater unity between its members 'by agreements and common action in economic, social, cultural, scientific, legal and administrative matters and in the maintenance and further realization of human rights and fundamental freedoms'.[1] As indicated in the Statute, it was originally envisaged that the Council could play a significant role in European harmonization of economic and social policies through its organs, namely a deliberative Consultative Assembly and an executive Council of Ministers. In his landmark study of the ECHR, Simpson notes that when the Council of Europe institutions began to function on 5 May 1949, the Consultative Assembly went through an initial phase of adopting a plethora of recommendations, proposals and resolutions in all

[1] Statute of the Council of Europe, London, 5.V.1949, Article 1(b).

fields of policy (economic, social, cultural, political, defence and security) alongside recommendations to amend the Statute to enlarge the Council of Europe's remit.[2] These proposals had no prospect of leading to any practical change without the consent of the Council of Ministers, and many of them were outside the remit of the Council of Europe. For instance, the Committee of Ministers highlighted that the Assembly's recommendations relative to the creation of a European army fell outside the scope of the Council of Europe.[3] Barely a year into the meetings, the Assembly's own standing committee rebuked it for the avalanche of what it perceived as ill-thought through, duplicated or overlapping suggestions which could not realistically be considered, let alone implemented.[4] Unlike most of the Assembly's recommendations, which were ignored or dismissed by the Council of Ministers, the Assembly succeeded in pressing ministers for the adoption of a European Convention on Human Rights coupled with the creation of a supranational court with the power to hear complaints of violations of human rights against member States. In retrospect, it turned out to be the Assembly's most significant achievement as the pursuit of social and economic European unity would be undertaken instead under the auspices of the European Economic Community (EEC) in 1956. However, the liberal ideals of political *and* economic European integration which had spurred the creation of the Council of Europe left a lasting imprint on the text of the ECHR. As shown in the rest of this chapter, the legacy is evident in the evolution of the substantive content of the Articles on rights of petition and property rights which ultimately secured the delegates' assent. The deep intersection between the two Articles is reflected in two ways in the evolution of the texts. Firstly, it is reflected in the identification of the subject of the substantive rights. Secondly, it is reflected in the identification of those vested with rights of petition to enforce the right. The evolution of the texts retraced and analysed below shows pervasive problems of definition, ambiguities and a disconnect between the drafters' moral ambition of securing protection of each human person's right to own property and the addition of 'legal persons' in the final iterations of the text.

2 See A. W. Brian Simpson, *Human Rights and the End of Empire: Britain and the Genesis of the European Convention* (Oxford: Oxford University Press, 2004) and Walter Lipgens and Wilfried Loth, *Vol 4 Transnational Organizations of Political Parties and Pressure Groups in the Struggle for European Union, 1945–1950: (Including 129 Documents in Their Original Languages on 3 Microfiches)* (Berlin, Boston: De Gruyter, 1991).

3 Ibid. (Lipgens), Doc. 136, p. 1132.

4 Ibid. (Lipgens), Doc. 137, p. 1133.

2.2 THE ORIGINAL TEMPLATE

2.2.1 *A Convention to Protect Human Rights or Economic Freedoms?*

Ahead of the First Session of the Council of Europe's Consultative Assembly (thereafter the 'Assembly') from 10 August to 8 September 1949, the Council of Ministers was sent 'unofficially and discreetly' a template draft for a European Convention on Human Rights.[5] The template had originally been prepared by the Judicial Committee of the European Movement (EM) under the leadership of Pierre-Henry Teitgen as Chair and David Maxwell-Fyfe as Rapporteur.[6] The two men were eminent jurists. They swapped roles at the Council of Europe's Legal Affairs Committee. The original EM text envisaged that the contracting States would be under a legal obligation to guarantee the right to 'freedom from arbitrary deprivation of property'.[7] It also contained a separate article on rights of petition which expressly envisaged that 'Any State a party to this Convention and *any natural or corporate person* in the territory of any such State, shall have the right to petition the Council of Europe in respect of any infringement of Part I of this Convention' (italics added).[8] The EM's draft became the template for the elaboration of the text of the Council of Europe's Convention on Human Rights by the Assembly under the auspices of Maxwell-Fyfe and Teitgen.

The Committee of Ministers, which controlled the Assembly's Agenda, originally rejected the Assembly's proposal to include human rights as a priority in the Agenda of the First Session of the Assembly. It relented under pressure from a letter signed by Winston Churchill, Maxwell-Fyfe and Teitgen. The letter drew attention to Article 3 of the Council of Europe's Statute's goal of achieving maintenance and further realization of human rights. The ministers had been divided. Ernest Bevin (UK) thought that the Assembly should be invited to define human rights before considering issues of enforcement. Robert Schuman (France) disagreed on the need to address definitional issues. In his view, definitional questions had already received considerable attention at the UN and there was a risk of two Declarations being issued (one universal, one European) which was clearly undesirable.[9] As a compromise, the Committee of Ministers approved the inclusion of

5 Council of Europe, *Collected Edition of the 'Travaux Préparatoires' of the European Convention on Human Rights*, 8 vols. (The Hague: Martinus Nijhoff, 1975), Vol. I, p. 296.

6 Ibid.

7 Ibid. Vol. I, Article 1.k.

8 Ibid., Vol. I, Part II, Article 7.a.

9 Ibid., Vol. I, p. 24, 5th meeting – 13 August 1949.

human rights in the Assembly's Agenda whilst expressing the hope that consideration would be given to issues of definition.[10]

2.2.2 *Whose Rights: Human Persons or Corporations?*

The Assembly, under the steer of Maxwell-Fyfe and Teitgen, had a different idea from the Council of Ministers on the Council of Europe's priorities: in their view, the priority was not definitional questions but the creation of a supranational court to enforce the Convention. At the Assembly's meeting of 19 August 1949, Teitgen and Maxwell-Fyfe took the lead in putting forward a joint proposal to be addressed to the Council of Ministers. The proposal was presented as giving rise to obligations arising from what they described as the principles of 'collective responsibility' and 'collective guarantee' in Article 1 of the Statute. There were no such obligations directly expressed in Article 1 and certainly nothing close to Teitgen and Maxwell-Fyfe's proposal that 'a European Commission of Human Rights and a European Court of Human Rights' should be set up for the purpose of ensuring observance of the Convention. This time, Churchill was not amongst the signatories. However, Churchill had previously said that, once the foundations of European human rights had been agreed 'on the lines of the decisions of the United Nations' (but, he trusted, in a much shorter form) 'we hope that a European Court might be set up'.[11] Churchill took it for granted that the jurisdiction of the Court would be optional and that the Court would not have the power to order sanctions against Member States.[12] By contrast, Maxwell-Fyfe and Teitgen's proposal went far beyond in seeking to establish a supranational court with compulsory jurisdiction.

In defence of the motion, Teitgen delivered an impassioned speech to the Assembly in which individual human rights, fundamental rights and economic freedoms all figured interchangeably. Europe was a land of freedom, said Teitgen, but freedom was in danger, not only from the 'scourges' of fascism, Hitlerism and communism but also from 'the economic and social conditions of the modern world'.[13] Freedom, Teitgen continued, implied liberalism, 'but the excesses of freedom of money, competition and profit threatened the crushing of the weak by the strong, leading some poor creatures to renounce their freedom'.[14] European democracies had to resist the

[10] Ibid., Vol. I, p. 26.
[11] Ibid., Vol. I, p. 34.
[12] Ibid.
[13] Ibid., Vol. I, p. 40.
[14] Ibid., Vol. I, p. 42.

temptation to secure social justice by renouncing freedom. In an ideal world, a complete list of all individual freedoms and rights, including the so-called social freedoms, was desirable. But this would take years to achieve. The urgent priority was to draw up a list of seven, eight or ten fundamental freedoms essential to a democratic way of life which could be sanctioned by the contracting States in a very short time and 'would be safeguarded by the Court of Justice'.[15] The problem, said Teitgen, was very simple. In signing the Statute of the Council of Europe, all States had bound themselves 'to respect the fundamental rights of the individual'.[16] This could only be done by a collective effort to 'immediately accept a common definition of these freedoms' and 'the creation of a guaranteeing organ, namely a European Court of Human Rights and a European Commission'.[17] The Commission would act as a filter to screen out frivolous petitions. Rights of petition would be enjoyed by 'Member States of the Council of Europe, *all corporate bodies and all individuals*'.[18] The elements of the proposals had been set out by the Legal Committee of the EM in a draft Convention which Teitgen said he had discreetly sent to the ministers and was now shared with the Assembly. Teitgen concluded his intervention with an emotional reference to his incarceration by the Gestapo and the death and internment of relatives at Buchenwald at the gate of which was the outrageous inscription 'Just, or Unjust, the Fatherland'. Henceforth, Teitgen said, all were agreed that there would only be *just* Fatherlands.[19]

The debates that followed reflected the blur in Teitgen's address between individual human rights and economic freedoms. On one view, the Convention was to be an expression of the foundational, moral values on which European unity would be built. On another view, the Convention was to express a liberal economic vision of European integration. The language of 'fundamental freedoms' traversed both visions and had very different meanings depending on whether the freedom in question related to the autonomy and dignity of the individual human person or whether it meant instead freedom of enterprise and market freedoms. The first implied, inter alia, that each individual human being should be free from torture and discrimination (religious and political). The second implied instead that corporate bodies and companies would have the freedom to operate in a European-wide market without State or trade restrictions. The first conception was the moral

15 Ibid., Vol. I, p. 44.
16 Ibid., Vol. I, pp. 48–49.
17 Ibid.
18 Ibid., Vol. I, p. 48.
19 Ibid., Vol. I, p. 50.

vision of human rights discussed in Chapter 1 and expressed in the UDHR. On that vision, the aim of the Convention would be to entrench protection of the rights required to enable full development of each individual human's personality. Only individual human beings would qualify as victims of violations of human rights and only natural, human persons would enjoy rights of petition to the Court in respect of violations of their human rights.

The alternative, liberal-economic vision of a united Europe founded on market freedoms was the vision pursued by Federalists in the EM, in which Teitgen and Maxwell-Fyfe had played a leading role.[20] Its practical implementation envisaged supranational judicial protection of corporations' freedom to invest and transfer property and capital cross-borders. In truth, a Convention on human rights based on the UDHR was not the appropriate legal framework to give effect to the EM's liberal vision of European political and economic integration. The two visions, moral and economic, were conceptually distinct. Their foundations had different normative implications for the substantive content of the enumerated rights and for the categorization of the victims of human rights who would have standing to secure enforcement of their rights in an ECtHR. The differences inevitably found expression in the formulation of the Convention's Article on property rights and in the Article on rights of petition to the Court. Whose property was the Convention to protect? Each individual human being's home and personal possessions or corporations' cross-border investments and capital? The delineation of property rights and rights of petition clearly depended on the answer. The EM's inclusion of corporate bodies in the Article on rights of petition effectively imported protection of economic freedoms into a Convention purportedly directed at protection of the fundamental human rights of individual human persons.

The delegates' response to Teitgen's address further illustrates the conflation of human rights and economic freedoms. Some delegates who had experienced the 'horrors of dictatorship' and 'wallowed in blood and filth' unequivocally asserted that the Convention should defend '. . .mankind's most precious possession, the 'freedom and the dignity of the human person", which they thought should be enforced by a Court with powers of sanction.[21] Others who concurred added that since the definition of human rights was already found in the Universal Declaration and in national constitutions, the time had come to take practical steps to secure enforcement. Yet, they went on to claim that rights of access to the Court should be enjoyed not only by

[20] See Simpson, *Human Rights and the End of Empire*.

[21] Council of Europe, *Collected Edition of the 'Travaux Préparatoires' of the European Convention on Human Rights*, Vol. I, pp. 62 and 64.

individuals but also by 'corporate bodies' without further explanation and without adverting to the incongruity of a Convention directed at protecting the dignity of the human person extending rights of petition to corporations.[22] Several doubted the value of adopting an abstract list of rights and feared their misapplication by a Court, citing the US Supreme Court's construction of the US Constitution as precluding State regulation of 'monster trusts'.[23] Fayat (Belgium) agreed and thought there was no need for a supranational court to protect fundamental freedoms as these freedoms were already protected in democratic national systems, including States without a written constitution.[24] Others were 'not thrilled' at the prospect of appointing a Commission and a Court to enforce abstract rights which have 'a thousand and one interpretation' and 'a thousand and one meanings'.[25] There was an evident political flavour to the debates. Those seeking more precise definitions of the enumerated rights, along others at the UN, were accused of following a 'more or less Marxist dialectic'.[26] One delegate suggested that if the Council of Europe wanted to make a real practical difference, instead of debating ideal abstract principles, its priority should be to address the misery of '600,000 to 700,000 European displaced persons and the 60,000 mutilated, invalids left in the concentration camps who had been deprived of almost all their freedom and rights'.[27] That route was not taken. Instead, the Assembly agreed to mandate the Assembly's Legal Affairs Committee to consider proposals for the adoption of a European Convention on Human Rights and its enforcement by a Court. The Committee was to report back to the Assembly with proposals for deliberation and approval before being remitted to the Council of Ministers.

2.3 RIGHTS OF PETITION

In advance of the first sitting of the Assembly's Legal Affairs Committee, Maxwell-Fyfe had asked Teitgen to draw up a questionnaire with a series of questions for consideration by the Committee. In response, in a letter dated 22 August 1949,

[22] Ibid., Vol. I, p. 74. Dominedo (Italy) distinguished substantive human rights, based on natural law which had already found legal expression in the UDHR and procedural questions relating to the implementation of the rights by a supranational institution, which undoubtedly required a transfer of States sovereignty. In his view, this was necessary to give effect to the rights. In order to work effectively, he added, access to court must be available to 'individuals and corporate bodies'.

[23] Ibid., Vol. I, p. 80 (Ungoed-Thomas).

[24] Ibid., Vol. I, p. 89.

[25] Ibid., Vol. I, p. 79 (Nally (UK)).

[26] Ibid., Vol. I, p. 94 (Foster (UK)).

[27] Ibid., Vol. I, p. 98 (Vallee de la Poussin).

Teitgen said that he had identified a 'list of guaranteed liberties' for possible inclusion in a European Convention on Human Rights.[28] The enumerated list included eleven substantive freedoms which were almost identical to the list in the EM's draft Convention.[29] The language of 'freedoms' without a specified subject was different from the language of the UDHR which begins with the proclamation that all human beings are born free and equal and then declares that 'everyone has a right to' or 'no one shall be . . .' By contrast, the proposed list of guaranteed freedoms was phrased as follows with the EM's list added in italics:

I. Security of the person (*security of life and limb*)
II. Immunity from arrest (*freedom from arbitrary unrest, detention and exile*)
III. Exemption from slavery (*freedom from slavery and servitude and from compulsory labour of a discriminatory kind*)
IV. Freedom of speech (*freedom of speech and of expression of opinion generally*)
V. Freedom of religious practice (*freedom of religious belief, practice and teaching*)
VI. Freedom of association and meeting (*freedom of association and assembly*)
VII. Natural rights appertaining to marriage, paternity and the family (*natural rights deriving from marriage and paternity and those pertaining to the family*)
VIII. Inviolability of domicile (*sanctity of the home*)
IX. Equality before the law – DITTO
X. Protection against all discrimination based on religion, race, national origin, profession of political opinion or other opinion (*freedom from discrimination on account of religion, race, national origin or political or other opinion*)
XI. Protection against arbitrary confiscation of property (*freedom from arbitrary deprivation of property*).[30]

If these freedoms were accepted, said Teitgen, the next question was whether a 'collective guarantee of fundamental rights should be backed by a Court of

[28] Ibid., Vol. I, p. 160.
[29] Draft European Convention on Human Rights, Vol. I, p. 296.
[30] Council of Europe, *Collected Edition of the 'Travaux Préparatoires' of the European Convention on Human Rights*, Vol. I, p. 160. Teitgen also asked whether the Committee should consider whether MS should bind themselves to hold elections at reasonable intervals and not to hinder 'the right of criticism and the right to organise a political opposition'. The corresponding articles in the EM draft were Article k. 2(a) and (b).

Justice instituted by and functioning within the Council of Europe'.[31] In the affirmative, the next question was:

> Who may appeal to the Court when a guaranteed right or liberty has been violated? Each one of the Member States? Corporate Bodies/personnes morales? Minorities? Individuals/personnes physiques?[32]

The Legal Committee met and considered these questions for six days from 25 August to 2 September 1949.[33] The Committee was chaired by Maxwell-Fyfe. The members included, inter alia, Lord Layton (Liberal, UK), Henri Rolin (Socialist, Belgium) and Ungoed-Thomas (Labour, UK). Pierre-Henri Teitgen, as Rapporteur, delivered the report of the committee's deliberations to the Assembly on 5 September 1949.

2.3.1 *Individuals, Collective and Corporate Bodies*

On the substantive rights, the Committee agreed unanimously that the rights guaranteed should be 'the principal human rights referred to in the *Universal Declaration of Human Rights* adopted by the UN'.[34] The reasons, Teitgen explained, were twofold. First, the Committee wished to demonstrate the technical and moral authority of this document and its worldwide significance. In addition, the Committee wanted 'to avoid making a distinction between European and world order'.[35] However, the Committee decided to leave out for the time being the social and economic rights in the UDHR and to limit the list to rights and essential freedoms 'which are practised, after long usage and experience in all the democratic societies'.[36] Everyone, said Teitgen, would understand that it was necessary to guarantee first 'political democracy in the European Union and then co-ordinate our economies, before undertaking the generalisation of social democracy'.[37] Teitgen then listed the rights identified by the Committee, including 'the right to own property, in accordance with Article 17 UDHR'.[38] At that stage there was no mention of corporate persons, corporate bodies or legal persons

[31] Ibid., Vol. I, p. 162.
[32] Ibid.
[33] Ibid., Vol. I, pp. 162–192. Teitgen's report to the Assembly was delivered on 5 September 1949 (pp. 192 ff).
[34] Ibid., Vol. I, p. 166.
[35] Ibid., Vol. I, p. 268.
[36] Ibid., Vol. I, p. 266.
[37] Ibid.
[38] Ibid., Vol. I, p. 230. Article 12 of Committee's Draft.

in the right to own property. The other rights included in the list were expressed in the language of *freedoms* rather than *rights*, although they expressly referred to their counterparts in the UDHR. For instance, security of the person was to be in accordance with Articles 3, 5 and 8 of the UDHR, and freedom of opinion and expression was to be in accordance with Article 19 of the UDHR. The more perplexing, dissonant note came from Article 7.a) on rights of petition which proposed that 'any person or corporate body' ('personne morale' in French) would have rights of petition.[39] If the rights protected in a European Convention were to reflect the rights contained in the UDHR, and the purpose of adopting a European Convention was to create an enforcement machinery for these rights, what was the rationale for corporate persons/bodies being granted rights of petition? The records of the Committee's deliberations give no indication of the rationale. Instead, the main controversy over the clause on rights of petition centred on the proposed creation of a supranational Court with the power to hear individual complaints against contracting States. As shown in Chapter 3, such a development was considered revolutionary in international law at the time, as a political and constitutional encroachment on State sovereignty. In addition, a European Court was seen as a potential competitor to the International Court of Justice (ICJ) at The Hague whose competence at the time was to hear inter-State complaints only.[40] Critics worried that States would be answerable to politically motivated individuals in an international court and that the Court itself could politically interfere with legislation adopted by States, particularly in relation to controls on property rights.[41] Thus, the critics' strategy was to focus on amendments which rejected the creation of a Court altogether (unsuccessfully as it turned out) or which limited the competence and powers of the Court and the filtering role of an intermediary Commission.[42] This is borne out in the debates which typically refer to the powers enjoyed by an undefined 'victim', 'aggrieved victim', 'individual' or 'any person' to bring a complaint against a State, whilst eluding the

39 Ibid., Vol. I, p. 298.

40 See Chapter 3.

41 These questions also formed the focus of discussions by the Committee of Ministers and their representatives – see Conference of Senior Officials (8–17 June 1950), Council of Europe, *Collected Edition of the 'Travaux Préparatoires' of the European Convention on Human Rights*, Vol. IV.

42 In the Committee of Ministers members' meetings of 2 to 8 February 1950, States opposed to the creation of a European Court of Human Rights were Luxembourg, Norway, Denmark, Turkey, Greece and the UK. The minority in favour were France, Italy, Belgium and Ireland. Ibid., Vol. III, p. 268.

question of why corporate bodies should have been granted rights of petition in Teitgen's proposed text.[43]

For instance, at the sitting of the Legal Affairs Committee on 1 September 1949, the Belgian socialist politician and eminent jurist Henri Rolin, who was opposed to the creation of a European Court, asked whether the committee was of the opinion that 'the individual should be entitled to address a claim to an international organization (Court or committee)'[44] and whether 'the individual, after exhaustion of local remedies should be allowed to present and discuss his claim before a Committee of Investigation though his legal representative'.[45] The minutes of the meeting show that a motion that 'any aggrieved person' should be entitled to submit a claim to an international organization, court or committee was approved by 13 ayes, 6 noes and 3 abstentions.[46] Another motion stated that 'any person after exhaustion of remedies should be allowed to present a claim to a committee' secured 14 ayes, 7 noes and 1 abstention. Both motions used the French term 'individu' rather than 'personne morale', the French for 'corporate bodies'.[47]

Yet the compromise text on rights of petition proposed by the Committee to the Assembly envisaged that 'any person or corporate body'/'personne morale' would have rights of petition:

> After all other means of redress within a State have been tried, any person, or corporate body, which claims to have been a victim of a violation of the Convention by one of the signatory States may petition the Commission in a request presented through legal channels.[48]

In his report to the Assembly, Teitgen did not explain the inclusion of corporate bodies but used obfuscating language instead,[49] stating that the Committee had deliberated on whether 'the injured person' (which he referred to interchangeably as 'victim', 'individual person' or 'corporate body') or 'a society or association' could bring a complaint directly to a Commission or Court.[50] If the complaint could be brought by the victim, he said, then a

43 The French term for 'individual' is 'individu' or 'particulier' rather than 'personne morale' used for the English 'corporation' or 'legal person'.

44 Council of Europe, *Collected Edition of the 'Travaux Préparatoires' of the European Convention on Human Rights*, Vol. I, p. 184.

45 Ibid.

46 Ibid., Vol. I, pp. 184 ff, Doc A. 259.

47 Ibid.

48 Ibid., Vol. I, Section III, Article 12, p. 210.

49 Ibid., Vol. I, p. 202. Sittings of the Assembly held from 5 to 8 September 1949, Ordinary Session, 5 September 1949.

50 Ibid., Vol. I, p. 286. The French version refers to 'personne physique ou personne morale' or 'simple particulier, ou societe, ou association'.

different Court from The Hague had to be created since the latter had no jurisdiction to hear individual complaints. Since the Committee agreed (by a majority) that victims of violations should be able to enjoy a direct right of petition, a novel international court would need to be created. He didn't explain, nor was he pressed on, the Committee's justifications for including corporate bodies.

In the debate that followed, there was no discussion of *who* should be granted rights of petition. Instead, the focus was on the implications for State sovereignty of the creation of a supranational Court with the power to hear complaints brought by individual victims of alleged violations. Ungoed-Thomas (UK) was one of the strongest critics opposing the creation of a European Court with jurisdiction to hear petitions from individuals against Member States.[51] He argued that 'we are not a federation here . . . we have no federal constitution'.[52] In his view, for a court to decide that the legislature and democratically elected government of a Country has violated any of the rights would be 'the most anti-democratic procedure that we could possibly conceive'.[53] He enjoined the other members of the assembly to look at what happened in the United States where the seemingly harmless provision that no person shall be deprived of life, liberty or property without due process of law was relied upon by the USSC to prevent States from taking action against monstrous trusts.[54] In his view, only States should be allowed to raise complaints/petition the Commission/Court.

Teitgen objected strongly to the comparison. The USSC, he said, had been able to strike down laws in the field of social and economic rights because its competence extended to ascertaining the compatibility of such laws with the US Constitution and in so doing 'give rise to what has been called the Government of judges'. By contrast, Teitgen asked, 'When a court is given competence to ensure only that States should respect *personal* security, freedom from slavery, freedom from arbitrary arrest, freedom of thought and conscience, freedom of assembly and association, do you really think that this Court is being given powers which would permit it to interfere in the economic policy of a State?'[55] Teitgen's reply was somewhat disingenuous. If the jurisdiction of the court related to *personal* civil rights, why did the Committee's Draft Convention contain an article on rights of petition which

51 Ibid., Vol. II, pp. 14 ff. Eighteenth Sitting of Consultative Assembly, Official report of the sitting.
52 Ibid., Vol. II, pp. 166–168.
53 Ibid., Vol. II, p. 168.
54 Ibid.
55 Ibid., Vol. I, pp. 178–180.

included corporate bodies? This question was not put to Teitgen. Instead, an amendment was put forward to delete the Article on rights of petition altogether. The movers were Ungoed-Thomas, Rolin, Lord Layton, Elmgren and Edberg. The proposal was unsuccessful. The amendment was cancelled as inappropriate, although it is not clear why.[56]

2.3.2 *Any Person, Non-Governmental Organizations and Groups of Individuals*

The draft Convention as approved by the Assembly was sent to the Committee of Ministers for their approval. The draft did not include the Article on property rights which had proved too controversial and had been remitted to the Assembly's Legal Committee for further consideration. As shown in Section 2.4, an alternative text on property rights in which the Legal Committee attributed the rights not only to natural persons but also to 'legal persons' was later adopted. Meanwhile, the text remitted to the Ministers contained the Article on rights of petition by 'any person or corporate body'.

The ministers referred the Assembly's draft to a committee of representative experts. The majority of representatives was initially opposed to the creation of a Court with compulsory jurisdiction and insisted that 'it was never proper for an individual to refer to the Court. The interests of the individuals would always be defended either by the Commission or … by a State'.[57] The Committee submitted two alternative proposals on rights of petition.[58] Under the first proposal, only States would have the power to refer individual claims to a Commission. The second proposal was a variation of the Assembly's Article 12 with corporate bodies removed and NGOs or any group of individuals added. The revised Article provided that

> Any person, any non-governmental organisation, or any group of individuals, which claims to be the victim of a violation by one of the High Contracting Parties of the rights secured by the Convention may petition the Commission.[59]

The committee stated that the rationale for the change was to give 'a wider definition of those bodies, other than individual persons, who will be qualified to petition the Commission' so as 'not to exclude any person or group of

[56] Ibid., Vol. I, p. 254.
[57] Ibid., Vol. III, p. 276.
[58] Ibid., Vol. IV, pp. 50 ff. Annex to the Report of the Committee of Experts on Human Rights: Draft Convention of Protection of Human Rights and Individual Freedoms of 16 March 1950.
[59] Ibid., Vol. IV, pp. 2 ff. Report to the Committee of Ministers, 16 March 1950.

persons from right of access to the Commission'.[60] In truth, 'corporate bodies' did not fall readily within the definition of NGOs or groups of individuals. Their inclusion was not explained either but suggested a likely different rationale from the inclusion of corporations.[61] The Committee's focus away from corporate bodies/companies was reinforced by its recommendation that instead of enumerating the list of rights by reference to the UDHR as the Assembly had done, the wording of the Universal Declaration should be included in the text of the Convention itself and scrupulously adhered to.[62] The implication was that neither corporate bodies nor companies could be subjects of human rights in the Convention nor, therefore, could they enjoy rights of petition as victims of violations of human rights.

The question of who could enjoy rights of petition as victims of violations of human rights was then lost in the intense controversy which arose about the jurisdiction of the Commission and Court empowered to hear the victims' claims. It was the creation of a Court with compulsory jurisdiction which took centre stage in the debates. The Committee thought that the creation of a supranational Court was a political decision which fell on the ministers. The ministers appointed a Conference of High Officials to lay the ground for the political decision.

The Report of the Conference of Senior Officials (8–17 June 1950) Right of Petition records that the majority of countries were opposed to the creation of a supranational court with compulsory jurisdiction.[63] However, nine countries out of twelve agreed that 'individuals should have the right to bring cases directly before the Commission of Human Rights, in accordance with the Proposal of the Assembly' subject to the consent of contracting States.[64] These countries were Belgium, Denmark, France, Ireland, Italy, Luxembourg, Norway, Sweden and Turkey. The French text uses the term 'particuliers'. Delegates considered that 'since it was a question of protecting the rights of individuals (le droit des individus) it was necessary to provide individuals with the possibility of safeguarding their rights by direct means'.[65] Those opposed (Greece, the Netherlands and the UK) feared that the right of petition could be easily abused by ideologically motivated groups for propaganda purposes. Similarly, in the ministers' deliberations on the right of individual petition, all

60 Ibid., Vol. IV, p. 38.
61 See Chapter 3 on Legal Personality.
62 Council of Europe, *Collected Edition of the 'Travaux Préparatoires' of the European Convention on Human Rights*, Vol. IV, p. 24.
63 Ibid., Vol. IV, pp. 252 ff.
64 Ibid., Vol. IV, p. 252.
65 Ibid., Vol. IV, p. 254.

the references are to 'individuals' ('individus'/'particuliers' in French). The outcome of the ministers' deliberations was an addition to the Article proposed by the Committee of Experts whereby States agreed not to hinder in any way the effective exercise of this right. The agreed text sent to the Assembly provided that

> Any person, non-governmental organisation or any group of individuals, which claims to be the victim of a violation by one of the High Contracting Parties of the rights secured by the Convention may petition the Commission in an application addressed to the Secretary-General of the Council of Europe. The High Contracting Parties undertake not to hinder in any way the effective exercise of this right. (Article 23)

The Draft Convention agreed by the Conference of High Officials was annexed to the report and sent to the Assembly.[66] The Assembly's Legal Affairs Committee met on 23 and 24 June 1950, chaired by Maxwell-Fyfe.[67] The discussion of Article 23 on Rights of Petition, summed up by the Chair, states that after considerable discussion between Rolin, Bastid, Persico, Azara, Pernot and McEntee, the committee had agreed to stress:

- The importance it attached of granting to individuals/individus the right to seek a remedy directly as an interested party.
- Its wish that the 'right of petition' should be retained but that the term should be changed and replaced by some such phrase as 'right of individual appeal' (droit de reclamation individuel ou de recours individuel).
- Its wish that Article 12 of the Assembly's recommendation should be retained 'after all means of redress within a State have been tried, any person or corporate body which claims to have been the victim of a violation of the Convention by one of the signatory States, may petition the Commission in a *request presented through legal channels*'. (italics added)

Following this meeting, Maxwell-Fyfe, as chair of Assembly's Legal Affairs Committee, sent a letter detailing these observations to the Chair of the Committee of Ministers.[68]

Whilst the Assembly insisted on the maintenance of their proposed formulation, ministers redoubled their opposition to rights of petition. At the

66 Ibid., Vol. IV, p. 274.
67 Ibid., Vol. V. Minutes of the Meeting of 23 June 1950.
68 Ibid., Vol. V, p.194. Letter dated 24 June 1950 from Sir David Maxwell-Fyfe.

meeting of 3 August 1950, the UK delegate stated that he had instructions to propose a reconsideration of Article 23 relating to the right of petition.[69] The Belgian and Greek delegations wished to delete Article 23 'relating to the right of petition of natural persons, non-governmental organizations or groups of individuals'.[70] The delegate from the Netherlands concurred with the UK that, as stated, Article 23 was not sufficient to protect States from ideologically motivated claims. The UK delegate reiterated the perceived 'great danger' of abuse, particularly from communists, in the current state of the work and proposed that the right of petition should be optional and subject to State consent.[71] The aim of the compromise agreed by all the ministers with one abstention (Ireland) on 5 August 1950 was to contain the threat of abuse by limiting the powers of the Commission and ensuring that the jurisdiction of the Court would be optional. There was no change to the category of subjects granted rights of petition. The agreed text on Rights of Petition (now Article 25) reiterated that

> The Commission may receive petitions . . . from any person, NGOs or group of individuals claiming to be the victim of a violation . . . provided that the High Contracting Party complained against has declared that it recognises the competence of the Commission to receive such petitions. Those of the High Contracting Parties who have made such a declaration declare not to hinder in any way the effective exercise of that right.[72]

The text was remitted to the Assembly.[73] The Assembly held a general debate on the text of the Convention proposed by the Committee of Minsters at their sixth sitting on 14 August 1950, chaired by M. Spaak.[74] Several members of the Assembly, notably Maxwell-Fyfe and Teitgen, objected to what they perceived as the ministers' dilution of rights of petition with the focus of their objections relating to the optional jurisdiction of the Commission and Court. Maxwell-Fyfe worried that the rights of the individual appeared to be entirely dependent upon States exercising their option of taking action.[75] In his view, the hurdles erected by the ministers were a 'retrogressive step in that the

69 Ibid., Vol. V, p. 54. It was agreed that government officials wishing to propose amendments should introduce them by the next day, 4 August 1950.

70 Ibid., Vol. V, p. 62.

71 Ibid., Vol. V, p. 68: 'The Commission may receive petitions from any person, non-governmental organization or group of individuals . . . subject to States recognizing the competence of the Commission to receive individual complaints.'

72 Ibid., Vol. V, p. 132.

73 Ibid., Vol. V, p. 144. Letter dated 7 August 1950.

74 Ibid., Vol. V, p. 216.

75 Ibid., Vol. V, p. 226.

general modern tendency of international law has been to emphasize the rights and duties of an individual as a subject of international law'.[76] As discussed in Chapter 3, Maxwell-Fyfe's claim was misleading insofar as the grant of individuals' right of petition to an international court was not being contemplated at the time, nor has it been since. Still, Maxwell-Fyfe's own preference was for a weak Convention 'as a milestone in the difficult road of international law' rather than no Convention at all.[77] He believed that, at a time when people 'were dying in support of the rule of law', the Convention offered the hope of 'a quiet life not interrupted by the knock at the door by the secret police'.[78] Lannung (Denmark) concurred that, if need be, the Assembly should accept the Convention as submitted whilst suggesting that amendments should be put forward to strengthen the 'individual right of petition' from individuals to avoid the harm caused by the optional clause.[79] Azara (Italy) was similarly inclined noting that the procedures concerned

> not merely a private matter . . . of two individuals . . . disputing about personal affairs but of . . . individuals with claims against States, which are accused of having violated one of the fundamental rights . . . upheld as being essential to the human personality.[80]

Mitchison (UK) was full of admiration for a document which he described as a 'most remarkable development in the history of international law' because, for the first time, a machinery had been set up to oblige contracting States to the Convention to make concessions on sovereignty to give effect to 'the individual rights of citizens, or most important, the fundamental rights of democratic communities'.[81] In his view, the Convention would provide the basis on which different conceptions of European unity could be pursued, whether on a functional or a federal basis.[82] Similarly, Lord Layton, whilst regretting that some of the Assembly's proposals had been lost, preferred to 'go for half a loaf' than facing a delay of several months.[83] Rolin, who had been one of the most persistent critics of the creation of a Court, ended up enthusiastically endorsing what he described as the revolutionary creation in international law of a right of individual appeal by the 'injured individual

76 Ibid., Vol. V, p. 227.
77 Ibid.
78 Ibid., Vol. V, pp. 218 and 226.
79 Ibid., Vol. V, p. 238.
80 Ibid., Vol. V, p. 248.
81 Ibid., Vol. V, p. 254.
82 Ibid., Vol. V, p. 256.
83 Ibid., Vol. V, p. 270. On Rights of petition, Layton also talks about 'right of individual petition'.

himself' ('l'individu lese lui-meme'), taking 'human rights out of the field of inter-state politics'.[84]

In all the views expressed on rights of petition, the references were to the 'individual right' or the rights of the individual (individu in French). There is no mention of 'corporate bodies'/'personnes morales' except by M. Teitgen and Foster (UK). In the longest address to the Assembly, Teitgen concurred that a partial 'even inadequate, guarantee of human rights and freedoms, is better than having no guarantee at all'.[85] But he thought that the Assembly should still seek to improve the text. He enjoined the Assembly not to give way on the right of petition and specifically on the optional jurisdiction of the Court and the limitations relating to the investigative and reporting powers of the Commission.[86] In the course of lamenting the discretionary power retained by States, he misquoted the ministers' text on rights of petition, stating incorrectly that petitions could only be raised by 'the victim of a wrongful act, whether the victim be an individual or a corporate body' if the accused State has consented.[87] Similarly, Foster (UK) shared Teitgen's regret that 'the right of an individual or juristic person (personne physique ou morale in French text) to petition the Commission' had been whittled down[88] but was nevertheless in favour of accepting the watered-down provision.[89] Both references to corporate bodies and 'juristic' persons/personnes morales were lost in the debate, without anyone adverting or questioning their inclusion.

Following the debate, the Assembly's Legal Affairs Committee reviewed the ministers' draft and put forward a series of amendments relating, inter alia, to the optional jurisdiction of the Commission and Court on rights of petition, whilst leaving the category of claimants (any person, NGOs and groups of individuals) unchanged. The Assembly also proposed that the right to own property should be added to the text as Article 10A. The proposed draft stated that 'every natural

84 Ibid., Vol. VI, p. 132.
85 Ibid., Vol. V, p. 282.
86 Ibid., Vol. V. Teitgen noted that the Commission's investigative powers are discretionary and that the Commission cannot publish its report without the Ministers consent (p. 296). Addressing the Assembly, Teitgen said that 'what we want to prevent is the re-establishment or the establishment in some countries, of totalitarian dictatorships such as we saw in Italy and Germany before the war . . . We are less concerned to set up a European juridical authority capable of righting isolated wrongs, isolated illegal acts committed in our countries, than to prevent from the outset, the setting up in one or other of these countries of a regime of the Fascist or Nazi type' (p. 294).
87 Ibid., Vol. V, p. 296.
88 Ibid., Vol. V, p. 318.
89 Ibid., Vol. V, p. 338. On Federalist aspirations see Becker (Germany) congratulating the Legal Affairs Committee as a result of whose works 'a part of the future constitution of the Federal State should have been made ready'.

and legal person is entitled to the peaceful enjoyment of his possessions'.[90] The Committee's recommendations were approved unanimously by the Assembly (111 to 0) on 25 August 1950 and remitted to the Committee of Ministers.[91] The Committee of Ministers accepted only one of the Assembly's amendments (which related to the Preamble) and couldn't reach agreement on the Assembly's proposal to include other rights, notably the right to own property.[92] As a compromise, the ministers proposed to open the Convention text for signature and to submit the proposals to a subcommittee of legal experts for further study. If agreement could be reached following the study, the Convention could be later supplemented by a protocol including the right to own property.[93] There was a shared sense of urgency between the ministers and the Assembly on the desirability of immediate signature. The ministers had met on 3 and 4 November 1950. The Convention was publicly signed at 4 pm on 4 November 1950 by Paul-Henri Spaak, President of the Consultative Assembly and David Maxwell-Fyfe, Chair of the Assembly's Legal Committee and the ministers of the contracting States.[94] The right of individual petition no longer included corporate bodies/personnes morales, but, in a new twist, the Assembly's revision of the proposed text on the right to own property was recast as the right of 'any physical or legal person/toute personne physique et morale to enjoyment of his possessions' later adopted as the text of A1P1.

2.4 PROPERTY RIGHTS

2.4.1 *Property as the Minimum Necessary to Live a Life with Dignity*

Despite claims that the list of substantive rights in the Convention were intended to be aligned with the UDHR, the Assembly's original draft text as remitted to the Committee of Ministers in September 1949 inexplicably envisaged that rights of petition would be enjoyed by 'any person or corporate bodies'.[95] Reference to corporate bodies/personnes morales was removed by

90 Ibid., Vol. VI, p. 192.

91 Ibid. Recommendation No. 24 to the Committee of Ministers on the Draft Convention for the Protection of Human Rights and Fundamental Freedoms, adopted 25 August 1950.

92 Ibid., Vol. VII. Six session of the Committee of Ministers (3–4 November 1950).

93 Ibid., Vol. VII, p. 44. As well as the right to education, the right to free elections and the right of individual appeal and colonial clause in an additional Protocol.

94 Ibid., Vol. VII, p. 46.

95 Ibid., Vol. I, p. 210. 'After all other means of redress within a State have been tried, any person, or corporate body, which claims to have been a victim of a violation of the Convention by one of the signatory States may petition the Commission in a request presented through legal channels' (Section III, Article 12).

the Committee of Ministers in what became the final text of Article 25 which declared instead that the Commission may receive petitions from 'any person, NGOs or group of individuals . . . claiming to be the victim of a violation'. Yet reference to corporate bodies/personnes morales/legal persons resurfaced in the alternative wording of the Article on property rights which the Assembly Legal Affairs Committee had been mandated to review in the absence of agreement at the end of the First Session of the Assembly in September 1949.

The Legal Affairs Committee had originally proposed that the basic list of rights should include 'the right to own property, in accordance with Article 17 UDHR'.[96] Reporting on the deliberations of the Legal Affairs Committee at the First Session of the Assembly, on 7 September 1949, Teitgen had explained that the committee had been divided. The inclusion of a right to own property had proved controversial.[97] Opponents had criticized the singling out of the right to own property, which they argued was an economic right, when other social and economic rights had not been included.[98] There was also concern at the prospect of an international court reviewing the legitimacy of State controls and restrictions on the use of private property for social or public purposes.[99] However, Teitgen said, a majority of the committee members had voted in favour of including the right to own property. In reality, the vote was very close with 10 ayes, 8 noes and 1 abstention.[100]

There is nothing in Teitgen's report to the Assembly to indicate that the delegates had corporate entities in mind as potential subjects or victims of violations of property rights in the discussions on the right to own property. On the contrary, according to Teitgen, the majority of the Committee had decided to include the right to own property because 'it is a pre-condition of personal and family independence'.[101] This was consistent with the Committee's approach which, he said, had been based on the UDHR for 'Who does not appreciate that these rights are fundamental, essential rights, and that there is no State which can, if it abuses them, claim to respect natural law and the fundamental principle of human dignity'.[102] The list of rights identified by the Committee were those 'without which personal independence

96 Ibid., Vol. I, p. 230, Article 2.12.

97 Ibid., Vol. I, pp. 250 ff.

98 Ibid., Vol. I, p. 270.

99 Ibid., Vol. I, p. 272.

100 Ibid., Vol. I, p. 182. The English wording of the motion which was the subject of the vote was slightly different and referred instead to 'the right of property'. The French version remained the same and referred to 'le droit de propriete'. The motion had been introduced by Mr Bastid.

101 Ibid., Vol. I, p. 272.

102 Ibid., Vol. I, pp. 268–270.

and a dignified way of life' could not be guaranteed.[103] As discussed in Chapter 1, the language of natural rights, personal and family development and human dignity used by Teitgen and other property rights advocates reflected the normative foundations of international human rights which took the individual human person as the subject of human rights. Equally, some of the concerns expressed had been presciently anticipated by Lauterpacht, who had warned that the inclusion of property rights in an international treaty on human rights was liable to raise complex economic, political and constitutional questions.[104]

Indeed, the concerns which had been raised in the Legal Committee were amplified in the debates of the plenary meeting of the Consultative Assembly. Rolin (Belgium) with Lord Layton and other delegates from the UK and Sweden were amongst the most vocal opponents of the inclusion of property rights. They proposed amendments either to delete the right to own property altogether[105] or to include other social and economic rights such as the right to work, the right to leisure and the right to an adequate standard of living.[106] Ungoed-Thomas (UK) was prepared to accept that 'you could not really have a complete life unless you had property and were able to use it in your way', but he argued that there is also an economic aspect to property which cannot be divorced from the personal.[107] There was a risk that including the right to property without the other social and economic rights in the UDHR would appear 'reactionary'.[108] Similarly, Elmgren (Sweden) feared that ordinary men and women in Europe would feel that the Council of Europe had disrupted the balance of economic and social rights in the UDHR by leaving out rights to work and to an adequate standard of living, which were as essential as the right to own property. Nally (UK) worried that inclusion of the right to own property as the only social and economic right would make the Council of Europe look as if it had used 'the right of average man to have little possessions of his own in order to defend a property structure in which a tiny handful of people own the means by which millions of others live'.[109] Philip (France)

[103] Ibid.

[104] See Chapter 1.

[105] Council of Europe, *Collected Edition of the 'Travaux Préparatoires' of the European Convention on Human Rights*, Vol. I, p. 254. Amendment proposed by MM Rolin, Layton, Ungoed-Thomas, Elmgren and Edberg.

[106] Ibid., Vol. I, p. 256. Amendment proposed by Mr Benvenuti.

[107] Ibid., Vol. II, p. 60.

[108] Ibid., Vol. II, p. 62.

[109] Ibid., Vol. II, pp. 79–80. See also Callias (Greece) who thought that for 'psychological and social reasons' the Council of Europe must not 'protect only and especially the right to own property, that is to say the right of the well-to-do, before establishing a complete list . . . guaranteeing . . . the rights of those who possess only their capacity and their will to work'. Ibid., Vol. II, p. 98.

was prepared to accept the inclusion of a right for 'each one of us to own as property for the owner's personal use – truly the projection of his person – those belongings which are tied to his being'.[110] But, Philip continued, beyond possession of goods for personal use, no one claimed that there was a sacred, fundamental human right to own the means of production or to own private companies. These were not natural, human rights but modes of ownership which were 'instrumental, social policies, aimed at ensuring the best development of the human personality'.[111] Because property had a social function, Philip said, it would be 'a grave error' to grant an international court the power to review national legislation affecting private companies without provisions protecting the social rights of workers.[112] Similarly, Edberg (Sweden), along with UK labour representatives, feared that nationalization programmes of private railways underway in Sweden or steel in the UK could be construed by an international court as 'expropriation by legal force'.[113] Pernot (France) disagreed and feared that restricting the right to own property to personal belongings, or 'clothing and lodging', would leave without protection 'the peasant, who cultivates his own land for himself and his family'.[114] In a similar vein, Sweetman (Ireland) 'violently' disagreed with proposals to delete the right to own property which he said was 'the fundamental dignity of the family'. Nor did he understand opponents' objections to vesting in a European Court the power to condemn arbitrary deprivation of property. To do so, he said, would leave the Court powerless after years of watching 'the dramatic spectacle of millions and millions of refugees being chased from their homes and being told: "you will have two hours in which to collect your belongings and go"'.[115] In Rolin's view, all the delegates were agreed in condemning the violations committed in recent years, but some were concerned that the right, as defined

> might have other consequences, which would encroach directly on the political life of our different countries and Parliaments. None of the courts of our countries would have the power to judge our laws in this field, and we deplore having to give to external organs a jurisdiction which we do not allow our national organs.[116]

[110] Ibid., Vol. II, p. 72 (French for 'belongings' is 'biens').
[111] Ibid., Vol. II, p. 74.
[112] Ibid.
[113] Ibid., Vol. II, p. 86.
[114] Ibid., Vol. II, p. 84.
[115] Ibid., Vol. II, p. 90.
[116] Ibid., Vol. II, pp. 130 and 132.

Thus, delegates along the left-right political spectrum concurred that the right to own property could be justified as a fundamental human right only to the extent that a *minimum* of *personal* possessions including home and personal belongings were necessary to enable the individual human being to live a life with dignity and to facilitate development of the human personality. On the broadest interpretation, favoured by Christian Democrats and delegates from Catholic countries, protection of the *minimum* necessary for personal, human self-development would extend to the land worked by labourers and the family home, as a nucleus for self-development of individual human beings. However, even some of those prepared to accept the minimalist, moral view of the right to own property had grave reservations about granting a supranational court the power to review compliance of national laws which regulated deprivation or limitations on use of property with Convention rights. The motivations and rationale for the inclusion of property rights in the Convention thus intersected with those relating to the grant of individual rights of petition and oversight of national laws by a supranational court.

2.4.2 *European Court's Review of Deprivations of Property*

Those who thought that property was a natural, human right admitted that property had a 'social function' and that the use of property could legitimately be curtailed for the benefit of society. Thus, the related critical question was whether controls on property rights in national laws, aimed at securing this social function, could be struck down by the proposed European Court as arbitrary deprivations of property. Could it be 'arbitrary' when 'a Parliament, duly elected under democratic rules, passes a law?' asked the President of the assembly (Spaak).[117] His government's view, he said, was that laws which were normally made by elected governments were not arbitrary laws.[118] However, Teitgen acknowledged that when it came to property rights, it was much more difficult to resolve whether complaints relating to nationalizations could be adjudicated by an international court.[119] Some delegates had told him that laws relating to leases should be subject to such review because they caused an excessive burden to private property.[120] Others had suggested that fiscal charges and rights of succession should also come under the supervision of the Court.[121] These, Teitgen said, were issues which had never been

[117] Ibid., Vol. II, p. 128.
[118] Ibid.
[119] Ibid., Vol. II, p. 126.
[120] Ibid.
[121] Ibid.

envisaged by the Legal Committee in its consideration of 'a general formula forbidding arbitrary, scandalous and illegal confiscation of property'.[122] They required detailed consideration because the disagreement between those in favour and those against the right to own property raised issues which were much more complex.

Smitt-Ingebretsen (Norway) suggested that the right to property should be removed from the text and referred to the Legal Committee for further consideration until the next Session.[123] The suggestion was immediately endorsed by Maxwell-Fyfe, who, as Chair of the Committee, said that the right to property had been included, 'not because of any arriere pense', but because it was part of the UN Declaration bearing in mind 'the withdrawal from large sections of humanity of surroundings which gave them the right to comfort and enjoyment'.[124] Nevertheless, Maxwell-Fyfe conceded that the right to property 'might appear to be prejudged' due to 'certain political questions in certain countries' in a veiled reference to socialist critics.[125] To dispel the misconception, he was strongly of the view that the right should be sent back to the Legal Committee to review the definition of the right. To have secured agreement on ten basic rights was a great achievement, said Maxwell-Fyfe. The text of the Convention should not be sacrificed but sent to the Committee of Ministers with a report explaining that the right to property was under consideration by the Legal Committee. This was overwhelmingly approved by the Assembly.[126] Some delegates had voted in favour despite the omission of the right to own property which was 'extremely dear to the heart of every inhabitant of our Western Countries' because 'a new barbarian invasion is at the gates of Europe' threatening the very core of Western civilization.[127] Others did so because it was a historic document, representing 'the emergence of Europe from the dark ages of the 20th century'.[128] Schuman (France) made very clear that he would have voted against the text in toto if instead of remitting the clause on property rights to the Legal Committee, it had been deleted altogether, as proposed in Lord Layton's amendment.[129] By contrast, those opposed to the inclusion of

[122] Ibid.
[123] Ibid., Vol. II, p. 112.
[124] Ibid., Vol. II, p. 114.
[125] Ibid.
[126] Resolution 38 from the Consultative Assembly with the revised draft Convention without a right to property was thus remitted to the Committee of Ministers.
[127] Council of Europe, *Collected Edition of the 'Travaux Préparatoires' of the European Convention on Human Rights*, Vol. II, pp. 264 and 266 (Moustier (France)).
[128] Ibid., Vol. II, p. 270 (McEntee (Ireland)).
[129] Ibid., Vol. II, pp. 252 and 254.

property rights as 'anti-democratic' and 'reactionary' would have been unable to vote in favour of the text had it included the right to property.[130] Thus, the decision to remit the text on property rights to the Legal Committee was a political compromise to facilitate review of the Assembly's Draft Convention by the Committee of Ministers in whose power the fate of the Convention ultimately lay.

2.4.3 *The Addition of Legal Persons*

The Assembly's Legal Affairs Committee waited to hear the ministers' views on the proposed Draft Convention before meeting to consider whether agreement could be reached on the wording of a text on the right to own property. As discussed in Section 2.3, the Assembly's Legal Committee had known since 23 June 1950 that the Committee of Ministers had introduced a significant change to the Assembly's Article on the Right of Petition, replacing 'any person or corporate body' with 'any person, non-governmental organization or group of individuals'. Upon receiving the Ministers' Draft Convention, the Committee had met to consider the Ministers text on 23 and 24 June 1950. The Chair, Maxwell-Fyfe, had sent a reply to the Committee of Ministers on 24 June 1950 raising the issues detailed in Section 2.3 on rights of petition and stressing that it was the Assembly's wish that an article on property rights should be added, in addition to other rights.[131] At the same meeting, a sub-committee was appointed, which composed of Rolin, Bastid, Pernot and Schmal, to deal with the Article on Property Rights.[132]

Thus, by the time the subcommittee met on 7 and 8 August 1950 to consider revisions to the text of the Article on property rights, the ministers' deletion of corporate persons from the Article on Rights of Petition was known to the members of the committee. The meeting was chaired by Bastid (France). Rolin proposed the following text:

> The property of *individual persons or collective bodies* shall not be liable to arbitrary measures of confiscation, subject to the legal provisions adopted by each State to ensure that the holding of such property is not in conflict with its functions in society.[133] (italics added)

[130] Ibid., Vol. II, pp. 250 and 252 (Ungoed Thomas).
[131] Ibid., Vol. V, p. 32.
[132] Ibid., Vol. VI, p. 232.
[133] Ibid., Vol. VI, p. 204.

The next day, 8 August 1950, in his absence,[134] Rolin's text was amended to

> All *individuals and corporate bodies* (French 'la propriete des individus ou des collectivites) are entitled to respect for their property. Such property shall not be liable to arbitrary confiscation. This shall not, however, in any way prejudice the right of the different States to enact such laws as may be necessary to ensure the use of the property for the public good.[135] (italics added)

There is no indication in the minutes of the meeting of the reasons for Rolin's proposal or for the subcommittee's alternative formula, nor were definitions of the terms 'collective bodies' and 'corporate bodies' given. In his report to the Assembly, M. Bastid said that the subcommittee had found itself 'in entire agreement with principles of the draft of M. Rolin' and only made amendments which were 'purely of form'.[136] Yet, absent definition, the terms 'collective bodies' and 'corporate bodies' in natural language would not necessarily be thought of as synonymous. Collective bodies/collectivities might include trade unions but not companies. The ambiguities were resolved in favour of companies by the subcommittee in another modification of Rolin's text introduced by Pernot (France) whereby:

> *Every person, whether physical or moral,* has the right to the respect of his property. His property may not be subjected to arbitrary confiscation. The present provisions cannot however be considered as infringing, in whatever way, the rights of States to pass the necessary laws with a view to the use of such property in conformity with the general interest.[137] (italics added)

The final and most significant amendment was proposed by Teitgen. His amendment urged the Committee of Ministers to adopt the following text:

> *Every natural or legal person* is entitled to the peaceful enjoyment of his possessions. Such possessions cannot be subjected to arbitrary confiscation. The present measures, however, shall not however be considered as infringing, in any way, the right of a State to pass necessary legislation to ensure that the said possessions are utilised in accordance with the general interest.[138]

[134] Ibid., Vol. VI, p. 158. Rolin: 'This morning Mr. Bastid stated that in my absence the Committee had amended the text which I had proposed to it, though only in form.'

[135] Ibid., Vol. V, pp. 205–206.

[136] Ibid., Vol. V, p. 202.

[137] Ibid., Vol. VI, p. 106.

[138] Ibid., Vol. VI, p. 6.

Teitgen was unable to attend the sitting of the Legal Affairs Committee but his text was approved by a majority of 15 to 4.[139] The records do not explain the aims or rationale for the various proposed changes. In his report to the Assembly's second session on 24 August 1950, Maxwell-Fyfe stated that, after much discussion, the Legal Affairs Committee had felt that the text was 'a fair definition of an essential right'.[140] The wording represented the efforts of the Committee 'to reconcile the divergent political views on the social conception of property with the prohibition on arbitrary confiscation'.[141]

Bastid (France) told the Assembly that the subcommittee had modified Rolin's literal wording but preserved both the spirit and intention.[142] In reality, as will be seen in Chapter 3, 'legal persons'/'personnes morales' is a technical term in law. A legal person/personne morale is not a person as ordinarily understood but a legal fiction to denote entities such as companies, corporations or groups of individuals. Yet those who spoke in favour of the motion in the Assembly persisted in claiming that the rationale for the inclusion of property rights was that property 'is bound up with the development of the human being. Property is an extension of the man, and man cannot feel safe if he feels exposed to arbitrary dispossession' (Bastid, France).[143] In France, Bastid added, men who fought in the war thought that they were defending 'their right to the possession of the soil, which is the fruit of their labour, the extension of their individuality and guarantee of their independence'.[144] Similarly, Pernot (France) talked about the natural right of workers and peasants to have a family home.[145]

Those who had originally opposed the inclusion of a right to property or whose approval was conditional on the addition of social rights relented. Mitchison (UK) explained that whilst, as a lawyer, he continued to have reservations about the inclusion of a right to property in the Convention subject to review by a European Court and about the lack of clarity in the wording, he was prepared to accept the provision without further amendments in order to avoid delays. He was doing so in deference to the spirit in which the Article was intended and in recognition of the 'remarkable achievement'

[139] Ibid., Vol. VI, p. 48.
[140] Ibid., Vol. VI, p. 60. Report of 24 August 1950 on the Draft Convention on behalf of Committee on Legal and Administrative Questions by Sir David Maxwell-Fyfe.
[141] Ibid., Vol. VI, p. 76.
[142] Ibid., Vol. VI, p. 116.
[143] Ibid., Vol. VI, p. 118.
[144] Ibid., Vol. VI, p. 120.
[145] Ibid., Vol. VI, p. 108.

that the overall text of the Convention represented.[146] Rolin, who had originally opposed the inclusion of a right to property, accepted that a great number of representatives were determined to include 'the right to own personal property' although he did not share their views.[147] He was sufficiently vain, he said, to believe that the formula which he had proposed had not been improved by the Committee's modification during his absence from Strasbourg.[148] Nevertheless, he was prepared to set aside his reservations in recognition of the 'revolutionary'[149] achievement that the Convention represented in substituting the declaratory text of the Universal Declaration on the protection of the human person with a legally enforceable one.[150] He thought it was important to pay tribute to the Committee of Ministers for agreeing to the creation of an enforcement machinery to hear individual complaints. Struye (Belgium) concurred in stressing the importance 'for the first time in the history of human law' of a right of individual complaint for the protection of those 'sacred rights'.[151]

2.4.4 *Property Rights as Enjoyment of Possessions*

There was another modification to the wording of the Article on property rights whose rationale was not explained by Teitgen. The word 'property' was replaced by the elusive expression 'enjoyment of possessions'. One of the delegates, Roberts (UK), commented on the uncertain meaning of the words. He agreed that everyone should have some property and personal belongings protected but he pointed out that the word 'possessions', in the English text, was not satisfactory: 'It is a word that would not be found in a British Act of Parliament or any other legal document.' He would have preferred property rights not to be included because of the difficulties in defining property. But he agreed that the Convention should be signed at the earliest date, even if the ministers rejected the Assembly's suggestion, because the draft Convention was 'a great landmark in the history of freedom' and might even one day form the preamble to a 'Constitution of Europe'.[152] Mitchison (UK) concurred with Roberts. He too had been opposed to the inclusion of a right to property, but he had come to the view that there was now 'very little difference' in the

146 Ibid., Vol. VI, pp. 96 and 98.
147 Ibid., Vol. VI, p. 123.
148 Ibid., Vol. VI, p. 124.
149 Ibid., Vol. VI, p. 132.
150 Ibid., Vol. VI, p. 134.
151 Ibid.
152 Ibid., Vol. VI, p. 92.

clause which had been redrafted with such care by other distinguished members of the profession. His objections had been 'fundamentally those of a lawyer', but lawyers 'also had hearts and a sense of responsibilities as citizens of the world'.[153] He too was 'fervently' in favour of approving the ministers' draft without delay.[154] De Valera (Ireland) was also of the view that the revised Article gave 'a very imperfect statement of the right to own property' but would still vote for the draft as a whole. In his view, the Article on property rights should have said flatly that 'an individual citizen is entitled to have and to own property'.[155] Lord Layton was one of only eleven delegates not to be swayed. He had originally opposed the inclusion of property rights. Like Roberts, he continued to have doubts about the definition of the rights and felt he could not defend the Article in the House of Lords. For this reason, he decided to abstain.[156] Another ten members also decided to abstain, but the text was approved by an overwhelming majority of the Assembly by 97 votes in favour and 11 abstentions.[157] Those who had originally objected to the inclusion of property rights in the Convention concurred with their opponents that it was better to have a weak and defective Convention than no Convention at all. There was a shared sense of urgency across the political spectrum that the moment had to be seized or the opportunity to adopt a European Convention on Human Rights would be lost. It was a triumph for the lawyers who had seized the political momentum to convince delegates to vote with their hearts in the shadow of mass confiscations of millions of people's homes and belongings by the Nazis, when the cold legal reality was that they were voting for a text which secured supranational protection of companies' assets and capital, tangible and intangible property, including debts, securities and intellectual property. The text was indeed revolutionary, not only because it included individual rights of petition to an international court, but also because these rights were implicitly extended to companies whose property would be protected under A1P1 on pretence that a home and minimum of personal belongings were required for each individual human being to live a life with dignity. In Chapter 3, the legal fictions embedded in the text of A1P1 are unmasked.

[153] Ibid., Vol. VI, p. 96.
[154] Ibid., Vol. VI, p. 100.
[155] Ibid., Vol. VI, p. 152.
[156] Ibid., Vol. VI, p. 148.
[157] Ibid., Vol. VI, p. 232.

3

Legal Persons and Legal Fictions

INTRODUCTION

As seen in Chapter 2, the addition of property rights to the European Convention on Human Rights (ECHR) was highly controversial and was delayed until the adoption of Article 1 of the First Protocol (A1P1). The opposition of large numbers of delegates at the Council of Europe's Parliamentary Assembly led to several iterations of the right to property and the addition of 'collectivities', 'corporate bodies' and legal persons in the final version of the text. Moreover, the final wording of A1P1 does not refer to ownership of property or property rights. Instead, A1P1 ambiguously declares that 'every natural and legal person is entitled to the peaceful enjoyment of his possessions'. As seen in Chapter 2, there is no evidence that in approving the text, delegates intended or understood that, insofar as A1P1 protected the rights of legal persons/personnes morales, Article 1 could be construed as extending human rights protection to companies. On the other hand, the Assembly had originally envisaged that corporate persons would enjoy rights of petition at the European Court of Human Rights (ECtHR). The clause on rights of petition was modified and corporate persons deleted by the Committee of Ministers in a revision criticized in the Assembly as a regressive step on the grounds that the trend in international law had been to emphasize the rights and duties of individuals. The aim of this chapter is to gain a deeper understanding of the conceptualization of the subject of rights and the grant of rights of petition in international law at the time.

This chapter shows that the concept of legal personality in international law was undergoing significant changes in the aftermath of WWII. There was a nascent debate on whether international organizations such as the United

Nations (UN) could acquire legal personality and file complaints on behalf of victims of injury at the International Court of Justice (ICJ) at The Hague. However, the extension of legal personality to corporations and grant of individual rights of petition to individual persons was not part of that debate. In contrast, this chapter shows that corporate bodies had historically enjoyed legal personality in civil and common law systems. The legal persona was a mask or legal fiction to facilitate ownership and transfer of property by groups of individuals. Legal personality was extended to monasteries, universities and trade associations in the Middle Ages, and later to trade unions as well as companies in the wake of the industrial revolution, to enable ownership of tangible and intangible assets, shares, profits and rents in national laws in Europe. At the same time, deep theoretical and political divisions emerged on the nature and aims of the corporation, free markets and the legal construction and regulation of property rights. The last part of this chapter details how these divisions were still alive at the end of WWII and formed the background to the political compromise which resulted in the addition of legal persons to the Article on property rights in the ECHR.

3.1 LEGAL PERSONALITY IN INTERNATIONAL LAW

3.1.1 *The Prevailing International Legal Order in 1949*

As seen in Chapter 2, the Assembly's original template for a European Convention on Human Rights contained a clause on standing whereby

> Any State a party to this Convention and any natural or *corporate person* in the metropolitan territory of any such State shall have the right to petition the Council of Europe in respect of any infringement of Part I of the Convention. (italics added)

Corporate persons were deleted from the clause on rights of petition by the Committee of Ministers and replaced by 'any person, non-governmental organization or group of individuals' in what became the final text of Article 25 ECHR.[1] The inclusion of corporate persons in the original text was not explained or discussed in the Assembly debates.[2] Nor was there any debate on the rationale and implications of conferring rights of petition to NGOs and

[1] Article 25: 'The Court may receive applications from any person, nongovernmental organisation or group of individuals claiming to be the victim of a violation by one of the High Contracting Parties of the rights set forth in the Convention or the Protocols thereto.' Subsequently Article 34 and then Article 44 further to Protocol 9 (1990).

[2] See Chapter 2.

other groups of individuals in the revised text. Instead, the focus of the Assembly debates was on the implications of creating a supranational Court with jurisdiction over complaints raised by individuals against contracting States.

Maxwell-Fyfe, in his address to the Consultative Assembly in August 1950, had described the Committee of Ministers' decision that rights of individual petition should be optional as 'a retrogressive step' because the trend in modern international law had been to acknowledge the rights and duties of individuals.[3] Maxwell-Fyfe's comment was somewhat misleading in conflating the ascription of substantive rights to individuals as subjects of law with the grant of rights of individual petition relating to enforcement of those rights. A close look at international law at the time indicates that there was no trend on whether individuals should be granted direct rights of access to the ICJ. The suggestion posed a threat to the traditional Westphalian model of international law whereby the ICJ could only hear complaints brought by one State against another. This was reflected in Article 34 of the Statute of the ICJ which declared that 'Only States may be parties in cases before the Court'. Contrary to Maxwell-Fyfe's claim, in 1949 (the same year as the Council of Europe was beginning to debate the adoption of the Convention), the ICJ had considered extending legal personality and rights of petition to international organizations but not individuals.[4]

3.1.2 *The Emergence of the Individual as a Subject of Law*

Jan Klabbers recounts how the discussions were prompted by the killing of a UN mediator in the Middle East in the late 1940s.[5] The question raised by the UN General Assembly at the ICJ was whether the UN had the capacity to bring an international claim on behalf of the victim for reparations of injuries.[6] The ICJ answered that the UN did have 'a large measure of legal personality' to bring international claims for damage caused to itself or to its agents, even though (according to traditional rules) diplomatic protection had to be exercised by the national state. Importantly, whilst the individual victim

3 See Chapter 2. See also Astrid Kjeldgaard-Pedersen, *The International Legal Personality of the Individual* (Oxford: Oxford University Press, 2018).

4 See Section 3.1.2.

5 Jan Klabbers, 'The Concept of Legal Personality' in Fleur Johns (ed.), *International Legal Personality* (London: Routledge, 2017).

6 Reparations for Injuries Suffered in the Service of the United Nations (Advisory Opinion) 1949 ICJ Reports 174. See also Rolin's reference to the failed attempt at the first meeting on Codification of International Law at The Hague in 1930 in Henri Rolin, 'Controle International des Juridictions Nationales' (1967) 3(1) *Le Revue Belge de Droit International (Belgian Review of International Law)* 1–23.

was implicitly recognized as a subject of rights in international law, it was not envisaged that the individual victim himself/herself could directly file a claim to enforce their rights at the ICJ. The question before the ICJ was not whether individuals could petition the Court but whether the protection of individuals by States could be complemented by protection by international organizations in circumstances where their personnel had suffered injury.[7] Moreover, corporate persons did not figure in that debate: the reason is evident from Klabbers' illuminating account of the history of legal personality. According to Klabbers, the ICJ s concept of legal personality and methodology owed much to Lauterpacht's seminal paper 'The Subjects of the Law of Nations', published in 1947.[8] In that paper, Lauterpacht had argued that the position of the individual as a subject of rights in international law had changed. Lauterpacht noted that the prevailing theory and practice of international law, with few exceptions, had been that international agreements could not create direct rights and obligations for private individuals.[9] In his view, the adoption of the Charter of the United Nations in 1941 had been a turning point in public international law because it was in the Charter that 'the individual human being first appears in his full stature as endowed with fundamental human rights and freedoms'.[10] Lauterpacht argued that whilst the rights were not fully enforceable by the individual, the effect of the Charter was nevertheless to recognize that the individual human person enjoyed *legal* rights in international law independently of the law of the State. However, whilst the Charter implicitly endowed the individual with substantive legal rights, there was no suggestion that the individual was thereby also endowed with individual rights of petition. Neither was there any indication that the subject of rights was anyone other than the individual human person.

Lauterpacht's view was that 'human dignity and considerations of utility alike rebel against the idea of the State as the sole guardian of the interests of man'.[11] It is the individual human being who provides the 'moral backbone' of international law,[12] shaping the contours of individual and State responsibility. Crimes against humanity, he stated, 'violate the sanctity of human

7 The author is grateful to Jan Klabbers for drawing her attention to this point.

8 Hersch Lauterpacht, 'The Subjects of the Law of Nations' (1948) 64(1) *Law Quarterly Review* 97–119. Note that Klabbers does not suggest that the ICJ shared Lauterpacht's substantive conclusions.

9 Ibid. Lauterpacht cites the Advisory Opinion of the ICJ to the contrary in Permanent Court of International Justice, Advisory Opinion No. 1.5; Series B, No. 15, pp. 17–21.

10 Ibid., p. 101.

11 Lauterpacht, 'The Subjects of the Law of Nations', p. 118.

12 Ibid., p. 112.

personality'. For that reason, 'unless responsibility is imputed and attached to persons of flesh and blood, it rests with no one'.[13] The implications of Lauterpacht's view that the individual human person formed the backbone of international law were twofold. On one hand, Lauterpacht welcomed what he perceived as the trend in modern international law to recognize the individual human person as a *subject* of legal rights in the UN system. On the other, because the individual human person was both subject and object of international law, Lauterpacht was also in favour of granting membership or consultative status to international public bodies or non-governmental agencies and organizations such as the International Labour Organization (ILO) and the World Health Organization (WHO) to represent the interests of individual human persons in recognition of the global social interdependence of individuals. These were not private corporations, but public international organizations whose goal was the improvement of the working conditions, life and health of human persons. As noted by Klabbers, it was precisely the global interdependence of human beings which lay behind the dictum of the ICJ in 1949 that 'the subjects of law ... are not necessarily identical in their nature or in the extent of their rights, and their nature depends upon the needs of the community'.[14]

Lauterpacht acknowledged that as a matter of State practice, in actions against a Foreign State, individuals had been able to directly file complaints against States which were parties to a Treaty such as the Upper Silesian Convention between Germany and Poland. The critical issue there was that the State retained full control to consent to international jurisdiction. For this reason, Lauterpacht could see no difficulty in States concluding ad hoc agreements with other States whereby the State would appear as a defendant in claims filed by individuals or corporations of foreign nationality. Neither could he see a difficulty in extending the jurisdiction of the ICJ to 'disputes between States, private and public bodies or private individuals in cases in which States have consented, in advance or by special agreement, to appear as defendants before the Court'.[15] Clearly the rationale for granting standing to corporations or private entities in these scenarios was not the *moral* rationale for securing the enforcement of individual persons' rights in international courts based on the sanctity of the human personality. The rationale in relation to corporations lay in State practices recognizing the jurisdiction of

[13] Ibid., p. 107.
[14] Klabbers, 'The Concept of Legal Personality', note 31.
[15] Ibid.

international tribunals to settle claims from foreign investors or foreign nationals in bilateral treaties.[16]

Thus, contrary to Maxwell-Fyfe's claim, the ministers' preference for a Court with optional jurisdiction was consistent with the prevailing thinking on State sovereignty at the time whilst the grant of individual rights of petition to an international court was not. On the contrary, as noted by delegates, this was a revolutionary development in international law.[17] But the revolutionary proposal was also disingenuous because the case for granting individual rights of petition to an international court was a moral case based on the emergence of the individual human person, (not corporations) as a subject of rights in international law.

Yet, as explained in Chapter 2, whilst corporate persons were deleted by Ministers from the ECHR draft text on rights of petition, corporate legal persons were reintroduced as subjects of rights by the Assembly's Legal Affairs Committee in the final iteration of the Article on property rights. From this it followed that legal persons could potentially suffer violations of their rights. Since the revised Article on rights of petition stated that the Court may receive complaints from 'any person' claiming to be victim of a violation of the rights set forth in the Convention, it followed that corporate legal persons could file complaints to the Court. By default, the words 'any person' include both natural and legal persons. Thus, the legal reality absent evidence to the contrary was that the Court could receive complaints from companies for breach of their right to 'enjoyment of possessions'.

3.2 THE SUBJECTS OF PROPERTY RIGHTS

Unlike Lauterpacht, State representatives at the Council of Europe did not address the normative and conceptual basis for granting individual rights of petition to companies in an international human rights treaty, focusing instead on the threat to State sovereignty posed by the creation of a supranational European Court. Nor were the reasons for the iterations of the Article on property rights explained. As seen in Chapter 2, the inclusion of property rights in the ECHR had been resisted by a majority of the Assembly which had nevertheless agreed to refer the Article back to the Legal Affairs Committee for further study. The Assembly's Legal Affairs Committee considered alternative

16 In respect of civil disputes relating to commercial or economic losses arising from contractual or tortious breaches, Lauterpacht's view was that liability for financial compensation should lie with the State as 'a corporation, a juristic person' (Lauterpacht, 'The Subjects of the Law of Nations').

17 See Chapter 2.

proposals whereby property rights would be enjoyed by 'collectivities', 'corporate bodies' and finally 'legal persons'. When the revised text was presented to the General Assembly, delegates were told that the text was the result of a compromise between members of different political persuasions after sustained deliberations. The text sought to reconcile some of the members' wishes to secure protection of the natural, sacred right to a home and personal possessions against those who feared the risk of political interference by an international court with States' regulation of private property. The substitutions which were made, the delegates were told, were purely in form; the substance and intent had been preserved.

Whilst this claim was not challenged in the debates, it sounds prima facie implausible as the terms 'collectivities', 'corporate bodies' and 'legal persons' are not synonymous in ordinary language. Moreover, we also know that Rolin, who had proposed the addition of 'collectivities', thought that the Committee's substitutions (made in his absence) were not an improvement on his text.[18] The following section investigates the possible meaning and rationale of Rolin's original proposal and the subsequent iterations of the text by Teitgen in light of the legal and political context at the time.

3.2.1 *Collectivities*

At the end of the Assembly's First Session in September 1949, the Legal Affairs Committee was mandated to consider how protection of property rights could be secured in a text which would accommodate the concerns of those who objected. At the meeting on 7 August 1950, Rolin introduced an amendment whereby property rights were to be enjoyed not only by individual persons but also by 'collectivities' (collectivités in French). The minutes don't explain the rationale behind Rolin's proposal, nor did Rolin offer a definition of the term. According to Simpson, in the 1940s the term 'collectivities' was used in Socialist and Christian Democrat pamphlets and proposals for Bills of rights which were critical of the classical individualist rights of the Enlightenment as artificially detaching individuals from their social community. For instance, Simpson recounts how the French exile Georges Gurvitch had drafted a Bill of Social Rights, Article 44 of which stated:

> Social property is owned simultaneously by collectivities, groups, and individuals, and has, so to say, a federal character (a kind of cooperative co-ownership). It can be neither divided nor alienated. Groups and individuals

[18] See Chapter 2, Section 2.4.3.

as joint owners have only the right to the redemption of their 'labour shares' when leaving the organization.[19]

The term 'collectivities' was also found in a Resolution from the League of Nations for Codification of World Laws adopted at the twenty-eighth Conference of the Inter-Parliamentary Union in Geneva on 20–26 July 1932. The recommendation was based on a report from the Belgian lawyer Henri La Fontaine which recommended that the title of the Code should be 'Rights and Duties of States, Collectivities and Individuals'.[20] The Code was to be divided into four titles. Chapter 1 of the second title concerned Collective and individual persons and was subdivided as follows: (I) States. Dominions. Colonies. (II) Regional collectivities. Minorities. (III) Other collectivities with world or extra-national interests. (IV) Natural persons (a) World citizenship (b) Right to vital liberties. The recommendation was that the terms should be further defined and content specified by a juridical committee. Absent definition, the term 'collectivities' in the proposed International Legal Code was vague enough to cover any type of collective entity, group or association, although private companies and corporations did not readily fit the nomenclature.

Rolin's legal expertise and political sympathies likely explain the rationale for his proposal. Rolin was a distinguished Belgian socialist lawyer who had been a delegate at the founding conference of the UN in 1945 and who had also built an impressive career as a barrister, successfully representing applicants at the ICJ in The Hague.[21] Rolin's proposal for the extension of property rights to collectivities as well as individuals makes sense in this light.

3.2.2 *Corporate Bodies*

The socialist connotations of the term 'collectivities', as proposed by Rolin, likely explain why, at the meeting of the Legal Committee the next day

19 A. W. Brian Simpson, *Human Rights and the End of Empire: Britain and the Genesis of the European Convention* (Oxford: Oxford University Press, 2004), p. 203.

20 'Twenty-Eighth Conference of the Inter-Parliamentary Union at Geneva, 20–26 July 1932: Resolutions Adopted' (1932) 95(2) *World Affairs* 124–128, www.jstor.org/stable/20662142.

21 Françoise Tulkens, 'A Propos de le Controle International des Juridictions Nationales de Henri Rolin' (2015) 48 *Revue Belge de Droit International (Belgian Review of International Law)* 465–471. On the contribution of Belgian judges see Dean Spielmann, 'La contribution des juges belges au rayonnement de la Convention europeenne des droits de l'hommes' (2015) 101 *Revue trimestrielle des droits de l'homme* 25–38. Tulkens notes that Rolin was elected by the Consultative Assembly on 21 January 1959 as a Belgian judge. He served in that capacity until 1973, then became Vice-president of the Court from 1965 to 1968 and President of the Court from 1968 to 1971.

(8 August 1950), it was replaced by Pierre-Henri Teitgen with the term 'corporate bodies': an expression which had a broader political resonance and was associated with variants of corporatism straddling the left–right divide.[22] In his study of the genesis of the ECHR, Duranti documents the multiple, and at times contradictory, variants of corporatism which animated the post-war movement for European integration.[23] He singles out the Union of European Federalists (UEF), which formed part of the Joint International Committee which organized The Hague Congress hosted by Churchill at The Hague in 1948, and the European Movement (EM) which drafted the original template for the ECHR. According to Duranti, it was some of the leading members of the UEF who first came up with the idea of a supranational court to enforce individual rights.[24] UEF's objective was to create a federal, united Europe overcoming 'bloc politics' to secure a lasting peace founded on 'respect for the rights of man, fundamental liberties for all and social justice'.[25] However, under the umbrella of a united Europe, there coexisted competing visions of European integration, ranging from a 'romantic' variant of corporatism to a technocratic neoliberal vision of free markets.[26] The political blur was reflected in the UEF's publications. On one hand, capitalism was denounced for perpetuating the hyper-individualism and materialism that afflicted modern societies, with particular vitriol aimed at

[22] For examples of trading corporations in the UK in 1948, see James E. S. Fawcett, 'Legal Aspects of State Trading' (1948) 25 *British Year Book of International Law* 34–51. Fawcett mentions the National Coal Board, British European Airways Corporation and British South American Airways, all statutory corporations created by the Civil Aviation Act.

[23] Marco Duranti, *The Conservative Human Rights Revolution: European Identity, Transnational Politics, and the Origins of the European Convention* (Oxford: Oxford University Press, 2017).

[24] Ibid., p. 267. Duranti attributes the proximate origins of the European Court of Human Rights to a single sentence in the French intellectual Bertrand Jouvenel's book *Quelle Europe?* (1947): 'The most indispensable international organ to be created is a Tribunal that would interpose itself between the national State and the citizen that disobeys it for a reason of conscience.' Also ibid. Duranti cites Salleron, explaining that 'The advantage of a European Tribunal of the Rights of Man is obvious. Besides constituting a precious safeguard for individuals, it recognizes them as subjects of supranational law, the strait gate through which the liberation from statist totalitarianism can pass'. Ibid.

[25] Cited by Duranti, *The Conservative Human Rights Revolution*, p. 256, note 5: Marc Alexandre, 'Une lettre et un bref rappel du "Programme" de l'U.E.F.', HAEU, European Union of Federalists Papers 91, 5.

[26] For instance, Duranti identifies Louis Salleron whom he describes as 'a social Catholic intellectual who had once directed the two other branches of the Institute for Corporatist and Social Studies. Salleron had been responsible for the development and implementation of Vichy's corporatist legislation, a central component of its National Revolution. He also sat on Vichy's National Council, a consultative assembly of notables selected from the country's cultural, economic, and political elites' in Duranti, *The Conservative Human Rights Revolution*, p. 259.

what its contributors termed 'neoliberalism'.[27] On the other, corporatism was presented as an alternative to both neoliberal individualism and socialist collectivism whereby 'intermediary communities', such as families and professional organizations mediating between citizens and the state, would form the basis of the European Federation.[28]

A Christian variant of corporatism, straddling the left–right divide, was embraced by the Christian Democrat Pierre-Henri Teitgen.[29] It was Teitgen as Rapporteur and member of the Assembly Legal Affairs Committee who substituted 'collectivities' first with 'corporate bodies' and then with 'legal persons' in the final iteration of what would become A1P1. Teitgen was a member of the Mouvement Républicain Populaire (MRP). In 1939, he founded the 'La Revue de droit sociale' whose aim was 'to find a happy medium between the need for business efficiency and the MRP desire for a more democratic and humanizing direction of the economy'.[30] This was reflected in the views expressed by Teitgen on the nationalization of the coal industry. Teitgen advocated the addition of a new category of members to the board of directors, 'not representing any specific interests but designated exclusively because of their ability to manage an industrial enterprise', to enhance efficiency.[31] Bouscaren described the recommendations as leaning toward 'the technique of the British Public Corporations, although with co-operatives of consumers and workers being shareholders together with the state'.[32] The technique had been endorsed to some degree by the Austrian Volkspartei.[33] The Volkspartei was a Christian, Nationalist, corporatist party which described itself as 'liberal-democratic' but acted as an umbrella for an Austrian variant of fascism.[34] In short, whilst the term 'corporate bodies' had a wider political appeal than 'collectivities', some of the political connotations

[27] Ibid., p. 257. Duranti cites examples of concerns that the UEF was coming close to the views of royalists from the ancien regime and initiatives by Brugmans, a leading advocate of Social Catholicism to integrate the Catholic authoritarian regimes of Portugal and Franco's fascist Spain.

[28] Duranti, *The Conservative Human Rights Revolution*, p. 259.

[29] See Anthony Trawick Bouscaren, 'The European Christian Democrats' (1949) 2(1) *Western Political Quarterly* 59–73.

[30] See Anthony Trawick Bouscaren, 'The MRP in French Governments, 1948–1951' (1952) 14 (1) *The Journal of Politics* 104–131.

[31] Cited by ibid., p. 114.

[32] Ibid.

[33] Ibid.

[34] Volkspartei, ahead of the 1949 elections, warned of the threat of communism, represented in an election pamphlet as a black octopus against a pool of red blood: www.cvce.eu/en/obj/the_austrian_people_s_party_ovp_and_the_dangers_of_communism_1949-en-c992b61d-7a29-4396-932c-e1eff1397e19.html.

of post-war variants of corporatism were decidedly negative as corporatism had become associated with fascism and Catholic authoritarianism in Austria, Italy and Spain.

3.2.3 *Legal Persons*

By contrast, the term 'legal person' did not carry controversial political connotations and was neutral in respect of competing political visions of European economic integration. It was a technical term with a specialist legal meaning and with no connection to the natural meaning of the words. A 'legal person' was not a professional lawyer; neither was a 'personne morale' a virtuous person. In natural language, it was unclear what the meaning of 'legal person'/'personne morale' precisely covered. But, for lawyers and jurists in civil and common law systems, 'legal person'/'personne morale' had a well-established meaning which was, to some extent, obscured by the natural connotations of the word 'person'. Section 3.3 shows how legal personality in domestic laws was a legal fiction: a legal device to facilitate ownership and transfer of property, tangible and intangible, by groups of individuals. The term 'legal person'/'personne morale' conveniently, included all types of 'collectivities', associations, corporations and 'corporate bodies', be they associations of natural persons or, in the words of the International Chamber of Commerce at the time, 'associations of capital'.[35] The analysis reveals how 'legal person'/'personne morale' had a malleable legal meaning in national laws which the ECrtHR could in due course draw upon to encompass the rights of companies to file claims which alleged violations of their fundamental right to 'enjoyment of their possessions'.

3.3 LEGAL PERSONS IN DOMESTIC LAWS

When the Court started to function on 21 January 1959, the customary practice on the interpretation of international law treaties had not yet been codified, although the distinguished former judge Françoise Tulkens recounts that the Court's approach was in line with the Vienna Convention on the Law of Treaties (VCLT) from its early days.[36] Accordingly, the meaning of the

[35] E. Wyndham White, 'Report by the Committee of the International Chamber of Commerce on the Legal Treatment of Foreign Companies' (1939) 3(1) *The Modern Law Review* 3, 54–58.

[36] Vienna Convention on the Law of Treaties (VCLT), Vienna, 23 May 1969, vol. 1155, p. 331. The VCLT did not become effective until 27 January 1980. Amongst the permitted *Supplementary Means of Interpretation* Article 32 lists 'the preparatory work of the treaty and the circumstances of its conclusion, in order to confirm the meaning resulting from the

ECHR clause on property rights would stand to be established in light of 'the object and purpose'[37] of the Convention. As expressed in the Preamble to the ECHR, the object and purpose of the Convention is, inter alia, to 'take the first step towards enforcement of certain rights in the Convention', reflecting the resolve of 'the governments of European countries which are like-minded and have a common heritage of political traditions, ideals, freedom and the rule of law'. The 'common heritage of' includes the legal traditions and cultures of the contracting States. In civil and common law jurisdictions at the time, the terms 'legal person'/'personne morale' had undoubtedly a meaning quite different from the natural meaning. An article published in 1948 by the advocate Maximilian Koessler noted that the term 'moral person' is the preferred expression used by French and other Romanic legal writers.[38] However, Koessler explained, it certainly has nothing to do with morality. Savigny considered it misleading and suggested its replacement by 'juristic person': the phrase commonly used by Germanic lawyers. The natural meaning of the English counterpart 'legal person' similarly bore little relation to the accepted legal meaning. As explained by the English jurist and politician William Blackstone in his Commentaries on the Laws of England (1765), legal persons are not persons as ordinarily understood but artificial legal constructs:

> Persons also are divided by the law into either natural persons, or artificial. Natural persons are such as the God of nature formed us: artificial are such as created and devised by human laws for the purposes of society and government; which are called corporations or bodies politic.[39]

The disjunction between the natural and legal meanings is illustrated in the work of Maitland who wrote that in England 'lately in the House of Commons the Prime Minister spoke of trade unions as corporations'. A distinguished lawyer on the Opposition benches interrupted him with 'The trade unions are not corporations', to which the Prime Minister responded, 'I know that …

application of article 31, or to determine the meaning when the interpretation according to article 31: (a) leaves the meaning ambiguous or obscure; or (b) leads to a result which is manifestly absurd or unreasonable'.

37 In accordance with Article 31(1), Section 3 of the Vienna Convention: *General Rules of Interpretation.*

38 Maximilian Koessler, 'The Person in Imagination or Persona Ficta of the Corporation' (1948) 9 *Louisiana Law Review* 435.

39 William Blackstone, *Commentaries on the Laws of England: A Facsimile of the First Edition of 1765–1769* (Chicago: University of Chicago Press, 1979), vol. 1, pp. 119–123, 157, 237–238, 243–244.

I am talking English, not law'. 'A long story…' Maitland adds, '… was packed into that admirable reply'.[40]

In short, there were technical layers of meaning attached to the terms 'legal person'/'personne morale in national laws which bore little relation to the natural meaning of the terms. Sections 3.3.1–3.3.3 outlines the origins, meaning and function of the terms 'legal person'/'personne morale' in civil and common law systems. A closer look reveals that 'legal persons'/'personnes morales' in national laws were legal fictions created to facilitate ownership and transfer of property by groups of individuals, including companies.

3.3.1 *Fictitious Persons as Owners of Property*

The distinction between natural and legal persons originates in Roman law and two interlinked assumptions about the subject of legal rights and the object of these rights. Under Roman law, only individual, physical persons could originally be subjects of legal rights, although the family head (or paterfamilias) was conceived as standing for all the family members in respect of rights relating, inter alia, to all family property. Over time, the rights enjoyed by the head of the family, notably property rights, were extended to all manner of associations and groups as legal persons or 'personae' – a term which in Latin denoted the mask of an actor.[41] The legal 'persona' was not a natural person but a fictional subject standing for and masking the members of the family/group. The purpose of the legal mask or fiction was to enable control and transfer of property from and to groups of individual persons.

Legal personality not only created artificial personhood, but conceptualization of the rights held by fictitious legal personae related to a separate anomaly in Roman law's conception of property rights. Roman law drew a distinction between 'rights in personam' and 'rights in rem'. Rights in personam were *private* civil rights, normally held by natural persons.[42] As such, rights in personam created binding legal obligations only between the individuals inter se. Typical examples of in personam obligations included a debtor's

[40] Frederic William Maitland, 'Moral Personality and Legal Personality' (1905) 6(2) *Journal of the Society of Comparative Legislation* 192–200.

[41] Otto Gierke, 'Persons: Fictitious and Real' in George Heiman (ed. and trans.), *Associations and Law: The Classical and Early Christian Stages* (Toronto: University of Toronto Press, 1977). Savigny and Gierke disagreed on whether legal personality denoted a subject with independent personality of its own. Gierke argued that the legal person can also be a group; Savigny argued that the legal person was a fiction. Gierke 'contends that the group-person, be it fellowship, association or corporation, has the same attributes as the personality derived from the individual'.

[42] For an overview, see Roscoe Pound, *Jurisprudence* (St. Paul, MN: West Publishing, 1959).

obligation to pay the debt to the creditor. By contrast, rights in rem were rights over physical, tangible things held in perpetuity against the whole world. Whilst the concept of 'res' formally referred to physical, corporeal things, towards the end of the Roman Republic the Roman concept of property evolved to include both physical and abstract objects and assets with economic value[43] or 'anything capable of reduction to personal possession and having value in exchange'.[44] Thus, under mature Roman law, the artificial legal persona was able to enjoy property rights over both tangible and intangible objects, laying the foundations for the modern legal concept of the corporation as a limited liability company and owner of financial assets, intangible property and, in due course, intangible 'intellectual' property.[45]

3.3.2 *Real or Unreal Corporate Bodies?*

Christian doctrine in the Middle Ages provided a religious justification for the legal construct of the corporation. The fictitious character of associations, corporate bodies or universities as legal constructs was affirmed in the thirteenth century by Pope Innocent IV.[46] Abbots, bishops and deans were able to act as single legal representatives of their ecclesiastic collegium or religious community and, subject to papal discretion, owned and controlled land and gifts donated to churches, abbeys and monasteries.[47] Internally, the fiction of the corporation as an abstract, undivided person was said to represent the unity of the body of Christ. Externally, it manifested the power of the Church.[48] The canon law view of the corporation was rejected in the aftermath of the French Revolution by legal realists seeking to assert the authority of the State

43 Barry Nicholas and Ernest Metzger, *An Introduction to Roman Law* (Oxford: Oxford University Press, 2008), pp. 98–99.

44 William E. Simonds, 'Natural Right of Property in Intellectual Production' (1891) 1(1) *The Yale Law Journal* 19.

45 See Chapter 4.

46 John Dewey, 'The Historic Background of Corporate Legal Personality' (1926) 35(6) *The Yale Law Journal* 655–673. Dewey cites Gierke's description of Pope Innocent IV as 'the father of the dogma of the purely fictitious and intellectual character of juridical persons which still rules' (p. 665, note 12).

47 T. Baty, 'The Rights of Ideas: And of Corporations' (1920) 33(3) *Harvard Law Review* 358–375.

48 Dewey, 'The Historic Background of Corporate Legal Personality', p. 665. Dewey states that 'It is hardly a coincidence that Pope Innocent was one of the strongest upholders of the supremacy of the spiritual over the temporal power, and that he was Pope immediately after the time of the greatest political power of the Papal Empire. In outward form the doctrine that corporate bodies are *persona ficta* was directed at ecclesiastic bodies'.

and by English common law pluralists opposed to codification and the idea of unlimited sovereignty. Two competing theories on the real or fictitious nature of corporate legal personality were developed by German jurists Von Savigny and Otto Von Gierke in the nineteenth century.[49] For Savigny, a Romanist legal realist, the legal person was a fictitious legal entity which derived its authority, as a subject of rights and duties by concession, from the state rather than the Church. Corporations were claimed to be creations of statute and subject to public law, but the regulatory potential of the theory was missed by Savigny and his followers. Savigny's fiction theory appeared to make it impossible to impute to corporations the requisite 'states of mind' for tort and criminal liability. The argument was that corporations could not be attributed the rights and liabilities attached to natural persons, except for property rights, the conferral of which (Savigny thought) constituted the essence of corporate legal personality.[50] By contrast, Otto Von Gierke developed an organic view of the legal person as a real entity symbolizing the association of individuals.[51] According to Gierke, the law did not create the corporation but recognized its existence as a real entity. Gierke was a fierce critic of what he perceived to be the 'rampant' individualism of Roman law in contrast to the embodiment of the communitarian goals of universities, trade unions and professional associations in German law.[52] Gierke's 'real entity' theory was imported into Britain by English pluralists to justify the regulation of the rights and liabilities attached to corporations.

3.3.3 *The Personification of Companies*

The historical context for the development of German real and fictional entity theories of the corporation was the seismic economic upheaval unleashed by the industrial revolution in nineteenth-century Europe. Legal personality and limited liability were attributed to companies in Britain, and constitutional protection extended to corporations in landmark judicial decisions in the

[49] Frederick Hallis, *Corporate Personality, a Study in Jurisprudence* (London: Oxford University Press; H. Milford, 1930).

[50] Ibid., p. 589.

[51] Ibid., pp. 173 ff.

[52] See Ron Harris, 'The Transplantation of the Legal Discourse on Corporate Personality Theories: From German Codification to British Political Pluralism and American Big Business' (2006) 63(4) *Washington and Lee Law Review*. At note 1, Harris cites Mathias Reimann, arguing that Gierke believed that the association was an expression of the collectivist character of German law, unlike the rampant individualism of Roman law.

United States.[53] Paddy Ireland[54] recounts how, around the mid-1830s, legislatures and courts in Britain began to redefine the legal nature of joint-stock companies. Joint-stock companies had previously been conceptualized as 'a collection of many individuals united in one body'.[55] This was to change with the adoption of the Joint Stock Companies Act 1844 which enabled incorporation by registration. The effect of the legislation was to alter the relationship between the shareholders of most companies and third parties. The contractual foundations of the relationship between corporate shareholders and directors were eroded with the reconstitution of the company as a property-owning legal person: 'Third-party creditors now dealt not with a collection of partners liable for each other, but with companies as separate, property-owning, legal (and corporate) entities.'[56] At the same time, shares were reconstructed as autonomous and freely transferable forms of property, relieved of any direct link to the assets of companies, enabling the rise of 'capitalism without the capitalist'.[57] As abstract legal persons, incorporated, large trading companies and railway corporations enjoyed extensive rights over tangible and intangible property, and limited liability for the damage, losses or injuries which they caused. By contrast, other corporate bodies (like trade unions) had legal personality ascribed to them 'both in order to make them more amenable to liability' or were 'pulverized into mere aggregates of separate persons ... to make more difficult their unified action in trade disputes, as in collective bargaining'.[58] In national laws, legal personality thus functioned as an umbrella term, signifying a multitude of public and private bodies including unincorporated trade unions as well as joint-stock companies, trusts, limited liability companies and 'associations of capital' whose

[53] See Carl J. Mayer, 'Personalizing the Impersonal: Corporations and the Bill of Rights' (1989) 41 *Hastings Law Journal* 577, noting that most important decisions of the USC were in the 1880s and 1890s, holding that corporations were persons enjoying equal protection under the fourteenth amendment (at p. 580). See also Morton J. Horwitz, 'Santa Clara Revisited: The Development of Corporate Theory' (1985) 88 *West Virginia Law Review* 173. Horwitz argues that under the fiction theory corporations could not assert constitutional protection because they owe their existence to the State.

[54] Paddy Ireland, 'Capitalism without the Capitalist: The Joint Stock Company Share and the Emergence of the Modern Doctrine of Separate Corporate Personality' (1996) 17(1) *Journal of Legal History* 41–73.

[55] Stewart Kyd, *A Treatise on the Law of Corporations* (London: J. Butterworth, 1793), vol. I., p. 1. Cited by Ireland, 'Capitalism without the Capitalist', note 15.

[56] Ibid., p. 462. The remaining indirect contractual links were eroded with the introduction of general limited liability in 1855. See Susan E. Woodward, 'Limited Liability in the Theory of the Firm' (1985) 141(4) *Zeitschrift Für Die Gesamte Staatswissenschaft (Journal of Institutional and Theoretical Economics)* 601–611.

[57] Ireland, 'Capitalism without the Capitalist'.

[58] Dewey, 'The Historic Background of Corporate Legal Personality', pp. 679–670.

contrasting rights and liabilities were set in charters or statutes interpreted by Courts. The German philosophical theories of corporate personality were particularly influential in shaping legal and political conceptions of the corporation in Britain in response to the excesses of liberal market freedoms.

3.4 CORPORATIONS AND FREE MARKETS

In Britain, the influence of Gierke's 'real entity' theory amongst jurists was at its most salient in the second edition of Pollock and Maitland, *The History of English Law before the Time of Edward I*.[59] A section in the first edition entitled 'Fictitious Persons' included 'Corporations and Churches'. In the space of five years, Maitland (who had translated Gierke's works into English) wrote five papers applying the real entity theory to towns and boroughs, the Crown, Trusts and to general corporate and unincorporated bodies.[60] At the turn of the century, corporations included a wide range of public and private entities enjoying legal rights over use and control of tangible and intangible property, attracting criticism directed at the excesses of economic market freedoms.[61] Maitland, described by Hager as a 'legal progressive', thought that real entity theory offered a 'liberation from common-law laissez faire jurisprudence'.[62] Other variants of British pluralism were favoured by Labour politicians, endorsing a radical left version of Gierkeanism which put 'special emphasis on the evils of corporate capital and tended toward a syndicalist brand of trade unionism'.[63] What united pluralist with radical-leaning Gierkeians was the idea that the fiction theory leaned towards protection of

59 Frederick Pollock and Frederic William Maitland. *The History of English Law before the Time of Edward I* (London: Cambridge University Press, 1898), vol. II.

60 Harris, 'The Transplantation of the Legal Discourse on Corporate Personality Theories', p. 1433. The papers are detailed in note 63.

61 For instance, Laski wrote that 'It is clear enough, that unless we treat the personality of our group persons as real and apply the fact of that reality throughout the whole realm of law, what we call justice will, in truth, be no more than a chaotic and illogical muddle'. In Harold J. Laski, 'The Personality of Associations' (1916) 29 *Harvard Law Review* 404 ff, 426.

62 Mark M. Hager, 'Bodies Politic: The Progressive History of Organizational Real Entity Theory' (1988) 50 *University of Pittsburgh Law Review* 575 cited by Harris, 'The Transplantation of the Legal Discourse on Corporate Personality Theories', p. 1422, note 4.

63 Hager, 'Bodies Politic', pp. 584–585 cited by Harris, 'The Transplantation of the Legal Discourse on Corporate Personality Theories', p. 1422, note. 4. Harris argues that the labour movement was thought as *incubator* of social and economic arrangements which would replace the capitalist state. British pluralists' ideal vision of society was a web of voluntary association. They rejected the liberal vision of a sovereign state and atomistic individuals. By contrast to Gierke, they did not see the state as the paramount association and the volk was not a meaningful entity. Despite their rejection of state-centred socialism and dislike of Fabianism, most British pluralists were on the left wing of the ideological map.

corporate capital and against attempts to regulate it.[64] They thought (naively as can be seen in retrospect) that corporations, conceived of as 'real entities', could be made liable in tort and crime by contrast to the Romanist-inspired 'fiction' theory which famously enabled corporations, lacking a mind or will of their own, to escape liability: *universitas non delinquit*.[65] Gierke himself became increasingly critical not only of liberalism and free market individualism but also of socialism and Marxism. Harris points out that Gierke's political beliefs veered towards conservatism and nationalism and shaped his analysis of the corporation: 'It was not only his personal war and unification experience, but also a fear of the rising tide of Socialism, Communism, Marxism and Revolution, that guided his later theory.'[66] An extreme-right version of corporatism, centred on land and nationally bounded communities under the central command of the state, surfaced in the following decades in Nazi and fascist ideologies. In short, by the end of WWII, the concept of legal personality had become associated with different, sometimes opposed, political conceptions of corporatism in Europe.

Thus, by the time the ECHR was adopted, there was a complex interwoven nexus of theoretical and political ideologies across the left–right political spectrum, underpinning ideas of the corporation and the concept of 'legal personality' in common and civil law systems. Arguably, the blurring of the left–right political divide in the language of corporatism facilitated the importation in the text of the ECHR of ideas originating in medieval, Catholic thinking and individual rights later adapted to the pursuit of ill-defined ideals of European economic and political integration. Only in the fictional language of national laws did 'legal persons' have rights, notably the right to own,

[64] See Harris, 'The Transplantation of the Legal Discourse on Corporate Personality Theories', p. 1442, arguing that British pluralists had affinity with trade unionism, guild socialism and even syndicalism. Two of their leading scholars, Cole and Laski, ended up among the principal intellectuals of the Labour Party. By contrast, Freund's shared an affinity with affinity with socialist and Fabian ideas and with European syndicalism.

[65] Albert J. Harno, 'Privileges and Powers of a Corporation and the Doctrine of Ultra Vires' (1925) 35(1) *The Yale Law Journal* 13–28, 18, note 11 citing Blackstone, *Commentaries on the Laws of England*: 'There are also certain privileges and disabilities that attend an aggregate corporation ... It can neither maintain, or be made defendant to, an action of battery or such like personal injuries; for a corporation can neither beat nor be beaten, in its body politic. A corporation cannot commit treason, or felony, or other crime in its corporate capacity.'

[66] Harris, 'The Transplantation of the Legal Discourse on Corporate Personality Theories', p. 1439. Harris argues that this fear blended well into his antagonism for Roman law, Latin culture, individualism, laissez-faire capitalism and universalism. He cites as an example Gierke's call for the inclusion in the Code of a separate property regime for landed property to replace the harmonized regime (that ordered both movable and immovable property) advanced by the Romanists.

use and dispose of property. There were no such persons in international human rights, only real individual human persons. The malleability of the technical concept of legal personality thus facilitated the inclusion of all types of corporate bodies, private and public, as subjects of property rights in the final version of the text of A1P1. The legal meaning of 'legal personality' accommodated a multiplicity of political conceptions of the corporation, enabling a consensus to be reached between Socialist, Christian Democrats and Conservative politicians in the Assembly. The term 'legal persons' literally meant different things to different politicians on opposite ends of the political spectrum in Europe. In short, the inclusion of companies in the ECHR in the form of 'legal persons' was not necessitated by a distinctive European liberal political conception of democracy. Instead, it was a semantic compromise between radically opposed political conceptions of the nature and function of corporations in a united Europe. Chapter 4 shows how the term 'possessions' had an equally fictional character in domestic civil and common law systems, standing for both tangible, real property and intangible debts, shares, assets, securities and 'intellectual' property.

4

Intellectual Property as Fictitious Possessions

Few, if any, of the terms in our legal vocabulary have always been technical terms. The licence that the man of science can allow himself of coining new words is one which by the nature of the case is denied to lawyers. They have to take their terms out of the popular speech; gradually the words so taken are defined; sometimes a word continues to have both a technical meaning for lawyers and a different and vaguer meaning for laymen; sometimes the word that lawyers have adopted is abandoned by the laity.[1]

INTRODUCTION

Article 1 of the First Protocol (A1P1) to the European Convention on Human Rights (ECHR) states that 'Every natural or legal person is entitled to enjoyment of their possessions'. As shown in Chapter 2, those in favour of including property rights in the ECHR argued that a home and minimum of personal belongings are required to facilitate development of the human personality. In ordinary language, 'possessions' include home and personal belongings such as furniture and clothes. This chapter shows that, by contrast, the term 'possessions' in law has a much wider technical meaning. Much like the fictitious 'legal persons' discussed in Chapter 3, 'intangible possessions' were created as legal fictions in civil and common law jurisdictions in Europe to accommodate shares, debts, securities and intellectual property as novel types of fictitious commodities.

Section 4.1 retraces the roots of legal fictions in European property law in Roman law's formal categories of rights in rem over tangible things and rights in personam, or personal rights over intangibles which could not

[1] Frederick Pollock and Frederic William Maitland, *The History of English Law before the Time of Edward I*, Reprint of 2nd ed. (Indianapolis: Liberty Fund, 2010), vol. II, p. 130.

accommodate the new economic interests of the industrial revolution. Section 4.2 shows how 'intellectual' property was added to the category of intangible fictitious possessions through legislative changes and judicial decisions in civil and common law jurisdictions in Europe. By the end of the nineteenth century, the legal meaning of the term 'possessions' had been firmly established in European national laws to include all types of intangible property, well beyond the types of personal possessions that advocates of property rights at the Council of Europe had argued were morally required to facilitate development of the human personality.

Overall, the analysis reveals a profound disconnect between the wide meaning and legal reach of the term 'possessions'/'biens' in A1P1 and the moral discourse on property rights which prompted its adoption at the Council of Europe. This chapter concludes that the constructive ambiguity and malleability of the term 'possessions'/'biens' opened the way for the European Court of Human Rights (ECtHR) to depart from the natural meaning of the words and embrace a technical, legal meaning based on statutory provisions and judicial precedents in European national laws. Overall, the obfuscation between the ordinary meaning and the technical legal meaning of 'possessions', combined with the assignment of fundamental rights to legal persons in A1P1, completed a virtuous fictitious legal circle, facilitating supranational judicial protection by a human rights court of the intangible assets, profits and intellectual property held by companies in Western capitalist market economies, justified as protection of a fundamental human right to property.

4.1 THE ORIGINS AND EVOLUTION OF LEGAL POSSESSIONS IN EUROPE

4.1.1 *Possessions in Roman Law*

In European law, property rights, ownership and possession are founded on a formal divide between tangible and intangible goods originating in Roman Law.[2] The classification reflected the land-based agricultural nature of Roman economy. Roman law drew a distinction between 'rights in personam' and 'rights in rem'.[3] Rights in personam were *private* civil rights, normally held by

[2] Peter Stein, *Roman Law in European History* (Cambridge: Cambridge University Press, 1999). See also David Johnston (ed.), *The Cambridge Companion to Roman Law* (Cambridge: Cambridge University Press, 2015).

[3] William Warwick Buckland, A *Text-Book of Roman Law from Augustus to Justinian*, 2nd ed. (Cambridge: Cambridge University Press, 1932). According to Buckland, 'Physical objects are

natural persons. As such, rights in personam created binding legal obligations only between the individuals inter se.[4] Typical examples of in personam obligations included a debtor's obligation to pay the debt to the creditor. The debtor A was only indebted to the creditor B and the debt could not be transferred to creditor C.[5] This related to another distinction drawn in Roman law between 'incorporeal' and 'corporeal res' or things. 'Res incorporales' were things that 'are not tangible, and are those consisting merely of rights, as, for instance, inheritances, usufructs, and obligations' and more generally rights conferred by law such as right to succession, right to the use and profit from another's property and rights conferred by contract.[6] By contrast, physical, tangible things were 'res corporales', defined as things that could be touched, for instance, land, a slave, silver or a garment.[7] Corporeal, tangible things were said to be alienable in that ownership could be conferred by delivery of the physical thing in possession of the holder. Possession formally required physical control of tangible things.[8] 'Rights in rem' were claimed to originate in possession of 'res nullius' or 'things which have not or never had an owner'.[9] For this reason, all property rights in Roman law were said by the German Jurist Savigny to have been 'founded on adverse possession ripened by prescription'.[10] The structural divide between rights over corporeal and incorporeal 'things' meant that rights to use another's land or the benefits of a contract could not be physically delivered or transferred. So alternative legal

given as illustrations of res corporales. Res incorporales were abstract conceptions, notional things, and, as res meant assets, res incorporales were rights. The illustrations given are rights of various kind' (p. 185).

4 Ibid. Buckland says, 'The Law of Obligations is, roughly speaking, the law of *iura in personam*, of rights and duties existing between two or more persons but having, prima facie, no bearing on their relations to other people' (p. 405).

5 Ibid. Buckland explains that 'The personal nature of obligation was one of its most marked characteristics. This was perhaps evidenced to some extent by the fact that it could not be assigned, but few rights were assignable. More significant is the fact that it was, in general, impossible at any stage in Roman law to acquire, directly, a right of this character through a transaction by a third party' (p. 407).

6 Francis de Zulueta, *The Institutes of Gaius: Commentary* (Oxford: Clarendon Press, 1946), Book II (14).

7 Ibid., Book II (13).

8 Buckland, *A Text-Book of Roman Law from Augustus to Justinian*, p. 197, citing Savigny's definition of possession as consisting 'of physical control (corpus) with the intention to hold as one's own'.

9 Henry Sumner Maine, *Ancient Law: In Connection with the Early History of Society, and Its Relation to Modern Ideas* (Kitchener, ON: Batoche, 1999): 'res nullius' included wild animals, fish, land newly discovered, jewels disinterred or land never cultivated and more generally, land and things which were either abandoned or in possession of defeated enemies (chapter VII).

10 Ibid., chapter VIII.

procedures were available in Roman law to facilitate the fictitious reduction to personal possession of intangible assets of economic value or anything having an exchange value.[11] Through the addition of artificial legal constructs, the 'res' was conceptualized as either the physical thing itself (e.g. the land) or the civil rights relating to the land (e.g. rent, use of the land). The conflation of the physical, tangible things or land as objects of rights, with the rights themselves relating to ownership and control, left a lasting imprint on the subsequent evolution of civil and common law in Europe.[12]

4.1.2 *Possessions in Civil Law Codes: France*

In the French Civil Code of 1804, the term 'biens' (French for the English 'possessions' in A1P1 ECHR) encompassed tangible and intangible goods.[13] The Code defined possession as:

> the detention or enjoyment of *a thing or of a right* which we hold or exercise by ourselves, or by another who holds and exercises it in our name.[14] (italics added)

Delivery was 'the *transfer of the thing sold into the power and possession* of the buyer' (Article 1604) whilst fulfilment of the seller's obligation to deliver immovables was fulfilled 'where he has handed over the keys, in case of a building, or *where he has handed over the instruments of title*'[15] (italics added). These include, for instance, rights acquired by adverse use which require '"peaceful" possession without the hindrance of the owner'.[16]

France's civil law system retained the formal original Roman divide between physical, tangible objects and incorporeal intangibles whilst resorting to legal constructs and fictions to reflect changes in economic and social modes of production in the nineteenth century. Adapting the legal principles was problematic because civil law could not, as a rule, formulate the right to

11 Barry Nicholas and Ernest Metzger, *An Introduction to Roman Law* (Oxford: Oxford University Press, 2008), pp. 98–99.

12 Roscoe Pound, *Jurisprudence* (St. Paul, MN: West Publishing, 1959). See also James E. Penner, *The Idea of Property in Law* (Oxford: Oxford University Press, 2003).

13 Article 516 Création Loi 1804-01-25 promulguée le 4 février 1804 'Tous les biens sont meubles ou immeubles'.

14 Ibid., Article 2228.

15 Ibid., Article 1605.

16 See Pound, *Jurisprudence*. See also Albert S. Thayer, 'Possession' (1905) 18(3) *Harvard Law Review* 196–213. Ownership was defined in the Civil Code as: 'the right to enjoy and dispose of things in the most absolute manner, provided they are not used in a way prohibited by statutes or regulations' (Article 544).

enjoy economic property. Continental systems always had to ask and answer the question: 'Who is the owner?'[17] They either had to divest the owner of his/her title and leave him/her with a mere beneficial right subject to the restrictions applying to personal property. The alternative was to leave the owner with a bare title but no economic interest. By contrast, the device of the Trust in English common law allowed multiple layers of 'property' rights over a 'thing' to coexist. For instance, 'ownership' of title to an estate or company could be vested in one entity/person whilst others (e.g. shareholders) could enjoy the profits as legal beneficiaries or trustees.

4.1.3 *Possession of Incorporeal 'Things' as 'Useful Fictions': England*

Following the Norman Conquest, complex legal fictions were also introduced in English law to overcome the legacy of the formal divide between ownership and possession of corporeal and incorporeal things.[18] Medieval England, the English jurists (Pollock and Maitland explained, was 'rich with incorporeal things'.[19] Having warned the reader that a complete list of incorporeal things would be exceedingly long and miscellaneous, they cite ten types of incorporeals, namely 'advowsons, tithes, commons, ways, offices, dignities, franchises, corodies or pensions, annuities and rents.'[20] The reader is further told that these are '*thing-like* rights and their thinglikeness is of their very essence' (emphasis added).[21] The form and type of remedy for these intangible rights were derived by analogy from the law on corporeal, tangible things and land. For instance, 'The landlord who demands the rent that is in arrear is not seeking to enforce a contract, he is seeking to recover a thing.'[22] The rent or 'thing' can be the object of a legal dispute between adverse claimants. One of the parties, is 'possessed of' it, the other 'claims possession and perhaps alleges that he has been unlawfully disseised'.[23] Since 'every sort of action that can be brought for the recovery of land can be brought for the recovery of rent; one has but to put in the writ ten shillingsworth of annual rent instead of ten acres of land'.[24] Similarly, if M has been paying his rent to A and is coerced into

[17] See Kahn-Freund's Introduction in Karl Renner, *The Institutions of Private Law and Their Social Functions* (London: Routledge & Kegan Paul, 1949), p. 22.

[18] Pollock and Maitland, *The History of English Law before the Time of Edward I.*

[19] Ibid., p. 74.

[20] Ibid.

[21] Ibid.

[22] Ibid., p. 75.

[23] Ibid., p. 78.

[24] Ibid.

paying the rent to X, A's remedy against X is not for malicious interference with a contract but with a possessory remedy protecting something that he possesses.[25]

The conflation of tangible 'possessions' with (intangible) rights is further evidenced in the legal definitions of the rights. The reader is told that 'a right' in a 'corporeal' thing is 'Any permanent right which is of a transferable nature ... (it) is *thought of as a thing* that is *very like a piece of land*'.[26] According to Maitland, this is 'because it is a thing, it is transferable'.[27] Of course, there is no literal transfer of anything, as such. In truth, the legal categories are legal fictions based on metaphors, figures of speech.[28] They are justified by Maitland on the grounds that they are

> no fiction invention by speculative jurists. For the popular mind these things are things. The lawyer's business is not to make them things but to point out that they are incorporeal.[29]

A similar conflation between the thing which is the object of the rights and the rights themselves is evident in Blackstone's Commentaries on the Laws of England.[30] In his discussion of corporeal and incorporeal hereditaments, Blackstone cites Sir Edward Coke's definition as the 'largest and most comprehensive' for it includes 'not only lands and tenements, but whatsoever maybe it corporeal or incorporeal, real, personal, or mixed'.[31]

In reality, as noted by Hohfeld: 'it is clear that only legal interests as such can be in the foregoing quotation; yet there is inextricable confusion of the physical or "corporeal" objects and the corresponding interests, all of which latter must necessarily be "incorporeal"'.[32] For Hohfeld, such confused use of language 'can but serve to mislead the unweary'.[33]

25 Notwithstanding, as acknowledged by Maitland in Pollock and Maitland, *The History of English Law before the Time of Edward I*, p. 76, 'receipt of money-dues or other services naturally gives rise to far more difficulties than such as are incident to a possessory protection of those who sit upon land'.
26 Ibid., p. 74.
27 Ibid.
28 As argued by Wesley Newcomb Hohfeld, 'Some Fundamental Legal Conceptions as Applied in Judicial Reasoning' (1913) 23(1) *The Yale Law Journal* 16–59.
29 Pollock and Maitland, *The History of English Law before the Time of Edward I*, p. 76.
30 William Blackstone and Thomas P. Gallanis, *The Oxford Edition of Blackstone's: Book II: Of Private Wrongs* (Oxford: Oxford University Press, 2016).
31 Ibid., p. 16.
32 Hohfeld, 'Some Fundamental Legal Conceptions as Applied in Judicial Reasoning', p. 23.
33 Ibid., p. 24.

Yet, for Blackstone, legal fictions were 'highly beneficial and useful'.[34] No doubt for this reason the fictitious class of intangible 'possessions' was further expanded in English law in response to economic changes brought about by the industrial revolution. As sources of wealth swung from land and chattels to intangible assets, shares, bonds, securities, investments, debts and patents, there followed a corresponding expansion of the legal categories of fictitious possessions.

4.1.4 *Company Shares as Intangible Possessions*

In eighteenth-century England, statutes were enacted to enable large joint-stock corporations to raise capital to finance trade at sea.[35] Exceptions were added to eighteenth-century statutes to enable the East India Company and South India Company to raise capital.[36] Outside these exceptions, the courts continued to apply the normal principles of the law of contract to shares which did not transfer liabilities. As explained by Ireland in his illuminating study on the origins of company law, as long as shares were treated as contractual objects, bound to the holder as a personal right, legal obligations and liabilities in respect of the shares or bonds remained with the holder.[37] This acted as an impediment to the sale and transfer of the shares. If the holder of shares in an unincorporated joint-stock corporation sold the shares, he/she remained personally liable up to the point of the sale. The personal legal bond between the share and its holder thus had to be broken to facilitate global trade and industrial expansion. The legal hurdle could be overcome if the share was treated in law as akin to a physical thing or commodity whose identity is independent of the holder and, as such, can be sold, alienated and

[34] William Blackstone, *Commentaries on the Laws of England* (D. Gallanis, ed., Oxford: Oxford University Press, 2016), Book III, p. 28. Blackstone acknowledged that legal fictions 'at first they may startle the student, he will find upon farther consideration to be highly beneficial and useful: especially as this maxim is ever invariably observed, that no fiction shall extend to work an injury; its proper operation being'.

[35] For instance 'An Act for better securing certain Powers and Privileges intended to be granted by His Majesty by Two Charters for Assurance of Ships and Merchandizes at Sea, and for lending Money on Bottomry, and for restraining several extravagant and unwarrantable Practices therein mentioned, 6 Geo I, c. 18, known as the Bubble Act'.

[36] Ibid., para. 9. The Act authorized the two corporations to raise capital by means of shares from members and non-members. The shares were declared to be transferrable and assignable – notwithstanding the fact that they were classified as part of the personal rather than the real estate of the holder upon his/her death (p. 329). See Lorraine Talbot's discussion in Lorraine Talbot, *Critical Company Law* (London: Routledge, 2015).

[37] Paddy Ireland, 'Property and Contract in Contemporary Corporate Theory' (2003) 23(3) *Legal Studies* 453–509.

transferred, much like the original Roman tangible 'res'.[38] By the second half of the nineteenth century, judges and legislators had effected the full commodification of the intangible share and its detachment from the personal tie to the holder. The legal transformation of intangible shares and investments into fictitious possessions detached from the equally fictitious legal holder completed the fictitious legal circle.

Thus, by the time the European Convention on Human Rights (ECHR) was adopted in 1950, corporations, as fictitious legal persons,[39] had enjoyed extensive powers and rights of enjoyment over equally fictitious 'possessions'. In contemporary Britain, legal scholars and senior judges disagree on whether debts and contractual liabilities should continue to be treated as 'possessions' and give rise to proprietary remedies.[40] The consequences of further relaxation or blurring of the legal definitions and boundaries of these seemingly archaic legal categories are critical. According to Bridge, as value chains are increasingly based on intangibles in global trade, the distinction between personal and property rights has become 'the testing-ground of insolvency where a claimant who can assert a real right against a trustee-in-bankruptcy, an administrator or a liquidator is in a superior position to the general body of unsecured creditors'.[41] Additional pressures forcing further adaptations and expansion of the fictitious legal categories are accelerating with the digital revolution.[42]

4.2 INTELLECTUAL PROPERTY AS FICTITIOUS POSSESSIONS

Much like investments and shares, intellectual property rights (IPRs) crystallized as fictitious legal 'possessions' in civil and common law systems in the nineteenth century. The consensus amongst historians of IP is that there is no evidence of the existence of a legal framework for the grant of exclusive rights

[38] Contrast Pretto-Sakmann's argument that alienability and transferability are not specific to rights in rem in Arianna Pretto-Sakmann, *Boundaries of Personal Property Law: Shares and Sub-Shares* (Oxford: Hart, 2005).

[39] On fictitious legal persons see Chapter 3.

[40] See, for instance, Lord Hoffman delivering the majority judgment in *OBG Ltd* v. *Allan* [2007] UKHL 21 and Lord Nichols and Lady Hale's minority judgments.

[41] Michael Bridge, et al., *The Law of Personal Property* (London: Sweet & Maxwell, 2021), pp. 1–5.

[42] See Law Commission's project *Adapting English Law for the Digital Revolution*, 2020 and Commissioner Sarah Green's comments: 'Smart contracts, digitised assets and electronic documents promise to revolutionise the way we do business, digitising existing processes and in some cases introducing entirely new concepts. There are, however, lingering uncertainties about whether and how English law can accommodate these.' www.lawcom.gov.uk/adapting-english-law-for-the-digital-revolution.

over inventions before the Middle Ages.[43] Some of the elements of modern conceptions of 'intellectual' property first emerge in medieval Europe.[44] Before then, there are some isolated examples of individuals being rewarded or granted special honours in antiquity, but there was no culture or practice in Ancient Greece or Rome of attributing property rights to individuals over novel creations or useful inventions. The grant of exclusive rights to individuals over their creations and inventions did not fit into the philosophical and cultural values of the time or the socio-economic organization of labour. Neither did it fit into Roman law's dual category of rights in personam over incorporeal intangibles and rights in rem over corporeal, tangible things. It took several centuries for the elements of modern conceptions of 'intellectual' property to crystallize and for patents, copyright and trademarks to settle as distinct bodies of law. The first turning point coincides with the rise of mercantilism in feudal Europe and the practice of granting individual privileges through charters, licenses and 'letters patent'.[45]

4.2.1 *Britain*

Venice is generally credited with the adoption of early forms of patent laws in the fifteenth century.[46] But by the eighteenth century it was the British model

[43] See, for instance, Pamela O. Long, 'Invention, Authorship, "Intellectual Property", and the Origin of Patents: Notes toward a Conceptual History' (1991) 32(4) *Technology and Culture* 846–884; Russ VerSteeg, 'The Roman Law Roots of Copyright' (2000) 59 *Maryland Law* Review 522; Oren Bracha, *The History of Intellectual Property Law* (Cheltenham: Edward Elgar, 2018).

[44] Long, 'Invention, Authorship, "Intellectual Property", and the Origin of Patents'. Long argues that some of the components of the notion of 'intellectual property' are evident in antiquity; the fully developed concept first emerges in the medieval period around the twelfth or thirteenth centuries.

[45] Oxford English Dictionary: from Latin *patent-* 'lying open', from the verb *patere*. The meaning of 'patentes' derives from the latin 'patere' which meant 'to lay open'.

[46] The Statute of Venice adopted in 1474, granting exclusive *privilegi* for new and ingenious devices of great utility to the commonwealth for a term ten years, did not lead to widespread practice. See Susan Sell and Christopher May, 'Moments in Law: Contestation and Settlement in the History of Intellectual Property' (2001) 8(3) *Review of International Political Economy* 467–500. See also Christopher May, 'The Hypocrisy of Forgetfulness: The Contemporary Significance of Early Innovations in Intellectual Property' (2007) 14(1) *Review of International Political Economy* 1–25 citing Braudel's claim that nine out of ten patents in Venice related to particular problems of the city (p. 5) in Fernand Braudel, *The Structures of Everyday Life: The Limits of the Possible. Civilisation and Capitalism. 15th–18th Century, Volume 1* (London: Collins, 1981).

from which American and French revolutionaries drew inspiration.[47] In medieval Britain, patent privileges granted by the monarch would typically entitle tradesmen or craftsmen with specialist skills to practice or teach the skills for a limited of time.[48] For instance, in 1331 Edward III granted a patent to John Kempe of Flanders and all his apprentices, servant dyers and weavers to settle in England, Ireland, Wales and Scotland in return for the practice and teaching of their skills.[49] Similar letters patent were issued to weavers to settle in York and to clockmakers from Delft to settle in England. Some elements of these early patent privileges carried over when patent privileges became exclusive rights in the seventeenth century.[50] But it was not until the seventeenth century that the elements of modern English patent law were put in place.[51] Until then there were no formal requirements. The grant of the patent privileges did not necessarily relate to a new 'invention' by an individual inventor. The original purpose was a public good, typically to incentivize the importation of trade and skills of benefit to the realm,[52] but the Crown's grant of monopolies was at odds with the 'common right' of all merchants to move and trade freely in England proclaimed in Magna Carta and recognized by the courts.[53] The monopolies were also intensely disliked by the trade

47 Gabriel Galvez-Behar explains that in France Stanislas de Boufflers stressed the English exemplar in his Rapport sur la propriété des auteurs de nouvelles découvertes et inventions en tout genre d'industrie presented to the Constituent Assembly in 1790. The law on patents, de Boufflers said, had made England 'a great corporation of arts and trades: a fearful association, where the most skilled craftsmen and the best manufacturers and above all the most inventive geniuses of all nations [rushed] to join'. Gabriel Galvez-Behar, 'The 1883 Paris Convention and the Impossible Unification of Industrial Property' in Graeme Gooday and Steven Wilf, *Patent Cultures: Diversity and Harmonization in Historical Perspective* (Cambridge: Cambridge University Press, 2020), p. 40, https://shs.hal.science/halshs-01009953/document.

48 Ramon A. Klitzke, 'Historical Background of the English Patent Law' (1959) 41 *Journal of the Patent Office Society* 615.

49 E. W. Hulme, 'The History of the Patent System under the Prerogative and at Common Law' (1896) 12 *Law Quarterly Review* 141, at 142.

50 Oren Bracha, 'The Commodification of Patents 1600–1836: How Patents Became Rights and Why We Should Care' (2004) 38 *Loyola of Los Angeles Law Review* 177.

51 Christine MacLeod, *Inventing the Industrial Revolution: The English Patent System, 1660–1800* (Cambridge: Cambridge University Press, 2002).

52 Bracha, 'The Commodification of Patents 1600–1836'. According to Bracha, Queen Elizabeth granted a total of fifty-five monopolies between 1561 and 1603, twenty-one of which went to foreigners.

53 Klitzke, 'Historical Background of the English Patent Law'. Klitzke defines a monopoly as 'a privilege consisting of the exclusive right to carry on a particular business or trade, manufacture a particular article, or control the sale of the entire supply of a particular commodity'. Magna Carta 1215, 40, proclaimed the freedom of all merchants to move and trade freely in England: 'All merchants shall have safe and secure exit from England, and entry to England, with the right to tarry there and to move about as well by land as by water,

corporations and guilds which had historically relied on trade secrecy to protect their skills and crafts, with the backing of the courts famously describing patent and copyright monopolies as 'odious'.[54] It was the arbitrary abuse of power by the Crown in the seventeenth century to grant monopolies for its own, rather than the public benefit which prompted Parliament to pass the Statute of Monopolies in 1623.[55] According to Machlup and Penrose's landmark article, the Statute of Monopolies established the principle that patent privileges should only be extended to the 'true and first inventor'.[56] With hindsight, the significance of the Statute appears much greater. Firstly, the Statute marked the beginnings of an institutional shift for the grant of patents from the Crown to what in due course would become a patent office charged with the registration and examination of patent applications. Secondly, the Statute contained the first legal definition of an invention as 'a manner of manufacture'. The definition proved extraordinarily influential and long-lasting. It was only left out of statutory changes to the Patents Act in 1977 when the UK acceded to the European Patent Organization (EPO). To date, the definition remains in force in Australia and other former English colonies. Thirdly, the Statute laid the foundations for the substantive legal requirements for an invention, namely novelty, utility and enhanced specification, which were to be further defined in later statutes.[57]

The main reforms took place in the nineteenth century with the Patent Law Amendment Act of 1852 and 1883.[58] The first reform was prompted by the British government's decision to sponsor the Great Exhibition of the 'works of

for buying and selling by the ancient and right customs, quit from all evil tolls, except (in time of war) such merchants as are of the land at war with us. And if such are found in our land at the beginning of the war, they shall be detained, without injury to their bodies or goods, until information be received by us, or by our chief justiciar, how the merchants of our land found in the land at war with us are treated; and if our men are safe there, the others shall be safe in our land.'

54 See Edward C. Walterscheid, 'Defining the Patent and Copyright Term: Term Limits and the Intellectual Property Clause' (2000) 7 *Journal of Intellectual Property Law* 315.

55 Joshua Williams, *Rights of Common and Other Prescriptive Rights: Being Twenty-Four Lectures Delivered in Gray's Inn Hall in the Year 1877* (London: H. Sweet, 1880), p. 289.

56 Fritz Machlup, and Edith Penrose. 'The patent controversy in the nineteenth century'. *The Journal of Economic History* 10.1 (1950): 1–29.

57 Statutory options to extend the term for another seven or fourteen years were introduced in 1835 and 1944. For a detailed account of legislative attempts to reform the law on patents, see Phillip Johnson, *Privatised Law Reform* (Routledge, 2017).

58 See Moureen Coulter, *Property in Ideas: The Patent Question in Mid-Victorian Britain* (Philadelphia: Thomas Jefferson University Press, 1991).

industry of all nations' to be held in 1851 in London.[59] British exhibitors feared that unless patent laws were strengthened, the public display of machines and processes would result in domestic piracy and/or foreign appropriation of new technology by industrial spies and Britain would suffer public humiliation in the eyes of European and American rivals.[60] The Act provided that an inventor applying for a patent (Petitioner) had to use a prescribed form which stated that

> Petitioner (who) is in possession of Invention for [the Title of the Invention,] which Invention he believes will be of great public Utility; that he is the true and first Inventor thereof; and that the same is not in use by any other Person or Persons, to the best of his Knowledge and Belief.

The term 'in possession of invention' was not defined.[61] Did the inventor have to be in physical possession of a new machine or physical process? Or was it sufficient for the applicant to have thought of or devised a new machine that had not yet been constructed but for which he/she could attach drawings and specifications? The statutory absence of further definition conveniently elided the difficult question of how patent rights fit into the formal categories of personal rights over intangibles and proprietary rights over tangible things. It also avoided controversial questions about the principled basis for the grant of the patent rights. In her insightful study of patent law reforms in Victorian Britain, Moureen Coulter shows how, in the following decades, the questions shifted from 'should the State protect the rights of inventors' to 'should the State recognize property in ideas?'[62]

Without exception, Coulter tells us, patent advocates in Britain endorsed the utilitarian, positivistic justification of patent rights as incentives to promote industrial progress and economic prosperity.[63] Some argued that 'In a market economy, where the profitability of an occupation determined its viability as a career choice, the artificial rights conferred by patents made invention profitable'.[64] Other patent advocates drew a distinction between the 'ideas' of theoretical science and practical applications:

59 See Aurora Plomer, 'Trading Intellectual Property Rights in Europe: From IP Nationalism to International IP' (16 June 2022), LSE Legal Studies Working Paper No. 12/2022.

60 Coulter, *Property in Ideas*, p. 64.

61 The Act repeated the definition of invention in the Statute of Monopolies 'The Expression "Invention" shall mean any Manner of new Manufacture the Subject of Letters Patent and Grant of Privilege within the Meaning of the Act of the Twenty-First Year of the Reign of King James the First, Chapter Three'.

62 Coulter, *Property in Ideas*, p. 155.

63 Ibid.

64 Ibid., citing patent agent Mathew Soul at p. 156.

> between ideas that are matters of science or common knowledge and ideas embodied in a description and illustration of means for carrying into practical effect a new manufacture.[65]

They accepted that 'it would not be just to give an individual the exclusive right to appropriate ideas already common and acted upon by others'[66] but argued that the grant of rights of exclusivity could be justified for new practical applications for industry:

> yet for all this it may be just, and on public grounds politic, to give him a temporary legal right to open some new channel of industry by a new practical application held by him in common with others.[67]

This was justified because the invention bore the personal imprint of the inventor. The inventors were said to give the common ideas from which they drew a unique expression. The inventor, they claimed, 'stamps the character of his mind on his invention as well as an author is known to do on his book'.[68]

Patent abolitionists rejected the analogy between inventions and artistic creations. They argued that inventions were not unique and, as such, could not be the object of exclusive possession and property rights.[69] They accepted that inventors applied existing ideas in ways that might be new, but they argued that this was because inventions resulted from the logical application of the existing laws of physics or chemistry. This meant that others following the same logic would similarly arrive at the same invention. Therefore, unlike artistic creations, inventions were not imbued with the personality of the inventor:

> If Milton had not written Paradise Lost, and Handel had not composed the Messiah, neither of those splendid productions of the creative powers of the mind would ever have seen the light; but if Watt had not invented his famous condensing steam engine, there can be little doubt that long ere this it would have been discovered.[70]

The patent controversy was ultimately resolved in favour of patent advocates, notwithstanding the fact that the new statutory rights of exclusivity did not fit into the formal division of rights in personam over intangibles and rights in

65 Ibid., citing patent agent William Spence at p. 158.
66 Ibid.
67 Ibid.
68 Ibid., p. 165.
69 Ibid.
70 William Mathewson Hindmarch, *Observations on the Defects of the Patent Laws of This Country: With Suggestions for the Reform of Them* (London: Wm. Benning, 1851) cited by Coulter, *Property in Ideas*, p. 141.

rem over tangible possessions. In law, IPRs emerged as a novel category of intangible property and fictitious possession.

In his widely cited textbook *Principles of the Law of Personal Property*, the nineteenth-century English barrister Joshua Williams described patents and copyrights as a new species of incorporeal property which, like shares and investment funds, were a source of wealth previously unknown to the common law.[71] For want of better classification, Williams said, these new rights 'are now usually spoken of as ... [things] in action. They are, in fact, personal property of an incorporeal nature'.[72] Although Williams added patents and copyrights to his book on 'personal incorporeal property', he acknowledged that, unlike personal rights, patents were assignable: 'The privileges granted by letters-patent are therefore plainly an instance of an incorporeal kind of personal property, different in its nature from a mere chose in action, which never has been assignable at law.'[73] Moreover, unlike contracts and debts which became extinguished at death, patents and copyright remained valid against the whole world for a limited time. Thus, in respect of alienability, patents and copyright shared the main features of in rem, proprietary rights attached to tangible possessions.[74]

Another author described patents and copyright as 'subjectless rights in rem', arguing that the time limitation was because

> Property in material products and commodities can be protected without interfering with the productive enterprise of others, but property in ideas cannot be protected without interfering more or less with the intellectual enterprise of others. Patent-right involves, from a practical or business point of view, a monopoly of ideas, and limits the field of invention.[75]

Others described patents and copyright as hybrid rights, sharing features of both personal rights (or 'choses in action') and property rights over tangible

71 Joshua Williams, *Principles of the Law of Personal Property: Intended for the Use of Students in Conveyancing*, 4th ed. (London: H. Sweet, 1860), p. 6. 'The funds now afford an investment, of which our forefathers were happily ignorant, whilst canal and railway shares, and other shares in joint stock companies, and patents and copy- rights, are evidently modern sources of wealth.'

72 Ibid.

73 Ibid., p. 201.

74 The 1852 Act expressly provided that patents whose term had not expired could be granted to executors and administrators at any time within three months of the death of the applicant. For a detailed bibliography of patent-related legislative reforms, see Phillip Johnson, *Parliament, Inventions and Patents: A Research Guide and Bibliography* (London: Routledge, 2018).

75 Jean Etienne Reenen de Villiers, *The History of the Legislation concerning Real and Personal Property in England during the Reign of Queen Victoria* (London: C. J. Clay and Sons, 1901), p. 127.

possessions.[76] Writing in the *Law Quarterly Review* in 1895, Spencer Broadhurst's answer to whether copyright was a chose in action was that

> An attempt to identify the division of property into choses in action and choses in possession, with the division into things corporeal and things incorporeal, can only lead to confusion, and therefore copyrights, patent rights, and rights of all kinds, if they must be classed as property at all, should be classed under the head, to which I submit that they more properly belong, of property in constructive possession.[77]

Constructive possession is another way of expressing that the subject of the property is not in fact in the possession of the holder but is fictitiously treated in law as if it was.

Thus, the debates that erupted in the nineteenth century over whether IPRs were a type of 'possession' had two distinct, but interlinked, dimensions. The first related to the assimilation of 'intellectual' property to the legal class of things that were capable of physical 'possession'. The second centred on whether the incorporeal, intangible objects of IPRs, the inventions or creative works, could be adequately distinguished from ideas. The assumption behind the forced assimilation of incorporeal 'intellectual' property to physical, tangible 'possessions' was that the objects or subject matter of IP were akin to physical objects. In truth, an invention or creative work cannot be identified and described in the same way as a piece of land or a table. As argued by contemporary IP scholars, the objects or subject matter of IPRs are of a

[76] Howard Elphinstone, 'What Is a Chose in Action' (1893) 9 *Law Quarterly Review* 314; Spencer Broadhurst, 'Is Copyright a Chose in Action' (1895) 11 *Law Quarterly Review* 64; T. C. Williams, 'Property Things in Action and Copyright' (1895) 11 *Law Quarterly Review* 223; C. Sweet, 'Choses in Action' (1895) 11 *Law Quarterly Review* 238. For a detailed discussion of legislative reforms see Phillip Johnson, *Privatised Law Reform: A History of Patent Law through Private Legislation, 1620–1907* (London: Routledge, 2017).

[77] Broadhurst, 'Is Copyright a Chose in Action', p. 75. Broadhurst cites Lindley L.J. in *Colonial Bank* v. *Whinney*, 30 Ch. D. 284 (CA) (1885) Lindley states that whatever the original meaning of 'choses in action' may have been, due to the lack of a word to denote a certain type of incorporeal property, its original meaning has been extended. Joshua Williams on Personal Property is quoted on choses in action including copyright and patents, 9th edition, 6 and 20. Broadhurst concludes: 'To sum up, then, there is this great distinction between debts, money in the funds, and perhaps shares, and such intangible forms of property as copyrights and patents, that while in the former cases there are two parties standing towards each other in the relation of debtor and creditor, the legal owner-the creditor-not having enjoyment of his property; in the latter there is a single person only, who is legal owner, and who has enjoyment of his property as far as he can ever have it. These various kinds of property "are so different in their nature and legal incidents, that care must be taken not to be misled by giving them all a common name which conceals their differences".'

different nature to the physical objects or 'possessions' of ordinary language in that their boundaries are defined by the nexus of users' rights.[78]

4.2.2 France

In France, letters patents had been issued by the King for at least two centuries before the French Revolution and the entrenchment of everyone's natural, inalienable sacred right to property in the French Declaration of the Rights of Man of 1789.[79] The justification for property rights over literary works was articulated by the philosophers of the Enlightenment. Unlike the utilitarian British advocates of IPRs, Diderot was firmly of the view that property rights were a natural, inalienable right, but he too shared the view that IPRs were like physical things capable of possession. In his 'Lettre sur le commerce de la librairie' (1763) Diderot objected to the Loi of 21 Mar 1749 which he said distinguished literary works from other possessions, limiting the duration of the rights.[80] An author's work, Diderot said, is an expression of his/her personal life, his education and his research; his ideas and feelings are immortalized in his/her work. They are not common property but *his/her* property and no less worthy of perpetual legal protection than his/her house,

78 See Ole-Andreas Rognstad, *Property Aspects of Intellectual Property*. Cambridge Intellectual Property and Information Law (Cambridge: Cambridge University Press, 2018); Alexander Peukert, *A Critique of the Ontology of Intellectual Property Law* (Cambridge: Cambridge University Press, 2021).

79 Jacques Isoré, 'De l'existence des brevets d'invention en droit français avant 1791' (1937) 16 *Revue historique de droit français et étranger (1922–)* 94–130. See also Long, 'Invention, Authorship, "Intellectual Property", and the Origin of Patents' and Jane C. Ginsburg showing that author's rights do not always occupy a central place within copyright legal history in Jane C. Ginsberg, 'A Tale of Two Copyrights: Literary Property in Revolutionary France and America' (1990) 64 *Tulane Law Review*. See Lionel Bently, et al., *Privilege and Property: Essays on the History of Copyright* (Cambridge: Open Book Publishers, 2010).

80 Denis Diderot, *Lettre Sur Le Commerce de La Librairie* (Paris: Librairies Fontaine, 1984): 'Les productions littéraires ont été distinguées par le législateur des autres possessions ; la loi a pensé à en assurer la jouissance à l'auteur ; L'arrêt du 21 mars 1749 les déclare non saisissables. Que devient cette prérogative si les vues nouvelles prévalent ? Quoi ! un particulier aliène à perpétuité un fonds, une maison, un champ, il en prive ses héritiers, sans que l'autorité publique lui demande compte de sa conduite. Il en tire toute la valeur, se l'applique à lui-même comme il lui plaît, et un littérateur n'aura pas le même droit ? Il s'adressera à la protection du souverain pour être maintenu dans la plus légitime des possessions ; et le roi qui ne la refuse pas au moindre de ses sujets quand elle ne préjudicie à personne, la limitera à un certain intervalle de temps, à l'expiration duquel un ouvrage qui aura consumé son bien, sa santé, sa vie et qui sera compté au nombre des monuments de la nation, s'échappera de son héritage, de ses propres mains, pour devenir un effet commun?'

chattels, land and other possessions. No one other than the author is entitled to the enjoyment of his possessions, their use, exploitation and disposal.[81]

Despite the French emphasis on natural, inalienable rights, French intellectual property (IP) laws promulgated after the Revolution expressly acknowledge the socio-economic value of IPRs. The Preambles of both the Loi of 7 Janvier 1791 and Loi of 25 May 1791 proclaim that 'each new idea whose expression or development could be useful to society, belongs in the first instance to the person who has conceived it' whilst asserting that 'it would be an attack on the rights of man, in their very essence, to deny the author ownership of an industrial invention'. Nevertheless, Article 1 in the Loi of 7 Janvier 1791 stated that enjoyment of the rights is not perpetual but time-limited and conditional:

> Any new discovery or invention, in any type of industry, belongs to its author; consequently, the law guarantees its full enjoyment for the duration and manner set out below.[82] (translated by the author)

The conditions and duration of the right were detailed in subsequent Articles which refer to authors and inventors interchangeably. Authors and inventors had an inherent right to exclusive use of their inventions or creations, but the right was time-limited, after which ownership ceded to the public:

> At expiration, the discovery or invention will belong to society, the specification will be made public, and its use permitted anywhere in the kingdom, so that each citizen may freely exercise and enjoy its use.[83] (translated by the author)

81 Ibid. 'En effet, quel est le bien qui puisse appartenir à un homme, si un ouvrage d'esprit, le fruit unique de son éducation, de ses études, de ses veilles, de son temps, de ses recherches, de ses observations ; si les plus belles heures, les plus beaux moments de sa vie ; si ses propres pensées, les sentiments de son cœur, la portion de lui-même la plus précieuse, celle qui ne périt point, celle qui l'immortalise, ne lui appartient pas ? Quelle comparaison entre l'homme, la substance même de l'homme, son âme, et le champ, le pré, l'arbre ou la vigne que la nature offrait dans le commencement également à tous, et que le particulier ne s'est approprié que par la culture, le premier moyen légitime de possession ? Qui est plus en droit que l'auteur de disposer de sa chose par don ou par vente ? Or le droit du propriétaire est la vraie mesure du droit de l'acquéreur.'

82 'Toute découverte ou nouvelle invention, dans tous les genres d'industrie, est la propriété de son auteur; en conséquence, la loi lui en garantit la pleine et entière jouissance, suivant le mode et pour le temps qui seront ci-après déterminés.'

83 Article 15. 'A l'expiration de chaque patente, la découverte ou invention devant appartenir à la société, la description en sera rendue publique, et l'usage en deviendra permis dans tout le royaume, afin que tout citoyen puisse librement l'exercer et en jouir, à moins qu'un décret du Corps législatif n'ait prorogé l'exercice de la patente, ou n'en ait ordonné le secret, dans les cas prévus par l'article 11.'

Thus, as argued by Gabriel Galvez-Behar, the French and English patent and copyright laws were justified by different philosophical cultures but overlapping utilitarian economic objectives which shaped the legal scope of the rights.[84] Authors and inventors were granted time-limited exclusive rights over new inventions or creations.

Much like British law, the objects of the exclusive rights were ill-defined. They were referred to as new ideas or inventions, or artistic works. They were classified in French law as rights over *movable* property, a category normally denoting tangible chattel.[85] The nature of the rights straddled the formal boundaries of rights in rem and rights in personam.

By the middle of the nineteenth century, the key elements of IPRs as a new type of fictitious possession in law had been laid in both the British and French legal systems.[86] The extension of property rights to new inventions and creative works had been achieved in both systems by assimilating the protected 'intellectual' works to physical, tangible things. It was the German law professor Josef Kohler who articulated the theory behind the construction of intellectual property as 'immaterial' possessions.

4.2.3 *Germany*

In Germany, prior to national unification in 1870–71, there were thirty-nine states and no single patent system until the adoption of the German patent statute of 1877 and establishment of the Berlin Patent Office.[87] The historian Karl Hall explains that in the 1870s, the prevailing view in Germany was that the inventor's right was a private, personality-based right rather than a property right.[88] This meant that legal protection of intangible inventions in the German patent statute of 1877 was difficult to accommodate within the formal categories of personality and property-based rights in German civil law, much like in French and British law. Leading figures such as Werner Siemens, who pressed for the adoption of the 1877 statute, had firmly rejected

[84] See Gabriel Galvez-Behar, 'The 1883 Paris Convention and the Impossible Unification of Industrial Property' (2020) *Patent Cultures: Diversity and Harmonization in Historical Perspective* 38–68.

[85] Article 14, l'inventeur '… pourra disposer de sa patente comme d'une propriété mobilière'.

[86] See Bently et al., *Privilege and Property*.

[87] Karl Hall, 'The Struggle over the Social Function of Intellectual Work in the Economy of Nations' in Graeme Gooday and Steven Wilf (eds.), *Patent Cultures: Diversity and Harmonization in Historical Perspective* (Cambridge: Cambridge University Press, 2020), vol. 52, pp. 201–220, citing Jan Vojáček, *A Survey of the Principal National Patent Systems* (New York: Prentice Hall, 1936), p. 202.

[88] Ibid.

the view that the statute created property rights over intellectual creations.[89] The statute avoided the controversy by leaving the term 'invention' undefined, ostensibly because the purpose of the act was not to grant inventors patent rights but 'to encourage inventors to disclose trade secrets'.[90]

It was the Berlin law professor Josef Kohler (1849–1919) who articulated the theory that patents were a sui generis species of property whose objects were not material, tangible things but 'intellectual' or 'immaterial' goods.[91] Kohler had begun to develop a theory of rights to intangible, 'immaterial' goods (Immaterialgüterrecht) in the 1870s, incorporating the theory into widely used textbooks of patent law. The rights of inventors and creators, according to Kohler, were not grounded in inherent natural rights to property.[92] Instead, Kohler maintained that whilst the invention may originate in the mind of an individual as an abstract, intangible idea, as soon as the idea entered the public domain it became 'as air and light, res communis omnium' and was no longer under the control of the individual.[93]

Kohler thought that jurists should accept the fortuitous industry-driven concept of patent rights in the 1877 statute and focus on developing the juridical science to accommodate it. According to Hall, what set Kohler apart from his rivals was his systematic appeal to comparative law. Keenly aware that French and American jurisprudence had little interest for German formalists, Kohler appealed to the Supreme Court of the United States decision in *Seymour* v. *Osborne* (1870)[94] as evidence that a property-like construal was

[89] Cited in Ibid., at note 21.

[90] Ibid., p. 206.

[91] Josef Kohler, 'Aus der Praxis' (1875) 41 *Annalen der badischen Gerichte* 100–104, cited at note 43 by Hall, 'The Struggle over the Social Function of Intellectual Work'.

[92] Ibid. But on a social contract between the individual and society. Kohler was a fierce critic of Kant on copyright. See Peukert's discussion in Peukert, *A Critique of the Ontology of Intellectual Property Law*, p. 8 citing Anne Barron, 'Kant, Copyright and Communicative Freedom' (2012) 31(1) *Law and Philosophy* 1–48. See also Abraham Drassinower, *What's Wrong with Copying?* (Cambridge, MA: Harvard University Press, 2015), p. 8.

[93] See Galvez-Behar, 'The 1883 Paris Convention and the Impossible Unification of Industrial Property' cited at note 43.

[94] In *Seymour* v. *Osborne*, 78 U.S. 516 (1870), the United States Supreme Court held that 'Inventions secured by letters patent are property in the holder of the patent, and as such are as much entitled to protection as any other property consisting of a franchise during the term for which the franchise or the exclusive right is granted. Letters patent are not to be regarded as monopolies, created by the executive authority at the expense and to the prejudice of all the community except the persons therein named as patentees, but as public franchises granted to the inventors of new and useful improvements for the purpose of securing to them, as such inventors, for the limited term therein mentioned, the exclusive right and liberty to make and use and vend to others to be used their own inventions, as tending to promote the progress of science and the useful arts, and as matter of compensation to the inventors for their labor, toil,

warranted. He invoked both British and French law as helpful models in recognizing the prior art.

Kohler argued that whilst inventions and creations have an undeniably individual character, they are also deeply embedded in the life of the community. As explained by Galvez-Behar, the implications of the German model were pragmatic. In contrast to the French model based on the eternal, inalienable rights of the inventor, for Kohler the legal delineation of IPRs had to address 'social and historical constraints' and, above all, the interests of industry.[95] As inventions and creations were reducible neither to personal contractual rights nor to alienable proprietary rights normally relating to material, tangible goods, what was required was the creation of a new category of proprietary rights whose objects were immaterial, intangible goods. In order to spread the benefits of the invention, the scope of the inventor's rights over these immaterial goods and their delineation had to respond to the needs of industry and capital. It was the need for law's adaptation to the economic pressures of the time which motivated the creation of a novel legal category of property rights whose objects were allegedly not legal fictions but 'immaterial', 'intellectual' goods.

The difficulty with IP as a type of 'immaterial' thing is that, since the objects of IP are not physical things, for example, the literary work is not the printed book and the anti-bacterial formula is not the liquid in a bottle, it is not clear how the 'immaterial' inventions or creative works and their legal boundaries are to be identified. For Rognstad and Peukert,[96] the idea of immaterial, intangible objects on which modern IP is founded rests on a flawed ontology. The objects or subject matter of IPRs are not immaterial goods akin to physical things: they are legal constructs and their identity is defined by the legal nexus of rights over use and exceptions. Rognstad draws on legislation and decisions of US and EU courts illustrating the endemic conflation of the objects of IPRs with the rights as objects. For instance, the US Supreme Court's *Monsanto* ruling on trade secrets and data regulation suggests that what is being protected against takings is the (intangible) data constituting the trade secret. However, Rognstad argues that it is clear from the Court's decision that it is not the data as such that constitutes the 'property interest'

and expense in making the inventions and reducing the same to practice for the public benefit, as contemplated by the Constitution and sanctioned by the laws of Congress' at p. 538.

95 Galvez-Behar, 'The 1883 Paris Convention and the Impossible Unification of Industrial Property', p. 54.

96 Rognstad, *Property Aspects of Intellectual Property* and Peukert, A *Critique of the Ontology of Intellectual Property Law*.

but the 'legal positions' protecting the data.[97] Similarly, the whole concept of distribution of a copy in EU legislation 'becomes a fiction in the peer-to-peer file-sharing situation where the copy received by the use of the file-sharing system is not identical to the copy uploaded by the file-sharer'.[98] Other illustrations of the enduring confusion of patents and copyrights with physical, tangible things or 'possessions' in relation to Artificial Intelligence (AI) are discussed by Oren Bracha.[99] Legal categories are stretched and legal fictions are created to accommodate social and economic changes, leading to conceptual tensions in the process. For Coulter, what took place in Britain with the conceptualization of patents as a species of fictitious, intangible possessions was a reciprocal adjustment of law and industrial capitalism.[100] A new wave of adjustments is underway with the digital and AI revolution.[101]

This chapter completes the comparative historical analysis of 'possessions' held by natural and legal persons in Europe by charting the emergence of 'intellectual' property as a novel type of intangible 'possession'. It shows that at the end of the nineteenth century, IPRs had been assimilated to rights over tangible, physical property in domestic European laws as a fictitious type of 'possession'. By the time the European Convention was adopted in 1950, French, English and German jurists would have been fully aware that in law 'possessions' were legal fictions. By contrast to natural language, the term 'possessions', in law, was an umbrella term for objects of property rights encompassing all manners of intangible, incorporeal and 'intellectual' property. In law, 'possessions' were not confined to the land, home or personal belongings of individual human persons which the advocates of property rights had argued required protection as a fundamental human right to enable development of the human personality. On the contrary, and unlike in natural language, the meaning of possessions in law had expanded over time to include company shares and 'intellectual' property as fictitious constructs and commodities which could be bought and sold like a house or a piece of land in capitalist market economies.

[97] Ibid., p. 145.

[98] Ibid., p. 121.

[99] Oren Bracha, 'The Work of Copyright in the Age of Machine Production' (24 September 2023) Legal Studies Research Paper, University of Texas Law.

[100] Coulter's thesis expressly draws on Landes *Unbound Promotheus*' view law as a reciprocal reflection of material, economic development: Coulter, *Property in Ideas*, p. 6.

[101] Robin Feldman, 'Regulatory Property: The New IP' (2016) 40 *Columbia Journal of Law & the Arts* 53.

5

Companies as Victims of Violations of A1P1

INTRODUCTION

As seen in Chapter 2, the drafting history of the right to property in the European Convention on Human Rights (ECHR) shows that the drafters did not discuss or contemplate the possibility of companies filing claims as victims of alleged violations of their right to property. Instead, those in favour of including property rights in the Convention justified protection on moral grounds in line with the Universal Declaration of Human Rights (UDHR). Protection of the home and a minimum of personal belongings/possessions were justified as necessary to enable full development of the human personality. For this reason, all sides of the debate concurred that arbitrary deprivation of an individual's home and possessions was a violation of the human right to property. Advocates of property rights also accepted that because property had what they described as a social function, property rights were not absolute but could be limited by the State in the public interest. This partly explains the drafters' intent in phrasing the right as relating to the ambiguous 'enjoyment of possessions'. However, this moral rationale does not justify extension of protection to companies' assets as 'legal persons'. Moreover, as seen in Chapters 3 and 4, the terms 'legal persons' and 'possessions' had a technical, legal meaning whose wide reach was not debated or clearly understood by State representatives in the Assembly. The final text of Article 1 of the First Protocol (A1P1) thus conceals an underlying tension between the universal moral ideal of protecting each individual human person's right to a home and a minimum of personal possessions and the political and economic ideal held by some of the key lawyers who drafted the document that protection of private property was necessary to the pursuit of a liberal European socio-economic order based on market freedoms. The potential tensions and contradictions between the natural and technical, legal meanings inevitably surface when looking for a coherent human rights ethos and principle behind the text. It was left to the now-defunct Commission and the Court to navigate through the ambiguities and tensions embodied in the text to distil the essence of the right to property. The analysis of the Court's case law in this chapter reveals that the decisions gradually became more distant from the moral reading and oriented towards a liberal economic reading of A1P1, ultimately anchoring supranational, constitutional protection of companies' Intellectual Property Rights.

The first wave of claims relating to Intellectual Property Rights (IPRs) was not filed until the early 1980s. Section 5.1 of this chapter shows that, by then, the Commission and Court had developed a set of rules and principles grounding the extension and expansion of A1P1 to IPRs. The early cases on A1P1 in the 1960s and 1970s were predominantly filed by companies. The Commission and Court's deference to national laws, which, as seen in Chapter 4, categorized intangible property as fictitious 'possessions', paved the way for an expansive reading of A1P1. The Court's landmark decision in *Sporrong* v. *Sweden* (1982)[1] entrenched transnational protection of private companies' financial interests as protected fundamental rights under A1P1, guarded by a supranational court applying an expansive 'autonomous' reading of the term 'possessions'. It was not until the early 1980s that the first claims relating to IPRs were filed, by which time the Commission and Court had no difficulty in hearing complaints from multinational global corporations claiming to be victims of State violations of their right to enjoyment of possessions.

Section 5.2 of this chapter examines the Commission and Court's case law on IPRs. In the first phase, from the 1980s until the early 1990s, deference is shown to national laws and a wide margin of appreciation is given to States to regulate IPRs under the second paragraph of A1P1. The next phase and turning point is the Grand Chamber's (GC) landmark judgment of *Anheuser-Busch Inc.* v. *Portugal* in 2007.[2] A detailed analysis reveals a tacit alignment of the scope of protection of IPRs under the Convention with the European Union's (EU) regulatory framework on IPRs, grounding a further extension of A1P1. The third phase has been led by the Court in the last decade. The analysis reveals that in a series of cases relating to patents, copyright and trademarks (TMs), the

[1] Application nos. 7151 and 7152/75, *Sporrong and Lonnroth* v. *Sweden*, decision 23 September 1982.

[2] Application no. 73049/01, *Anheuser-Busch* v. *Portugal* (Grand Chamber), decision 11 January 2007.

Court has adopted a 'rule of law' approach to the construction of A1P1, eluding a substantive application of the 'fair balance' test. Overall, the review of the case law suggests that the future will bring an inevitable tilt of the Court's construction of A1P1 towards the European Union (EU) legal order, consolidating and deepening the liberal economic reading of the right to 'enjoyment of possessions' and supranational protection of companies' IPRs, with little trace left of the original moral intent of entrenching protection of the right of each individual human person to a minimum of personal belongings and home to enable full development of the human personality.

5.1 COMPANIES AS VICTIMS OF VIOLATIONS OF A1P1

Article 1 – First Protocol

1. Every natural or legal person is entitled to the peaceful enjoyment of his possessions. No one shall be deprived of his possessions except in the public interest and subject to the conditions provided for by law and by the general principles of international law.
2. The preceding provisions shall not, however, in any way impair the right of a State to enforce such laws as it deems necessary to control the use of property in accordance with the general interest or to secure the payment of taxes or other contributions or penalties.

The ambiguous wording of the text of A1P1 embodies an uneasy, even contradictory, mix of moral, political and economic perspectives on who is entitled to claim protection for their human right to property and why, opening the way for a multiplicity of interpretations. At one end of the spectrum, a moral reading would limit protection to the home and tangible 'possessions' of the individual human person. At the other end, a liberal economic reading would encompass private ownership of tangible, real property and intangible, personal property including the assets, profits, patents and other IPRs owned by national and transnational corporations. As seen in Chapter 2, the drafting history shows that the latter wide reading, construing companies as subject of human rights and intangible profits as the objects of fundamental rights, was not part of the spectrum contemplated in the debates or expressly defended by property rights advocates. Nor was it consistent with the alleged moral basis of the right reflecting a basic human need for a home and personal belongings. Unsurprisingly, the case law of the now-defunct Commission and Court evidences the ambiguity and tensions in the text, eluding a coherent, principled basis.

Records show that companies were filing applications alleging violations of their human rights under A1P1 from the very beginning. There are thirteen cases on A1P1 reported in the HUDOC database spanning the first ten years of the now-defunct Commission (1959–69) and another thirty-seven cases before the Court issued the first judgment on A1P1 in *Handyside* v. *United Kingdom* (1976),[3] followed by a landmark decision on the meaning of 'possessions' in *Marckx* v. *Belgium* (1979).[4] Until then, the Commission and Court had adopted a deferential approach to national laws in the construction of A1P1, based on a liberal economic reading of A1P1, whereby companies and their intangible assets were assumed to fall within the scope of A1P1 whilst States were allowed a wide margin of discretion in limiting the rights.[5]

In the vast majority of cases, the Commission found the claims inadmissible on procedural grounds, for instance when the applicant had not exhausted all national routes.[6] Alternatively, the application was dismissed on the merits, with the Commission deferring to the contracting State on the alignment of national law measures with the Convention.[7] A rare instance of a decision on the merits relates to a complaint raised jointly by an Icelandic national and a company in which he had a majority shareholding: *Gudmundsson* v. *Iceland* (1966).[8] The applicants complained, inter alia, that tax measures relating to large properties and companies' assets, imposed by legislation adopted by the Icelandic government in 1957, were a violation of their constitutional right to property in the Icelandic constitution and their right to property under A1P1. The claimants

[3] Application no. 5493/72, *Handyside* v. *the United Kingdom*, decision 7 December 1976. The right to dispose of one's property was said to be a traditional and fundamental aspect of the right of property (p. 29, para. 62).

[4] Not all cases heard by the Commission are reported.

[5] See for instance Case No. 511/59, *Gudmundsson* v. *Iceland*, decision 20 December 1960.

[6] Some claims were declared inadmissible because they related to a period prior to the State's ratification of the Protocol: Case No. 150/56, X. v. *German Federal Republic*. The report in International Law Reports, vol. 24, pp. 355–356 cites 'Report: Documents et Décisions, 1955–56–57', p. 181 (in French).

[7] Dismissal of claims on the merits typically concerned legislation adopted by States regarding taxation, redistribution of land and other measures found by the Commission to be consistent with the power granted to States to control use of property in the general interest under A1P1.2. See for instance Case No. 551/59, X v. *Germany*, decision 31 May 1959 holding that the claim was inadmissible because 'The Liability Equalisation Act complied with the conditions in Article 1(1) of the First Protocol to the Convention in that it had been introduced as part of the financial and monetary reforms in Germany after the war, which were considered necessary for establishing a sound basis for the new democratic society. An express purpose of the Law was to distribute the resultant economic burdens proportionately among the citizens'. See also the Commission Plenary's dismissal of a barrister's complaint of the imposition of taxes on employers in Case No. 6087/73, X v. *Austria*, decision 13 May 1975. Other similar dismissals under the second paragraph of A1P1 include Case No. 6837/74, *X. and others* v. *Belgium*, decision 2 October 1975 on redistribution of land or redistributive measures affecting landowners.

[8] Case No. 511/59, *Gudmundsson* v. *Iceland*.

alleged that the tax burden was politically inspired by 'a Communist-influenced' Parliament and Government 'to take over private enterprise for the purpose of suppressing the institution of private property'. The complaint further stated that 'A pursuit of a policy of nationalisation would eventually lead to a complete denial of the human rights which were fundamental for the preservation of Western Democracy'.[9] The application was dismissed in the national courts and by the Commission on the substantive merits of the claim. The Commission stated that A1P1 was not intended to provide a ground for constitutional review of domestic legislation involving the taking of property affecting nationals. The principles of general international law referred to in A1P1, the Commission said, were directed at 'the confiscation of the property [424] of foreigners'. From this, the Commission concluded that

> measures taken by a State with respect to the property of its own nationals are not subject to these general principles of international law in the absence of a particular treaty clause specifically so providing.[10]

The complaint was dismissed by the Commission on the merits, as the taxes introduced by Law No. 44 of 1957 were found to be 'in every way consistent with what are contemplated in paragraph one of A1P1, as permissible interferences with a person's right to the peaceful enjoyment of his possessions'.[11] The Commission also rejected the company's claim that the differential tax treatment of cooperatives and joint-stock companies was discriminatory considering the room for manoeuvre left to Member States under the second paragraph of A1P1.[12]

Two years later, the Commission's economic reading of A1P1 is again evident in X v. *Austria* (1962).[13] The claimant had been granted licenses for

9 Ibid., para. 22.

10 Ibid., p. 266. Something worthy of note is that notwithstanding the Commission's claim that the references to international law were intended by the drafters to apply only to deprivation of property owned by foreigners, it is by no means clear that the travaux preparatoires support this interpretation. Moreover, the Commission's interpretation at a stroke de jure barred claims from national applicants whose property may have been confiscated on arbitrary, discriminatory grounds, for instance claims from German Jews whose homes and personal belongings were seized under the Nazi regime. There is no evidence in the travaux preparatoires that such an outcome was intended. A similar liberal economic reading is evident in a Commission decision the following year: the claimant had deposited bank notes in Pays Bas bank. Currency was devalued after the war causing C loss. Commission held that State had acted within P1.A2, impliedly accepting that A1P1 applied to Case No. 1017/61, X v. *The Netherlands*, decision 18 September 1961.

11 Ibid.

12 Ibid.

13 Case No. 1008/61, X v. *Austria*, decision 5 March 1962.

the prospecting of hydrocarbon. Following Anschluss, the licenses were revoked and X was sent to a concentration camp. When he was freed, he went to live in France and sought compensation from Austria. This time, the Commission dismissed the claim on the grounds that it had no jurisdiction to hear the complaint because the claims predated Austria's accession to the Convention in 1958 and Austria had entered a reservation in respect of measures relating to war claims under A1P1.[14] The Commission also dismissed on procedural grounds a claim from a company called Retimag created by the German Communist party to safeguard property which stood to be confiscated following the banning of the Communist party. The claimants argued that the refusal to indemnify was a violation of A1P1. The claim was held inadmissible on the grounds that the claimant had not exhausted all available routes of appeal at the German Constitutional Court.[15]

Muller v. *Austria* is a rare instance of a claim found to be admissible by the Commission.[16] The Commission held that an obligation to contribute to a social security scheme may in certain circumstances give rise to a property right under A1P1. The Commission cited a previous decision in X v. *the Netherlands* where the existence of such a right was said to depend on the way in which the assets were used for the payment of a pension.[17]

5.1.1 *Companies' Property: The Renvoi to National Fictitious 'Possessions'*

As late as 1976, the Commission was still assuming that intangibles were 'possessions' within the meaning of A1P1 whilst dismissing applications on procedural or substantive merits. For instance, a claim against Austria by four companies[18] was dismissed on the assumption that 'even assuming that losses of property or income suffered by the applicant companies in connection with their above obligations can be regarded as deprivations of possessions within the meaning of A1P1(1), they are covered by the exception provided for in A1P1 (1.2) as being necessary to secure the payment of taxes and contributions'.

14 For an example of a similar other earlier dismissal based on the fact that the defendant State (Germany) had not ratified the protocol at the time of the complaint see Case No. 712/60, *Retimag S.A.* v. *Federal Republic of Germany*, decision 16 December 1961.

15 Case No. 5849/72, *Muller* v. *Austria*, decision 16 December 1974.

16 Ibid.

17 Case No. 4130/69, *X* v. *The Netherlands*, decision 20 July 1971. Contrast Case No. 6572/74, X. v. *Federal Republic of Germany*, decision 4 March 1976. The applicant had contributed to social security fund in Germany prior to emigrating and taking Argentinian nationality in 1953. Legislation barring payment of pension to non-nationals deemed in accordance with A1P1(1.2).

18 Case No. 7427/76, *W., X., Y. and Z.* v. *Austria*, decision 27 September 1976. The legislation imposed on employers an obligation to deduct taxes from the employees' salaries.

It was not until 1978 that the Commission examined the scope of the term 'possessions' in *Wiggins* v. *UK*,[19] confirming the earlier expansive reading which had assumed that intangible assets, licenses and pensions could fall under the umbrella of the term 'possessions'. In *Wiggins*, the applicant had claimed that a local authority's refusal to issue a license to occupy the home to which he had title, following divorce, was a violation of A1P1. The Commission rejected the UK government's submission that 'possessions' included only movables, referring to the French word 'biens' which it said clearly encompassed both movable and immovable property:

> The Commission furthermore does not accept the view of the Government that the term 'possessions' within the meaning of that provision should be limited to moveable property only. The French text is clear in this respect. It refers in both paragraphs of Article 1 to 'biens', which clearly means both moveable and immoveable property version of the text.[20]

As seen in Chapter 4, it is true that the terms 'biens' and 'possessions', at the time the Convention was drafted, had a legal meaning in European domestic laws which covered all kinds of intangibles, stocks, assets, debts and securities. But, as argued in Chapter 4, there is a disconnect between the legal meaning of the terms 'biens'/'possessions', which was not brought to the attention of State representatives, and the natural meaning of the terms 'biens' and 'possessions' in ordinary language. Moreover, the drafting history of the debates shows that the choice of words 'enjoyment of possessions' in the final version of the text reflected the drafters' intention to limit the type of property protected to an individual's home and his/her tangible, personal belongings to further human dignity.[21]

5.1.2 Marckx v. Belgium: *A Divided Court on 'Possessions'*

The first time the Court addressed the meaning and scope of the terms 'biens'/ 'possessions' is in the landmark judgment of *Marckx* v. *Belgium* in 1979.[22]

Three years earlier, in *Handyside* v. *United Kingdom*,[23] the Court had stated, without further elaboration, that the right to dispose of one's property

19 Case No. 7456/76, *Wiggins* v. *the United Kingdom*, decision 8 February 1978.
20 Ibid.
21 See also A. Grear, 'Challenging Corporate "Humanity": Legal Disembodiment, Embodiment and Human Rights' (2007) 7(3) *Human Rights Law Review* 511–543.
22 Application no. 6833/74, *Marckx* v. *Belgium*, decision 13 June 1979.
23 Application no. 5493/72, *Handyside* v. *the United Kingdom*.

was 'a traditional and fundamental aspect of the right of property'.[24] In *Marckx*, the claim related to the inheritance rights of an illegitimate child and the rights of the mother to dispose of her estate in favour of the child. Under Belgian law, an illegitimate child was excluded from the family in respect of inheritance rights on intestacy whilst the mother was precluded from bequeathing the whole of her estate to the child.[25] Neither of these limitations applied to legitimate children and their parents. The Commission had found, by a majority of 9 to 6, that Belgian law violated the mother's but not the child's right to 'enjoyment of their possessions' under A1P1 in isolation and in conjunction with Article 14.[26] In respect of the mother, the Commission had stated that the right to dispose of her property by will was 'without doubt' one of the incidents of the right to property protected by A1P1.[27] The reasoning of the dissenting minority is not reported.

By contrast, the judgment of the five dissenting judges in the Plenary decision of the Court sets out in some detail their reasoning on the scope of application of A1P1 and the term 'possessions'. The majority of the Court had reasoned that

> By recognising that everyone has the right to the peaceful enjoyment of his possessions, A1P1 is in substance guaranteeing the right of property. This is the clear impression left by the words 'possessions' and 'use of property' (in French: 'biens', 'propriété', 'usage des biens'); the 'travaux préparatoires', for their part, confirm this unequivocally: the drafters continually spoke of 'right of property' or 'right to property' to describe the subject-matter of the successive drafts which were the forerunners of the present Article 1. (Series A no. 31, p. 27, para. 63)

[24] Ibid., p. 29, para. 62.

[25] Application no. 6833/74, *Marckx* v. *Belgium*. At para. 17 'A recognised "illegitimate" child's rights of inheritance on intestacy are less than those of a "legitimate" child. As appears from Articles 338, 724, 756 to 758, 760, 761, 769 to 773 and 913 of the Civil Code, a recognised "illegitimate" child does not have, in the estate of his parent who dies intestate, the status of heir but solely that of "exceptional heir" ("successeur irrégulier"): he has to seek a court order putting him in possession of the estate (envoi en possession).'

[26] Application no. 6833/74, *Marckx* v. *Belgium*: The court concurred with the Commission's report that '… l'article 1er du Protocole, s'il garantit à toute personne le respect de ses biens, ne garantit par contre aucun droit à acquérir des biens par voie de succession ou de libéralité.' Commission's Report 31 – 10th December 1977, p. 44. The Court reasoned that A1P1 'applies only to a person's existing possessions and that it does not guarantee the right to acquire possessions whether on intestacy or through voluntary dispositions' applies only to existing possessions *Marckx* judgment, Series A no. 31, p. 23, para. 50.

[27] Application no. 6833/74, *Marckx* v. *Belgium*; Commission's Report 31 – 10th December 1977, p. 45.

The five judges who dissented held that A1P1 was not applicable to rights of inheritance.[28] In their view, the language of the text, whilst confusing, did not point to a clear intent by the drafters to extend the scope of protection to rights of inheritance.[29] In his partly dissenting judgment, Sir Gerald Fitzmaurice pointed out that

> The apparent interchangeability of the terms 'possessions', 'property', 'biens' and 'propriété' in different contexts and without evident reason is confusing. The French 'biens' is best translated into English by 'assets' not 'possessions'. But the best French rendering of the English 'assets' is 'avoirs'. In addition, there is no really satisfactory French equivalent of 'possessions' as such, and in the plural. These anomalies of translation add to the difficulties. But they also thereby reduce the value of the Court's interpretation.[30]

Sir Gerald Fitzmaurice, formerly judge at the International Court of Justice (ICJ),[31] thought that it was inconceivable that the drafters would have used the language of 'enjoyment of possessions' or 'use of property' if the intent was to bring rights of inheritance within the scope of A1P1. To read these rights within the scope of A1P1, he said, was to inflate A1P1 'beyond its true proportions'. It was obvious that

> the chief, if not the sole object of Article 1 of the Protocol was to prevent the arbitrary seizures, confiscations, expropriations, extortions, or other capricious interferences with peaceful possession that many governments are – or frequently have been – all too prone to resort to. To metamorphose it into a vehicle for the conveyance of rights that go far beyond the notion of the peaceful enjoyment of possessions, even if they are connected with property, is to inflate it altogether beyond its true proportions.[32]

[28] The Court held at para. 13: by ten votes to five that A1P1 is applicable to Paula Marckx's claims; at para. 14: by nine votes to six that there has been no breach of this Article (P1–1), taken alone, with respect to the same applicant; at para. 15: by ten votes to five that there has been breach of Article 14 of the Convention, taken in conjunction with 1P1 (art. 14+A1P1), with respect to this applicant.

[29] Judge Matscher, Pinheiro Farinha and Sir Gerald Fitzmaurice specifically dissented from the majority on the applicability of A1P1 which, in their view, did not reflect the drafters intent and was not supported by the Travaux Preparatoires.

[30] Application no. 6833/74, *Marckx v. Belgium*, p. 44, footnote 8.

[31] Between 1967 and 1973. Previously also judge at the Permanent Court of Arbitration (1964–1973).

[32] Application no. 6833/74, *Marckx* v. *Belgium*, p. 45, para. 20.

Judge Matscher referred to the travaux preparatoires for confirmation that rights of disposition and inheritance between relatives were covered not by the right to the peaceful enjoyment of possessions within the meaning of A1P1. In his view:

> this provision has completely different aims (the protection of the right of property against interference by the public authorities, the form of expropriation or other restrictions on the use of property similar in their effects). Moreover – and contrary to the opinion expressed on this matter in the reasons set out in the judgment (paragraph 63) -, the travaux preparatoires on Article 1 of Protocol No. 1, although not very explicit in this respect, also seem to confirm this opinion.[33]

Judge Thor Vilhjalmsson stated that, in his opinion, A1P1 did not deal with the financial side of the relationship between the two applicants, although he did not elaborate further.

It followed from the five dissenting minority judgments that since A1P1 was not applicable, there could be no violation of Article 14 taken in conjunction with A1P1.

It is possible that the majority's expansive reading of the scope of 'possessions' in *Marckx* had been influenced by the judges' condemnation of the lack of 'objective' or 'rational' grounds for the social discrimination suffered by natural children and their mothers in Belgian inheritance law. However, there were no such social and moral considerations of justice in the next landmark judgment of *Sporrong and Lonnroth* v. *Sweden* delivered three years later in 1982.[34]

5.1.3 Sporrong and Lonnroth *v.* Sweden: *Entrenching Companies' Financial Interests*

Sporrong and Lonnroth v. *Sweden* marks the beginning of the Court's departure from deference to national laws and assertion of its authority on the 'autonomous' meaning of Convention terms, setting out a novel three-step approach to the construction of A1P1. By contrast to *Marckx* where the applicants were both natural persons, the applicants in *Sporrong and Lonnroth* included a legal entity which held the estate of the deceased Sporrong. They complained that delays and uncertainty relating to expropriation orders had caused them inconvenience and substantial losses. The Commission had reasoned that paragraph 1 did not apply because, until the

33 Ibid., p. 55.

34 Application nos. 7151 and 7152/75, *Sporrong and Lonnroth* v. *Sweden*.

orders were enforced, the applicants remained in possession of the estates. In the Commission's view, it was clear that the applicants had not yet been deprived of their possessions, therefore there was 'no appearance of a violation of the rights set forth in the second sentence of the first paragraph of Article 1 of the Protocol'. The Commission reasoned that the issue of whether or not the prolonged existence of the restrictions was legitimate and proportionate under paragraph 2 involved complex questions concerning the interpretation of the Convention, noting the wide margin of appreciation enjoyed by States. Accordingly, the application was deemed admissible and remitted to the Court. The decision assumed without further analysis that the financial benefits enjoyed by the applicant owners and legatees of two estates also fell within the scope of 'possessions'.

A bare majority of the Court, by ten votes to nine, disagreed with the Commission's analysis of A1P1 and set out an alternative groundbreaking three-step approach. Paragraph 2 was claimed not to apply because 'the applicants were … not formally "deprived of their possessions" at any time: they were entitled to use, sell, devise, donate or mortgage their properties'.[35] Instead, the Court considered the application of the first sentence of the first paragraph in isolation from both its second sentence and the second paragraph, and laid down three novel rules to guide the construction of A1P1 whereby

> The first rule, which is of a general nature, enounces the principle of peaceful enjoyment of property; it is set out in the first sentence of the paragraph. The second rule covers deprivation of possessions and subjects it to certain conditions; it appears in the second sentence of the same paragraph. The third rule recognises the States are entitled, amongst other things, to control the use of property in accordance with the general interest, by enforcing such laws as they deem necessary for that purpose, it is contained in the second paragraph.[36]

The majority then applied a 'fair balance' test to the first sentence of the first paragraph and reasoned that the delays and inconvenience suffered by the applicants constituted an unjustified interference with the applicant's right to peaceful enjoyment of their possessions. The legislative framework and construction prohibitions were said by the majority to have 'upset the fair balance which should be struck between the protection of the right of property and the requirements of the general interest'.[37]

35 Ibid., para. 62.
36 Ibid., para. 61.
37 Ibid., para. 73.

The rationale for the majority's three rules scheme is unclear; neither is it clear why a 'fair balance' test should be imported into the first sentence of A1P1 instead of the proportionality test in the second paragraph. There is little doubt that the application of a separate first rule was to the benefit of the applicants whose claim would not otherwise have succeeded under the more natural interpretation of A1P1 adopted by the Commission and the minority.[38]

The dissenting minority thought that the majority's interpretation of A1P1 was inconsistent with the drafters' 'underlying intention and the real meaning of that provision'.[39] The exclusion of paragraph 2 was 'hardly convincing' since 'the deprivation in reality never took place'.[40] The use of the property by the owner was never terminated by State action; it was temporarily restricted. In the minority's view, the natural interpretation would be to construe the planning restrictions as States measures directed at controlling the use of property under paragraph 2 and as such, subject to a 'general interest' test. Moreover, citing the *Marckx* case, the minority noted that paragraph 2 'sets the Contracting States up as sole judges of the "necessity" for such a law'.[41] The emphatic language 'shall not ... in any way impair the right of a State' showed a clear intent by the drafters to leave to States a wide margin of appreciation, acknowledging the complexity of modern States' obligations to regulate the use of private property in the interest of the community. For the minority, it was evident that the Swedish planning laws for a big city like Stockholm were directed at the 'general interest'. Like the Commission, the minority found there was no good reason to doubt that the measures taken in the present case were lawful. Nor was the length of the proceeding disproportionate. There was thus no violation of A1P1.

The only judgment expressly addressing the extension of 'possessions' to financial losses is the separate dissenting judgment of Judge Walsh. In his

38 See Tom Allen, *Property and the Human Rights Act 1998* (Oxford: Hart, 2005), p. 106.

39 Joint dissenting opinion of judges Zekia, Cremona, Thór Vilhjálmsson, Lagergren, Sir Vincent Evans, Macdonald, Bernhardt and Gersing with regard to A1P1, p. 28, para. 2.

40 See also Application no. 5493/72, *Handyside* v. *the United Kingdom*, where the court stated that the wording originates in a Belgian amendment to the effect that deprivation entailed loss of ownership: 'In these circumstances, the Court thinks that the second sentence of the first paragraph of Article 1 (P1–1) does not come into play in this case. Admittedly the expression "deprived of his possessions", in the English text, could lead one to think otherwise but the structure of Article 1 (P1–1) shows that that sentence, which originated moreover in a Belgian amendment drafted in French (Collected Edition of the "travaux préparatoires", document H (61) 4, pp. 1083, 1084, 1086, 1090, 1099, 1105, 1110–1111 and 1113–1114), applies only to someone who is "deprived of ownership" ("privé de sa propriété").' So a temporary seizure did not constitute deprivation.

41 Application no. 6833/74, *Marckx* v. *Belgium*.

view, the applicants' alleged losses consisted primarily of the 'loss of possible prospective profit'[42] caused by the adverse impact of the planning laws on the market value of the properties.[43] However, by contrast to the minority in *Marckx*, Judge Walsh's analysis stops short of questioning whether financial losses fall within the scope of 'possessions'. Instead, his judgment acknowledges that development plans might cause financial losses to property owners but notes that A1P1 does not create an absolute right to the protection of private property but contemplates that the private interest may yield to the public good. In this instance, the planned development was thought by Judge Walsh to be legitimate. Moreover, compensation would have been payable when, and only if, the expropriation had taken place (which in the end did not happen). In his view, the applicants were not entitled to compensation under A1P1 for the very existence of the development: 'Justice does not require that compensation must be paid for profits which might have been gained if there was no development of the area.'[44] He concluded that, as the development plans were legitimate, the expropriation never took place so there was no violation of A1P1.

By contrast, the majority's subsumption of financial losses into 'possessions', combined with the three-step reading of A1P1, enabled the applicants to receive compensation for a breach of the alleged general rule in the first sentence, widening even further the scope of protection of property rights, contrary to the drafters' original intent. The travaux preparatoires indicate unequivocally that several countries were not prepared to entrench a right to compensation in A1P1.[45] The wording that deprivation of possessions should be 'subject to the conditions provided for by … the general principles of international law' was suggested by Germany and Belgium as a compromise on the clear understanding that there was no international law obligation for States to compensate their own nationals or to provide compensation for nationalisations, absent a specific clause to that effect in a Treaty.

Thus, by a bare majority of one, the three rules test in *Sporrong and Lonnroth* v. *Sweden* entrenched private companies' financial interests as a protected possession under A1P1(1), independently of the public and general interest considerations expressly mentioned in the other sentences in the second paragraph, and at odds with the intention of the drafters to allow

42 Dissenting opinion, Judge Walsh, para. 41.
43 Ibid., para. 40.
44 Ibid.,
45 Vol. VII, 194. For a detailed discussion see Danny Nicol, *The Constitutional Protection of Capitalism* (London: Bloomsbury, 2010), pp. 142 ff.

States a wide margin of appreciation in regulating property rights in recognition of the social function of property.[46]

5.1.4 *Possessions as an 'Autonomous' Concept: Legitimate Expectations*

The court's inversion of the text of A1P1, giving primacy to the protection of companies' financial interests under the guise of 'enjoyment of their possessions', reflected the fictitious legal categorization of intangible property as a type of 'possession' in domestic laws. A renvoi to domestic laws facilitated a broad reading of the term 'possessions', encompassing not only tangible personal belongings but also shares, assets, profits and intellectual property (as seen in Chapter 4). Judicial deference to domestic laws lent some legitimacy to the majority's decision to interfere with planning laws limiting the use of companies' private property in the general interest adopted by democratically elected governments,. The early decisions of the Court deferring to national laws reflect this dual aspect. Possessions were said by the majority in the landmark judgment of *Marckx* in 1979 to include patrimonial and intestacy rights, but only provided that the rights were recognized in domestic laws. A1P1 was held to apply only to existing possessions and did not guarantee the right to acquire property.[47] The applicant's natural daughter did not enjoy inheritance rights under existing Belgian law. Accordingly, she had no right to 'enjoyment of possessions' under A1P1. The Court's construction limiting rights over 'possessions' to those vested in national laws was reiterated in *Van der Mussele* v. *Belgium* (1983)[48] and *Inze* v. *Austria* (1988).[49]

As the Court grew in confidence in the following decade, it began to relax its deference to national laws, invoking the doctrine of the autonomy of meaning of key terms in the Convention.[50] The doctrine was applied to property rights in *Gasus* v. *the Netherlands* in 1995. The Court stated that

> 'possessions' ... has an autonomous meaning which is certainly not limited to ownership of physical goods; Certain other rights and interests constituting assets can also be regarded as 'property rights', and thus as 'possessions', for the purposes of this provision P1(1).[51]

46 Application nos. 7151 and 7152/75, *Sporrong and Lonnroth* v. *Sweden*.
47 Application no. 6833/74, *Marckx v. Belgium*, para. 50.
48 Application no. 8919/80, *van der Mussele* v. *Belgium*, decision 23 November 1983, para. 48.
49 Application no. 8695/79, *Inze* v. *Austria*, decision 28 October 1987.
50 For a detailed discussion see Allen, *Property and the Human Rights Act 1998*, pp. 42 ff.
51 Application no. 15375/89, *Gasus Dossier und Fordertechnick GmbH* v. *the Netherlands*, decision 23 February 1995.

The range of 'possessions' was said to extend not only to assets but also included 'claims, in respect of which an applicant can argue that he has at least a "legitimate expectation" that they will be realised'.[52] The Court said that 'a legitimate expectation … must be of a nature more concrete than a mere hope and be based on a legal provision or a legal act such as a judicial decision'.[53] However, in *Pressos Compania Naviera S.A. and Others* v. *Belgium* (1995),[54] the Court found a violation of A1P1 in circumstances where the government had introduced legislation which effectively overruled the decision of lower courts before the applicants' claim had reached the highest court. The Belgian government had disputed the application of A1P1 as the applicants had, at best, a hope that their claim might succeed; nor was the value of the claim assessed. Yet in other cases, the Court has found no violation in reliance on formalistic and procedural grounds or dismissed claims where determination of the applicants' rights had not been decided in the highest courts.[55] As noted by Tom Allen, the principles advanced by the Court to identify 'legitimate expectations' and 'possessions' are neither clear nor coherent.[56] The lack of clarity and consistency in the decisions has left considerable uncertainty as to the precise legal contours of 'possessions', particularly in respect of rights or claims asserted by the applicant when their legal status is contested in national laws. As will be seen in Section 5.2, there is a similar lack of clear principled basis and consistency in the Commission and Court's jurisprudence on IPRs.

The main points emerging from the historical analysis of the case law on A1P1 so far are threefold. Firstly, the construction of A1P1 by the Commission and Court took a critical turn in the early 1980s when a divided court, by a bare majority, adopted a liberal economic reading giving primacy to companies' financial interests under the first sentence of A1P1. Secondly, the Court was able to expand the natural meaning of 'possessions' beyond the drafters' intent, to include intangible, personal rights, by leaning unto national laws' fictitious categorization of assets, securities, shares and IPRs as 'possessions'. Thirdly, the Court's application of the doctrine of the 'autonomous' meaning of key terms in the Convention enabled it to widen the range of protected interests in A1P1 beyond those vested in national laws which were

52 Application no. 44912/98, *Kopecky* v. *Slovakia* (Grand Chamber), decision 28 September 2004, para. 35.

53 Ibid., para. 69.

54 Application no. 17849/91, *Pressos Compania Naviera SA and Others* v. *Belgium*, decision 20 November 1995.

55 See Allen, *Property and the Human Rights Act 1998*.

56 Ibid., p. 56.

coupled with the ambiguous notion of 'legitimate expectations'. In each of these aspects, the Court arguably departed from the intent of the drafters who had pressed for the inclusion of property rights in the Convention on moral grounds, arguing that protection of personal belongings and home were necessary for each human being to live a life with dignity, whilst conceding property rights could legitimately be limited by States for social purposes. By contrast, by the early 1980s, the Convention institutions had entrenched companies' financial interests and privileged their protection, laying the grounds for companies to file claims alleging violation of their intellectual IPR as protected rights under A1P1.

5.2 COMPANIES' INTELLECTUAL PROPERTY

In this light, unsurprisingly, when the first claims relating to IPRs were filed by large multinational corporations with the capacity and legal resources to test the boundaries of A1P1in the late 1980s, the Commission had no difficulty in admitting the complaints. Companies, including majority shareholders, were undoubtedly legal persons with standing to claim violation of their right to enjoyment of their 'possessions' under A1P1. As noted above, this had been firmly established in the decisions of the Commission and Court early on.[57]

The Commission's and Court's decisions had also recognized as A1P1 'possessions' the intangible assets, investments and shares which were classified as fictitious possessions in domestic laws. The addition of IPRs, patents, TMs, copyright and designs to the class of protected 'possessions' in A1P1 was similarly facilitated by their categorization as fictitious 'possessions' in national laws. As seen in Chapter 4, national laws had wrestled to accommodate IPRs within the established dual categories of real property and personal rights originating in Roman law. The difficulty with IPRs was that, unlike personal property and much like real property or rights *in rem* over 'possessions', IPRs were transferrable and enforceable against the whole world. National legislatures and courts had resolved the legal conundrum by carving out a hybrid category of rights which straddled the real property and personal rights divide. By the end of the nineteenth century, civil and common law systems were resorting to legal fictions to align IPRs with other personal rights (such as contracts, securities or debts) whose subject matter was intangible, and the

[57] For instance, in Case No. 12742/87, *Pine Valley Developments Ltd. and Others* v. *Ireland*, decision 3 May 1989, the Commission noted that 'both a company and a majority shareholder can be regarded as victims within the meaning of this provision'; citing *Kaplan* v. *the United Kingdom*, Comm. Report 17.7.80, D.R. 21 p. 5 at p. 23.

term limited. IPRs were categorized in French, British and German law as fictitious 'possessions'/'biens'. The Commission and Court could thus find ample support in national laws to construe patents, TMs, copyright and designs as a type of 'possession' notwithstanding the original moral intent to limit protection to the home and tangible personal possessions needed by each individual human person for self-development. Moreover, deference to national laws had the advantage of allaying critics' concerns that the creation of a supranational court to enforce the Convention carried a risk of constitutional overreach. Section 5.3 analyses the Convention case law on IPRs, detailing how the Commission and Court first drew on domestic laws to bring IPRs within the scope of 'possessions' in the 1980s, and, subsequently in the 1990s, invoked the Court's own doctrine of the autonomous meaning of the Convention to controversially expand the scope of supranational protection of IPRs, privileging neoliberal policies, free trade and cross-border protection of companies' IPRs.

5.2.1 *Existing IPRs in National Laws*

The first wave of Intellectual Property (IP) claims in the 1980s and early 1990s tested the Commission's and Court's view of the scope of IPRs as possessions and their willingness to interfere with national laws which regulated the grant and control of IPRs. The first reported IP application was filed in 1986 by the University of Illinois, a corporate body under US law.[58] The applicants' agents had failed to pay the prescribed fees to the Dutch patent office to maintain the patent. As a result, the patent was voided in accordance with provisions in the Dutch Patents Act. The applicants sought to have the patent reinstated, alleging, inter-alia, breach of A1P1 and Article 6. The Commission dismissed the applicants' claim that they had a 'right' to have the patent restored. Recalling the *Marckx* judgment of 13 June 1979,[59] the Commission stated that there was no legal basis for such a right under A1P1 which deals with acquired rights only:

> A right to restoration of a patent would essentially entail a right to acquire property, which is not guaranteed by Article 1 of Protocol No. 1.[60]

The Commission recalled that the Court had held that the term 'right' has an autonomous meaning in the sense that it is not decisive that a given privilege

[58] Case No. 12048/86, *University of Illinois Foundation v. the Netherlands*, decision 2 May 1988.
[59] Application no. 6833/74, *Marckx v. Belgium*, p. 23, para. 50.
[60] Case No. 12048/86, *University of Illinois Foundation* v. *the Netherlands*.

or interest is not described or classified as a 'right' in a domestic system. However, there was no room for application of the doctrine of the autonomous meaning of 'right' when the effect was to create a new substantive right which had no legal basis in the Contracting state. In the instant case:

> by finding that the applicant could claim a 'right' to have his patent restored, the Commission would in fact be creating a new substantive right which has no legal basis under Dutch law.[61]

In the same year, the multinational pharmaceutical corporation Smith Kline filed an application against the Netherlands which also alleged violation of their right to enjoyment of possessions under A1P1.[62] Although Smith Kline were registered in the UK, they were the owners of a Dutch patent whose use was required by a competing Dutch company (Centrafarm) to develop a therapeutic product. Smith Kline had refused to grant a license to Centrafarm, and the Dutch patent office had issued a compulsory licence in favour of Centrafarm. Smith Kline complained that the grant of the compulsory licence 'interfered with the applicant's peaceful enjoyment of its patent and deprived it of the exclusive right to the use of the patented invention contrary to Article 1 of Protocol No. 1'. The Commission declared the application inadmissible. This time, the Commission specifically considered whether a patent fell within the meaning of the term 'possessions', holding that

> under Dutch law the holder of a patent is referred to as the proprietor of a patent and that patents are deemed, subject to the provisions of the Patents Act, to be personal property which is transferable and assignable. The Commission finds that a patent accordingly falls within the scope of the term 'possessions' in Article 1 of Protocol No. 1.[63]

The Commission then reasoned that the grant of the compulsory licence constituted an interference with the use of the property and proceeded to consider whether the control was 'lawful, in accordance with the general interest and pursues a legitimate aim in a proportionate manner' in the second paragraph of A1P1', citing the Court's Tre Traktörer AB judgment of 7 July 1989, Series A no. 159, pp. 22–24, paras. 56–63. It noted that many States limited the rights of the patentee to prevent 'long-term hampering of technological progress' and 'to prevent abuse of monopoly situations'. The

61 Ibid.

62 Case No. 12633/87, *Smith Kline and French Laboratories Ltd* v. *the Netherlands*, decision 4 October 1990.

63 Ibid.

legislative framework setting out limitations was found to be within the margin of appreciation of the Contracting State. The Commission thus held that, on the facts, the aims pursued were legitimate and the means proportionate. Accordingly, there was no violation of A1P1.

In the next case of *British-American Tobacco* v. *the Netherlands* (1995),[64] the applicant's claim related to the invalidation by the Netherlands Patent Office Appeals Division of a patent granted by the Examining Division. British-American Tobacco (BAT) no longer had a patent. Consequently, the Commission reasoned that the company had not been deprived of its existing property, nor had it suffered an interference with its rights under A1P1, recalling that A1P1 applied only to existing possessions and did not guarantee any right to acquire property.[65] The Court left open the question of whether a patent *application* constituted a 'possession' under A1P1, stating that there was no need in the instant case to decide, as the Commission had done, 'whether or not the patent application lodged by the applicant company constituted a "possession" coming within the scope of the protection afforded by Article 1 of Protocol No. 1'.[66] In retrospect, the Court's decision in *BAT* to leave open the question of whether the contested IPRs fell within the scope of 'possessions' may have been indicative of a lack of consensus amongst the judges at the time. The question was settled in favour of companies a decade later in the landmark Grand Chamber (GC) judgment of *Anheuser-Busch* (discussed below).

Notwithstanding , as late as 1998, the Commission was reiterating that 'a patent is a possession for the purposes of Article 1 of Protocol No. 1' citing *Smith Kline* and continuing to defer to national laws.[67] In *Lenzing* AG v. *UK* (1997),[68] the applicant's patent had been invalidated on appeal by the European Patent Organization (EPO) boards. The applicant had sought judicial review, in the UK courts, of the EPO's decision and correction of the UK patent register. Justice Jacob, in the UK High court, add dismissed the claim on the grounds that UK courts lacked jurisdiction to review the EPO's decisions. Lenzing appealed to the European Court of Human Rights

64 Application no. 19589/92, *British-American Tobacco Company Ltd* v. *the Netherlands* (Grand Chamber), decision 20 November 1995.

65 Report of the Commission, *British-American Tobacco Company Ltd v. the Netherlands*, adopted 9 May 1994, para. 72. The Court considered that no separate issue arose under A1P1 as the claim under that heading was, in substance, identical to the claim under Article 6.1.

66 *British-American Tobacco* v. *the Netherlands*, para. 91.

67 Case No. 12633/87, *Smith Kline and French Laboratories Ltd* v. *the Netherlands*, decision report 66, p. 79.

68 Case No. 38817/97, *Lenzing AG* v. *the United Kingdom*, decision 9 September 1998.

(ECtHR).[69] In line with the reasoning of Justice Jacob, dismissing the applicant's claim, the Commission observed that 'The possession at issue was therefore not the patent itself, but the applicant company's right to pursue a legal claim in the domestic courts'. However, the Commission also noted that possessions may include a claim.[70] Since the applicant's claim had been dismissed by the UK Court, there was no right which had been the subject of interference under A1P1.

5.2.2 *Contested IPRs in National Laws: Anheuser-Busch*

As noted above, by contrast to the Commission, the Court had left open the scope of application of A1P1 to IPRs in *BAT* in 1995. Until then, the Commission had construed existing IPRs in domestic laws as 'possessions' protected under A1P1 by contrast to voided IPRs which had been categorized instead as civil rights, protected under Article 6(1), when the applicant was seeking to overturn a national court's decision to void the IPR. 'Possessions' did not include claims or rights to have a voided patent restored without a legal basis in the domestic system as this was deemed to amount to the acquisition of a new substantive right. This approach was radically altered by the Grand Chamber's exceptional intervention in the landmark judgment of *Anheuser-Busch Inc.* v. *Portugal* in 2007.[71] The case is of seminal importance in setting out a new, expansive approach to the construction of the scope of IPR protection in the Convention, including not only existing IPRs but IPR applications too. The Grand Chamber also expressly extended its analysis to all types of intellectual property rights beyond the TMs and geographical indications under dispute in the instant case.

The case concerned a dispute between a US company, Anheuser-Busch (AB), and a Czech company, Budejovicky Budvar (BB). AB had been producing and selling beer around the world under the name 'Budweiser' since 1876. BB produced a beer in the town of České Budějovice in Bohemia (Czech Republic), also called 'Budweiser', using special methods. The two companies had agreements in 1911 and 1939 concerning the distribution and sale of 'Budweiser' in the United States but not in Europe. AB's entry into the European markets in the 1980s led to legal disputes over the use of the mark in various European countries and with BB over use of the mark in Portugal.

69 Ibid.

70 Citing Application no. 17849/91, *Pressos Compania Naviera SA and Others* v. *Belgium*, Series A no. 332, p. 21, para. 31.

71 Application no. 73049/01, *Anheuser-Busch* v. *Portugal*, Grand Chamber decision 11 January 2007.

BB had registered 'Budweiser Bier' as an appellation of origin (AO) in 1958. In 1981, AB applied to Portugal's National Institute of Intellectual Property (NIIPI) to have 'Budweiser' registered as a TM. The application was opposed by BB and NIIPI did not grant the application because of BB's prior registration of the AO. The two companies then entered negotiations over the use of the mark. They were unable to reach agreement, and in 1989, AB applied to the Lisbon Court of First Instance to have BB's AO struck out. AB's application was successful. The Lisbon Court held that 'Budweiser Bier' did not fall within the category of products whose quality and characteristics are due exclusively to the geographical environment, as defined in the Lisbon Agreement of 31 October 1958.[72] Consequently, the Lisbon Court cancelled BB's AO registration on 8 March 1995. The NIIPI then registered Budweiser as a TM on 8 November 1995, despite BB's opposition. BB appealed NIIPI's decision to the Lisbon Court of First Instance, in reliance on a bilateral agreement between Portugal and Czechoslovakia on the Protection of Indications of Source, Appellations of Origin and Other Geographical and Similar Designations (the 'Bilateral Agreement'), signed in Lisbon on 10 January 1986. The application was dismissed and the TM maintained on the grounds that there was no risk of confusion over the TM (as consumers thought of Budweiser as an American beer) whilst the 1986 Agreement was no longer in force due to disappearance of one of the parties (Czechoslovakia). The decision was overturned by the Lisbon Court of Appeal on 21 October 1999. The Court held that the Portuguese public would not be misled as to the origin of Budweiser beer, but registration of the TM would infringe the 1986 Agreement which had remained in force by agreement of the Portuguese and Czech governments. The decision was upheld on appeal to the Supreme Court in 2001.

AB appealed to the ECtHR, alleging violation of their rights under A1P1. The appeal was dismissed by the Chamber in 2005. The majority found no violation of A1P1 by five votes to two. In line with the Commission's decision in *Lenzing*, the majority reasoned that whilst IPRs as such fell within the scope of protection of A1P1,[73] when the IPR in question had been invalidated by the

[72] "Under the terms of the Lisbon Agreement of 31 October 1958, such protection was reserved to the geographical name of a country, region or locality, which served to designate a product originating therein, the quality and characteristics of which were due exclusively or essentially to the geographical environment, including natural and human factors. 'Budweiser' did not come within this category. The registration was therefore cancelled." Application no. 73049/01, *Anheuser-Busch* v. *Portugal*, para. 18.

[73] Case No. 38817/97, *Lenzing* AG v. *the United Kingdom* and Application no. 73049/01, *Anheuser-Busch* v. *Portugal*, decision 11 October 2005, para. 43.

national courts, the applicant did not have an existing 'possession'. The Court accepted that an application to register a TM had a definite financial value, it could be assigned or licensed and it created a priority right which warranted a degree of legal protection. However, until final registration, in accordance with the national laws of the State concerned, the applicant did not have a sufficiently strong interest to amount to a 'legitimate expectation' protected under A1P1:

> In the instant case, the applicant company could not be sure of being the owner of the trademark in question until after final registration and then only on condition that no objection was raised by a third party. In other words, the applicant company had a conditional right, which was extinguished retrospectively for failure to satisfy the condition, namely that it did not infringe third-party rights.[74]

The Court noted that the applicant company was engaged in a commercial enterprise which, by its very nature, carried a degree of risk. AB was, or ought to have been, aware that by the time it filed its application to invalidate the Czech company's AO in 1989, the Bilateral Agreement of 1986 had already been in force for two years so its application may not succeed. For these reasons, the majority concluded that there had been no violation of A1P1.

By contrast, in a joint dissenting judgment, the two minority judges (including the President of the Court, J.P. Costa and I. Cabral Barreto) reasoned that the company's 1981 application to register the Budweiser TM created a 'legitimate expectation' which was 'sufficiently strong to attract the protection of A1P1'. This was because the applicant was the owner of a pecuniary interest recognized by Portuguese law. The refusal to register the mark following the adoption of the 1986 Bilateral Agreement, whilst pursuing a legitimate aim to protect national products, had the effect of harming the company's financial interests. The State's interference with the applicant's pre-existing rights failed to strike a 'fair balance' between the private company's fundamental right to property and the general interest. The absence of compensation resulted in an excessive burden being born by a non-national, contrary to the decision in *Lithgow and others*.[75] Accordingly, the minority concluded that there had been a violation of A1P1.

[74] Ibid., para. 50.

[75] Ibid., para. 7. "The State's right to enter into international agreements that are necessary for the protection of certain products cannot be disputed, but in this context the State must also take into account any rights of private parties, especially if, like the applicant company, they are non-nationals. Although a taking of property must always be effected in the public interest,

The decision was referred to the Grand Chamber which concurred with the Chamber, by fifteen votes to two, that there has been no violation of A1P1, but on different grounds. The GC agreed with the Chamber that 'intellectual property was protected as such' under A1P1 but by contrast to the Chamber, the majority took the view that an application for a TM was a protected 'possession' which gave rise to a set of proprietary rights, albeit conditional rights, until final registration. The rights enjoyed by the owner of a TM application included the right to sell and license the TM application. These rights were recognised in domestic Portuguese law, even though they could be revoked under certain conditions.[76] In the GC's view, the rights relating to an application for a TM were 'proprietary' because, in a market economy, an application for a TM possessed, or was capable of possessing, a definite financial value. The GC also noted that under Portuguese law, fraudulent or illegal interference with an application for a TM could give rise to compensation.[77] Having established that AB's application for a TM was a possession, the Court then considered whether the retrospective application of the 1986 Bilateral Agreement constituted an interference with the applicant's right to enjoyment of its possessions. The Court started by noting that even in cases involving litigation between individuals and companies, the State's obligations entailed by A1P1 is to take the measures necessary to protect the right to property A1P1(83). It further noted that in certain circumstances the retrospective application of legislation may 'upset the fair balance' between the general interest and protection of enjoyment of possessions A1P1(82), citing prior cases. But it distinguished the instance case where the meaning and scope of application of the 1986 Agreement was under dispute. The Court further noted that at the time the 1986 Agreement was signed, the only registered IPR was the AO of 1958. In the absence of arbitrariness or manifest unreasonableness in the decision of the Portuguese Supreme Court, it was not for the ECtHR to review the decision of that court. For these reasons the GC concluded that there was no violation of A1P1.

different considerations may apply to nationals and non-nationals and there may well be legitimate reason for requiring nationals to bear a greater burden in the public interest than non-nationals."

76 Ibid., para. 78.

77 It is notable that in setting out the relevant law, the Grand Chamber noted that under EU law, and application for a TM is an object of property, giving rights in rem. See detailed discussion in Section 5.3.

There were two dissenting judgments (Judges Caflisch and Cabral Barreto) and two dissenting judgments in part (Judges Steiner and Hajiyev). Judges Steiner and Hajiyev concurred with the majority that there had been no violation of A1P1, but, in their view, the AB's TM application was not a 'possession', because until final registration it was not an existing right: 'Our settled case-law denies the quality of "possession" to a conditional claim which has lapsed as a result of a failure to fulfil the condition' (A1P1(6)). The applicant's filing of the TM application in 1981 did not give rise to a 'legitimate expectation' because the applicant knew that it was likely to be opposed by BB. The applicant was engaged in litigation throughout Europe and AB and BB were in negotiations about use of the marks. Thus, at the onset, the legal outcome of AB's TM application was uncertain. Judges Steiner and Hajiyev thus concluded that, on the facts of the case and by contrast to *Pine Valley Developments and Others* v. *Ireland* (1991), 'there was no justified reliance on a legal act which had a sound legal basis'.[78]

Judges Caflisch and Cabral Barreto arrived at the opposite conclusion, starting from the opposite premise that the TM application gave rise to a legitimate expectation that registration would follow. In their view, the retrospective application of the 1986 Agreement without compensation was a violation of A1P1.

Altogether, A1P1 was thought *not* to apply to IP applications by seven of the Court's judges, including a majority of five in the Chamber and a minority of two in the GC. Their analysis was in line with the previous decisions of the Commission and the Court which had consistently ruled that possessions included only existing rights. By contrast, a total of fifteen judges in the GC thought that IP applications fell within the category of 'possessions' and left open the question of whether they may be categorised as legitimate expectations. The alternative analysis of the minority of two judges in the Chamber and two judges in the Grand Chamber was that IP applications gave rise to legitimate expectations. Judges Caflisch and Cabral Barreto questioned why the majority had bothered to engage in a lengthy analysis of the applicability of A1P1 when they appeared to view the main issue as 'akin to Article 6'. Their concern about the intersection of A1P1 with Article 6(1) was to prove prescient in light of the Court's subsequent turn to a 'rule of law' approach to the construction of A1P1.

78 *Anheuser-Busch* v. *Portugal*, Grand Chamber decision, at para. 9.

5.3 IPRS IN THE ECHR THROUGH THE LENS OF EU LAW

The significance of the Grand Chamber's judgment arguably lies in the Court's express references to European Union law to justify the extension of the European Convention to IP applications. The relevant sources of law listed in the Chamber and Grand Chamber's judgments, informing their construction of A1P1 include, inter alia, the European Union's regulation on the Community trade mark whose aim is acknowledged to be 'to promote the development, expansion and proper functioning of the internal market by enabling Community undertakings to identify their products or services in a uniform manner throughout the Union' (A1P1 (36)). The list of relevant international law instruments specifically mentions Article 24 of Council Regulation (EC) No. 40/94 of 20 December 1993,[79] which describes a community TM as 'an object of property' and specifies that the provisions relating to the community TM are also applicable to applications for registration. The rights conferred by the Community TM and applications include transfer (Article 17), the right to be given as security or be the subject of rights in rem, independently of the undertaking (Article 19) and licensing for all or part of the goods for which the mark is registered (Article 22). Article 9(3) further provides that an application for registration may found a claim for compensation. Finally, Article 17(2) of the Charter of Fundamental Rights guarantees the right to property and provides that 'Intellectual property shall be protected' (para. 38). Drawing on the aims of the Community TM and rights conferred, the Grand Chamber concurred with the Chamber that there is a bundle of financial and legal interests attached to TM applications, whose value (in a market economy) will vary depending on a number of factors. Consequently, the majority dismissed the submission of the Portuguese government that the value of the applicant's TM application was negligible. In the Grand Chamber's view, it was 'impossible to assert at the outset that the assignment of an application for the registration of a TM will have no financial value' (para. 77). When read in the light of EU law, the category of protected 'possessions' under A1P1 could encompass not only granted TMs but also TM applications. The Grand Chamber's approach in *Anheuser-Busch* thus denotes an alignment of Convention rights in A1P1 with the European Union's legal framework on IPRs and fundamental rights.

[79] Amended by Council Regulation (EC) no. 422/2004 of 19 February 2004.

At first sight, this may seem perplexing and problematic because the two legal orders have distinct normative logics. As seen in Chapter 1, the entrenchment of rights over enjoyment of 'possessions' in the Convention was instrumental and aimed at protection of the minimum of home and personal belongings required by each individual to lead a life with dignity. The moral ideal expressed in the Convention was consistent with the existence of different types of economic orders. By contrast, the European Union legal order and EU Charter of Fundamental Rights have a different aim altogether, expressly directed at promoting integration of a single market.[80] Conceptually, the Grand Chamber's reading of A1P1 in the light of the EU's market-oriented regulation of IPRs and the EU Charter blurs the normative basis of the EU and Convention legal orders. This is all the more problematic in relation to TMs because of their commercial character and the absence of a more salient personal dimension which is reflected in some of the moral justifications for copyrights and patents and the language of Articles 27 UDHR and Article 15 ICESCR.[81]

On the other hand, a closer look suggests that, with the evolution of EU law into a legal order which has supremacy over domestic laws, the intrusion of EU law in the construction of A1P1 is likely unavoidable. The reasons are twofold. As seen above, the case law of the ECtHR clearly establishes that A1P1 protects only existing rights in domestic laws or at least those which give rise to legitimate expectations. For the twenty-seven countries which are members of the EU, the nature and scope of IPRs protected in domestic laws will inevitably be closely defined by EU Directives and Regulations on patents, copyright and TMs as interpreted by the EU court which has supremacy over national laws. From a constitutional perspective, the deep structural links between domestic laws and EU law cannot therefore be ignored in the ECtHR's application of the Convention. As *Anheuser-Busch* shows, domestic (Portuguese) law on TMs and TM applications was brought in line with EU law once Portugal had become a member of the EU. Technically, the obligations imposed on States by the European Convention are independent of those imposed by the EU. Formally, the ECtHR remains the ultimate

[80] There is a vast body of literature on the interface between the EU single market and human rights, including the seminal paper by Philip Alston, and Joseph H. H. Weiler, 'An "Ever Closer Union" in Need of a Human Rights Policy' (1998) 9(4) *European Journal of International Law* 658–723 which preceded the adoption of the EU Charter of Fundamental Rights.

[81] See for instance Peter K. Yu, 'Reconceptualizing Intellectual Property Interests in a Human Rights Framework' (2006) 40 *UC Davis Law Review* 1039 and Aurora Plomer, *Patents, Human Rights and Access to Science* (Cheltenham: Edward Elgar, 2015).

arbiter on the interpretation of the European Convention and the scope of application of the category of 'possessions', whose meaning the court has declared to be 'autonomous'. The ECtHR has reiterated on numerous occasions that Member States are under an obligation to implement Convention law in their domestic laws. The difficulty with the existence of a dual system for the protection of fundamental rights in Europe is that States could potentially face conflicting obligations in the event of divergence between the two systems. It was hoped that the conundrum would be resolved through the EU's accession to the ECHR. This hope was dashed after the EU Court's rejection of the joint proposal for the EU's accession to the ECHR in the landmark Opinion 2/3 of the Court of Justice of the European Union (CJEU) on 18 December 2014. In the absence of a formal integration of the two legal orders, the ECtHR remains formally free to develop its own 'autonomous' interpretation of the nature and scope of IPRs protected under A1P1. But the constitutional reality is that European Union law on the rights vested on IPR owners and their limitation must of necessity substantially inform, if not formally dictate, the legal contours of IPRs under the Convention. For commercial applicants, this could mean that there may no longer be clear strategic advantage in filing claims for violation of their IPRs at the ECtHR rather than the EU Court. The EU's system arguably offers an enhanced and less uncertain level of legal protection for IPRs. Alongside unequivocal protection of IPRs as fundamental rights in the EU Charter, the EU legal system comprises dedicated legislation on IPRs coupled with an extensive body of case law from the EU Court.[82] By contrast, the European Convention system was not designed to promote European market integration, nor was A1P1 drafted with a view to protecting companies' IPRs of as economic tools to achieve that goal. Consequently, there is no legal infrastructure to secure protection of IPRs; neither are there dedicated laws or policy guidance defining the nature and scope of the rights, nor their limits or exclusions in the Convention legal order. Compared to the EU legal system, the legal lacunae on protection of IPRs as 'possessions' in the European Convention system are substantial, systemic and pervasive. The future thus points to an inevitable tilt of the ECtHR jurisprudence towards the EU legal order, at least for States which are members of the EU. However, the ripple effects of the ECtHR's acquis could well reach out to cases involving States which are not (or no longer are) members of the EU, as the principles developed by the Court are formally grounded on the text of the Convention.

[82] For an overview, albeit somewhat outdated, see Justine Pila and Paul Torremans, *European Intellectual Property Law* (Oxford: Oxford University Press, 2019).

Nevertheless, the Court remains the final authority on the meaning of A1P1 and retains discretion on the determination of the legality of national laws delineation of IPRs by Member States and the limitations on the rights conferred thereof. The structural deficits on IPRs in the Convention system are to be filled by the Court in line with the text of A1P1 and the 'fair balance' and proportionality tests laid down in the Court's case law. Section 5.4 details how, in a new phase following the GC decision in *Anheuser-Busch*, the Court is leaning towards a rule of law approach, eschewing the earlier substantive internal balancing of private and public interests.

5.4 INTERNAL BALANCING OF IPRS AND THE PUBLIC INTEREST

Once an applicant's IPRs or IPR applications are categorized as 'possessions', the key question is whether applicant's have suffered a violation of their A1P1 rights as a result of States' interference with, limitations on or deprivation of the applicant's IPRs.[83] In the absence of a dedicated legal framework on IPRs dovetailing the Convention system, the limits on the applicant's IPRs are in the text of A1P1 and the Court's case law. The second sentence of A1P1 stipulates that no one may be deprived of their rights except in the public interest and subject to the conditions provided for by law and by the general principles of international law. The third sentence in the second paragraph of A1P1 states categorically that rights over enjoyment of possessions 'shall not, however, in any way impair the right of a State to enforce such laws as it deems necessary to control the use of property in accordance with the general interest or to secure the payment of taxes or other contributions or penalties'.[84] As shown earlier, the Court laid down a three-rule test for the construction of A1P1 in *Sporrong*. The first sentence was said to enunciate the right to peaceful enjoyment of possessions which requires the Court to determine whether 'a fair balance was struck between the demands of the general interest of the community and the requirements of the protection of the individual's fundamental rights' (paragraph 69 of the judgment). In *Sporrong*, the 'fair balance' test in the first sentence was applied by the Court independently of the second and third sentence of A1P1 which were held not to apply on the

[83] Christophe Geiger and Elena Izyumenko, 'Shaping Intellectual Property Rights through Human Rights Adjudication: The Example of the European Court of Human Rights' (2020) 46(3) *Mitchell Hamline Law Review*.

[84] Application nos. 7151 and 7152/75, *Sporrong and Lonnroth* v. *Sweden*. In *Sporrong*, the wording was said to be 'emphatic' by two of the dissenting judges.

facts of the case.[85] The majority held that the fair balance had been upset by the long planning process which had caused excessive delays and inconvenience to the applicants. Consequently, Stockholm City County was found to have violated the applicants' rights to peaceful enjoyment of their possessions.[86] The fact that the decision was reached by a divided Court with a bare majority of one is arguably indicative of the uncertainty attached to the application of the fair balance test by the Court. In this light, it is not surprising that in the latest cases, the Court is leaning towards a 'rule of law' approach.[87]

5.4.1 *Rule of Law*

In a series of cases relating to patents, copyright and TMs, since the early 2020s, the ECtHR has taken a 'rule of law' approach to the construction of A1P1, eschewing the 'fair balance' test. In *Tokel* v. *Turkey* (2021)[88] the Court determined, as it did in *Sporrong*, that the alleged interference did not fall within the second and third categories and had to be examined under the general rule in the first sentence.[89] In 1991, the applicant had been granted a patent for a mechanized system for drying tea leaves. The patent was in force until 2008 and was declared valid by the domestic courts when the applicant, Tokel, sued Caykur, a State-owned company, seeking compensation for unauthorized use of the invention.[90] Tokel was denied compensation by the civil courts and took his complaint to the ECtHR. The ECtHR approached the construction of A1P1 from a 'rule of law' perspective, stating that 'the first and most important requirement of Article 1 of Protocol No. 1 is that any interference by a public authority with the peaceful enjoyment of possessions should be lawful' (para. 73). The principle of lawfulness was said to be

85 The second sentence did not apply because the applicants had not been deprived of their property, nor did the planning process fall within the rules on control of use in the third sentence.

86 A majority of 12 to 7 also found a violation of Article 6 (1).

87 See Laurence R. Helfer, 'The New Innovation Frontier-Intellectual Property and the European Court of Human Rights' (2008) 49 *Harvard International Law Journal* 1, advocating a 'rule of law' approach.

88 Application no. 23662/08, *Tokel* v. *Turkey*, decision 9 February 2021.

89 Ibid., para. 72. 'The Court observes that the interference at issue in the present case cannot be classified in a precise category. The case should therefore more appropriately be examined in the light of the general rule laid down in the first sentence of the first paragraph of Article 1 of Protocol No. 1.'

90 Ibid., para 1. Caykur had started using the same system two months before the applicant had the patent registered for the invention. In domestic proceedings, Caykur successfully relied on a prior use exemption incorporated in a Decree of 1995 following Turkey's accession to TRIPS.

reflected in the second sentence of A1P1 that deprivation of property should be 'subject to the conditions provided for by law', and in the second paragraph which recognises that States have the right to control the use of property by enforcing 'laws' (para. 73). The term 'law' in A1P1 was said to allude to the same concept elsewhere in the Convention, namely that interferences should be 'sufficiently accessible, precise and foreseeable in their application'.[91] In particular, the ECtHR added, a legal rule is 'foreseeable' when it affords a measure of protection against arbitrary interferences by the public authorities.[92] Applying these principles, the Court found that Turkey's laws did not meet the lawfulness requirement as there was no legislation or case law on prior use before the Decree of 1995, even though Turkey had been a member of the Paris Convention, which had anticipated such a right, since 1925. Since the interference was unlawful, the Court held that there was no need to consider whether the aims pursued were legitimate, nor whether a fair balance had been struck between the general interest and the protection of the individual's fundamental rights.[93] Consequently, the Court found that Caykur's unauthorised use of Tokel's patented invention was a violation of A1P1. Turkey was ordered to pay Tokel's legal costs, and the applicant was referred to the Compensation Commission in respect of compensation for his losses.[94] Similarly, in *Safarov* v. *Azerbaijan* (2022),[95] the Court held that the domestic courts had failed to provide reasons which established that the digital reproduction by a non-governmental organisation (NGO) of the applicant's book online without his consent fell within the range of exceptions in the domestic laws on copyright relating to 'exclusively personal purposes',[96] educational purposes[97] or exhaustion of rights of distribution.[98] The Court held that 'elaborate reasoning by the (domestic) courts was needed' to justify, inter-alia, the application of Article 18 of the Law on Copyright to libraries, archives and educational institutions due to the fact that the defendant had made a

[91] Ibid., para. 74, citing among many other authorities *Beyeler v. Italy* [GC], no. 33202/96, § 106, ECHR 2000-I.

[92] Ibid., citing Application no. 38433/09, *Centro Europa 7 S.R.L. and Di Stefano v. Italy* (Grand Chamber), decision 7 June 2012.

[93] Ibid., para. 79.

[94] Ibid., paras 86–90.

[95] Application no. 885/12, *Safarov* v. *Azerbaijan*, decision 1 September 2022. For a review of the judgment see Elena Izyumenko, 'Ineffective Investigation into Making a Book Available for Illegal Download Breaches Copyright Holder's Right to Property, Rules the European Court of Human Rights' (2023) 18(4) *Journal of Intellectual Property Law & Practice*.

[96] *Safarov* v. *Azerbajan*, para. 17, citing Article 17.1 of the Law on Copyright.

[97] Ibid., para. 17.

[98] Ibid., para 35.

digital version of the applicant's book freely available online 'and therefore – practically to a world-wide audience, not to visitors of a library building'.[99] Neither had the Supreme Court explained its application of the exception in Article 15 of the Law on Copyright which relates to exhaustion of rights of distribution of lawfully published physical books.[100] Significantly, the Court added that the effective implementation of A1P1 gives rise to a positive obligation[101] for States to ensure that in their domestic legal systems 'property rights are sufficiently protected by law and that adequate remedies are provided whereby the aggrieved party can seek to defend his or her rights, including, where appropriate, by claiming damages in respect of any loss sustained'.[102] The Court reiterated that the role of the ECtHR in overseeing domestic courts' implementation of the Convention was limited. It was not to take the place of the national courts but to verify that the Convention has been correctly interpreted and that the decisions of the courts 'are not arbitrary or otherwise unreasonable'.[103] In this instance 'the respondent State had failed to discharge its positive obligation under Article 1 of Protocol No. 1 to protect intellectual property notably through effective remedial measures'.[104] Consequently, there was a violation of A1P1. There was therefore no need to examine the complaint under Article 6.[105] *Safarov* thus consolidates the rule of law approach to A1P1 taken by the Court the previous year in *Tokel*. In addition, the protection of IPRs under A1P1 is further enhanced by the

99 Ibid., para. 34.

100 Ibid., para. 35.

101 On positive obligations see Application no. 33949/05, *Potomska and Potomski* v. *Poland*, decision 29 March 2011, para. 74. "The Court reiterates that the genuine, effective exercise of the right protected by A1P1 does not depend merely on the State's duty not to interfere, but may give rise to positive obligations (see Application no. 48939/99, *Öneryıldız* v. *Turkey* (Grand Chamber), decision 30 November 2004; and Application no. 22279/04, *Plechanow* v. *Poland*, decision 7 July 2009. Such positive obligations may entail the taking of measures necessary to protect the right to property, particularly where there is a direct link between the measures an applicant may legitimately expect from the authorities and his effective enjoyment of his possessions, even in cases involving litigation between private entities. This means, in particular, that States are under an obligation to provide a judicial mechanism for settling effectively property disputes and to ensure compliance of those mechanisms with the procedural and material safeguards enshrined in the Convention. This principle applies with all the more force when it is the State itself which is in dispute with an individual (see Application no. 73049/01, *Anheuser-Busch* v. *Portugal*, and Application no. 22279/04, *Plechanow* v. *Poland*)."

102 Application no. 885/12, *Safarov* v. *Azerbaijan*, para. 31.

103 Ibid., citing Application no. 39544/05, *Zagrebačka banka d.d.* v. *Croatia*, decision 12 December 2013, and Application no. 6169/13, *Mindek* v. *Croatia*, decision 30 August 2016).

104 Ibid., para. 36.

105 Ibid., para. 37.

Court's unqualified assertion that States have a positive obligation to ensure effective protection of property rights, including (inter se) disputes between private applicants, without reference to fair balance between private and public interests. The shift to a 'rule of law' approach in the recent case law of the Court is evident when compared to the approach taken in the previous decade in the cases of *Balan* v. *Moldova* (2008) and *Dima* v. *Romania* (2005). In *Dima* v. *Romania*,[106] the applicant had been commissioned in 1990 by the Romanian Parliament to work with other appointed experts to design a state emblem and seal. The applicant's design was adopted with some modifications and he was mentioned as the author of the graphic design in the Official Journal on 24 September 1992. On an unspecified date, the Office for Patents and Trademarks rejected the applicant's request for registration of his design, citing unpublished guidance on Article 11 of law 129/1992 which precluded copyright on designs for State emblems. A law adopted in 1996 expressly excluded copyright on designs for State emblems and seals. Unlike the other experts, and for unclear reasons, the applicant was not paid a fee for his work. The Supreme Court of Romania dismissed the applicant's claim for compensation. The applicant appealed to the ECtHR, alleging breach of Article 6(1) and A1P1. The ECtHR rejected both claims. In relation to Article 6.1, the applicant had claimed, inter-alia, that the domestic courts had unlawfully retrospectively applied the law of 1996 to deny him compensation.[107] The ECtHR disagreed, noting that the Romanian Supreme Court had instead based its decision on the law of 1956 which did not include models amongst the enumerated list of subjects of copyright. Consequently, there was no violation of Article 6(1). The claim under A1P1 also failed because the domestic courts had held that the applicant's design did not meet the originality requirements for copyright under the law of 1956. According to the domestic courts, the applicant's work was not an original creation because it was the outcome of a collective effort in which Parliament had a determining role. The ECtHR reiterated that it was not for the Court to revisit the decisions of the domestic courts which had access to the facts. In the absence of manifest arbitrariness, the Court found that there was no violation of A1P1. Yet, on the facts as stated, it is not obvious that the scope of application of the law of 1956 on originality and the domestic institutions' and courts' reasoning was any clearer than in the latter case of *Balan* v. *Moldova* (see below), not

[106] Application no. 58472/00, *Dima* v. *Romania*, admissibility decision 26 May 2005.

[107] Ibid., para. 2(a). The ECtHR noted that the applicant, like the other experts, had been offered remuneration under a contract and could have pursued a claim under that heading in the civil courts.

least because the applicant was expressly mentioned as the author of the graphic design in the official journal.

In *Balan* v. *Moldova* (2008),[108] the domestic courts had rejected the applicant's claim for compensation for the unauthorised State use of a photograph, which he had taken, as background for ID cards. The ECtHR found that there were discrepancies in the domestic authorities' and courts' interpretation of the applicable exclusions on IPRs over ID cards/government property in domestic laws. This, the Court said, suggested that the relevant legislation had not been 'sufficiently foreseeable' adding that this 'in itself might be a sufficient basis for the conclusion that the interference was not "lawful"'. However, the Court determined that it was not necessary to decide that point in view of its conclusion that the refusal to compensate the applicant for the unauthorised use of the photograph, whilst pursuing a legitimate aim, was disproportionate. In the Court's view, the public interest could have been served without violating the applicant's rights. Unlike in *Tokel*,[109] the Court did not specify which of the three rules had been applied, although the language of the conclusion is reminiscent of *Sporrong* 'the domestic courts failed to strike a fair balance between the interests of the community and those of the applicant, placing on him an individual and excessive burden' (para. 46).[110]

5.4.2 *Overlapping Illegality under A1P1 and Article 6*

A key area of uncertainty with the Court's shift to a 'rule of law' approach to A1P1 is the unclear relationship of A1P1 with Article 6(1).[111] The case law of the Court on IPRs is not consistent. IPR applicants typically frame their complaint as either a violation of A1P1 and/or a violation of Article 6. Historically, an A1P1 claim has been dismissed by the Court and the concurrent Article 6 claim not examined or vice-versa. As seen earlier, in *Safarov*, the Court decided that there was no need to examine the complaint under Article 6, having found a violation of A1P1. However, in other cases, the claim is examined under Article 6 instead. Article 6(1) of the Convention provides that

[108] Application no. 19247/03, *Balan* v. *Moldova*, decision 29 January 2008.

[109] Application no. 23662/08, *Tokel* v. *Turkey*.

[110] Application nos. 7151 and 7152/75, *Sporrong and Lonnroth* v. *Sweden*. The applicant had claimed 20,267 euros (EUR) for pecuniary damage and EUR 5,000 for non-pecuniary damage and was awarded EUR 5,000 for pecuniary and non-pecuniary damage.

[111] Article 6(1) of the Convention provides that 'In the determination of his civil rights and obligations ... everyone is entitled to a fair and public hearing ... by an independent and impartial tribunal....'

'In the determination of his civil rights and obligations . . ., everyone is entitled to a fair and public hearing . . . by an independent and impartial tribunal.' In *British-American Tobacco Company Ltd* v. *the Netherlands* (1995),[112] the applicant company had alleged a breach of both A1P1 and Article 6(1). The Court first examined the complaint under Article 6(1). The applicant had complained, inter alia, that the institutional structure of the Netherlands Patent Office fell short of the requirements of independence and impartiality under Article 6(1) and did not guarantee a fair and public hearing. The Court rejected the claim, noting that the applicant could have appealed the decision of the Patent Office in the ordinary civil courts of the Netherlands but had decided not to pursue that option 'for whatever reason'.[113] Had this option been pursued, the Netherlands civil courts would have had full jurisdiction to review the refusal to grant the patent application on the merits and afford an appropriate remedy,[114] and the applicant company would have had access to a classical judicial remedy under Article 6(1).[115]

Having rejected the applicant company's claim under Article 6, the Court then found it unnecessary to examine the claim for alleged violation of A1P1. The applicant had argued that 'the denial of access to an independent and impartial tribunal for the determination of its entitlement to a patent meant that they had been deprived of a "possession" without any judicial examination'.[116] In the Court's view, that claim was 'in substance identical to that already examined and rejected in the context of Article 6(1) of the Convention'. There was no need to examine whether a patent application was a 'possession' under A1P1 because 'no separate issue arises under Article 1 of Protocol No. 1 (P1–1) in relation to the matters complained of'.[117] By contrast, as discussed earlier, in *Anheuser-Busch*, the GC examined the claim under A1P1 instead of Article 6.[118] The difficulty, as pointed out by two of the dissenting judges, is that it is unclear why the majority had opted to construe the applicant's complaint as falling under A1P1 when it could have been dealt with under Article 6.

Until the GC's decision in *Anheuser-Busch*, once invalidated in legal proceedings in domestic courts, A1P1 did not protect an applicant's existing 'possession' or property rights. Unless the applicant could establish a legitimate

[112] Application no. 19589/92, *British-American Tobacco Company Ltd* v. *the Netherlands*.
[113] Ibid., para. 86.
[114] Ibid., para. 84.
[115] Ibid., para. 85.
[116] Ibid., para. 91.
[117] Ibid., para. 91.
[118] Application no. 73049/01, *Anheuser-Busch* v. *Portugal*.

expectation, the ECHR complaint was treated as an Article 6(1) type claim which required the applicant to establish that the domestic courts had acted unlawfully.[119] Since the Court's turn to a 'rule of law' approach to A1P1, it is unclear when the claims will fall under A1P1 or Article 6(1).

Another difficulty with the overlap of A1P1 and Article 6 is illustrated in the case of *Kamoy Radyo Televizyon Yayincilik Ve Organizasyon A.S.* v. *Turkey* (2019).[120] The case also concerned a dispute relating to two companies' TMs. The name 'Vadan' had been used by a daily newspaper since 1977 but registered by Turkey's Patent Office following an application in 1998 by a company subsequently taken over by the applicant. The applicant's complaint to the ECtHR alleged that national courts had erred in invalidating the applicant's mark in applying a legislative provision which was subsequently declared unlawful by Turkey's constitutional court. For this reason, the Court found, by a majority of 5 to 1, that there had been a violation of A1P1. The majority had distinguished the facts of *Anheuser-Busch* and *Moldova* in which, it said, there had been a dispute about title to the IPRs by contrast to the instant case. The trouble with the majority's reasoning is set out in the separate dissenting Opinion of Judge Lemmens. Judge Lemmens could not see how the majority could find that that there was no dispute in *Kamoy*, since the applicant company's TM rights had been declared null and void by the domestic courts, independently of the invoked legislation. In Lemmens' opinion, the applicant's complaint should have been dismissed by the Court as there was no basis for holding that a property right existed. At first sight, the different opinions appear to be based on different constructions of the facts. However, a closer look suggests that the issues are more complex as the ECtHR's majority judgment rests on a different assessment from that of the domestic court of the combined legal effect of a range of national IP laws on the validity of the applicant's IPRs. *Kamoy* thus points to a possible blur of the Court's jurisdiction and constitutional role vis-à-vis domestic courts. The ECtHR has stated in numerous cases that it is not a last instance court of appeal. But the majority's decision in *Amoy* appears to contradict this, opening the way for powerful private companies to launch claims at the ECtHR to

[119] Despite categorizing AB's application for a TM as a 'possession', the majority of the GC in *Anheuser-Busch* found that there had been no violation of A1P1 noting that the Supreme Court's interference with the applicant's TM was not arbitrary, was in the public interest, and struck a fair balance, partly because the validity of the applicant's registered TM had been under dispute in the domestic courts before and independently of the retrospective application of the dispute Bilateral Treaty.

[120] Application no. 19965/06, *Kamoy Radyo Televizyon Yayincilik Ve Organizasyon A.S.* v. *Turkey*, decision 16 April 2019.

secure supranational protection of IPRs which have been invalidated in the national courts.

Notwithstanding the turn to a 'rule of law' approach, the Court retains formal discretion to engage in a substantive balancing exercise to determine whether a fair balance has been struck between the applicant's private interests and those of the public. A good illustration is the decision in *SIA AKKA/LAA* v. *Latvia* (2016),[121] where the ECtHR unanimously held that an order from the national courts, which set out the terms of a licensing agreement and equitable royalties between the applicant organisation (AKKA) and two Latvian radio stations, was both in the public interest and in the interests of the authors represented by AKKA. AKKA managed the copyright of musical works of two thousand domestic and two million international authors and had failed to reach an agreement with the radio stations.[122] The legal rights relating to the copyrighted works were found by the Court to fall within the 'autonomous' meaning of the term 'possessions' under A1P1 because of the associated financial rights and economic value of the interests.[123] On the facts of the case, the order of the Court's interference with the organization's A1P1 rights was found not to be arbitrary, to pursue a legitimate aim and to strike a fair balance.

Overall, the direction of the Court's jurisprudence on IPRs in the last two decades has been to consolidate and expand protection of companies' IPRs under A1P1 based on what the Court describes as its autonomous construction of the term 'possessions' to include intangible assets, anything of financial value or legal relations giving rise to financial rights. Behind the laconic reasoning of the Commission's and Court's decisions, this chapter shows there lies a complex web of domestic and international laws underpinning the

[121] Application no. 562/05, *SIA AKKA/LAA* v. *Latvia*, decision 12 July 2016.

[122] The Court dismissed the government's claim that the dispute was contractual and did not fall under A1P1 at para. 41. "The Court reiterates that the protection of IPRs, including the protection of copyright, falls within the scope of Article 1 of Protocol No. 1 to the Convention (see Application no. 73049/01, *Anheuser-Busch* v. *Portugal* and Application no. 28743/03, *Melnychuc* v. *Ukraine* (admissibility) decision 5 July 2005. The Court observes that the domestic courts in the course of the impugned civil proceedings acknowledged, among other issues, the infringement of the copyright of authors represented by the applicant organisation. The protection of musical works and the economic interests deriving from them thus fall within the scope of rights protected under Article 1 of Protocol No. 1."

[123] At para. 54. The Court reiterates that the concept of 'possessions' referred to in the first part of Article 1 of Protocol No. 1 has an autonomous meaning. In the case of non-physical assets, the Court has taken into consideration, in particular, whether the legal position in question gave rise to financial rights *SIA AKKA/LAA* v. *Latvia* judgment 13 and interests and thus had an economic value (see, for example, Application no. 9074/07, *Mullai and Others* v. *Albania*, decision 23 March 2010).

construction of companies' IPRs as 'possessions' in the ECHR. The classification of IP as fictitious possessions in European domestic laws facilitated the subsumption of IPRs under A1P1 in the early decisions of the Commission and Court, whilst EU law was the basis of the subsequent consolidation and expansion of protection of IPRs in the ECHR. Thus, the story of the ECtHR's protection of companies' IPRs is the story of the internalization by the Court of the neoliberal values of free trade, market integration and cross-border protection of transnational companies' capital in the EU. These were not the values that the ECHR founders thought they were entrenching in a treaty aimed at securing protection of the rights required to enable each individual human person to live a life with dignity. Chapter 6 shows how the Court's balancing of A1P1 with other substantive rights in the ECHR forms part of the same story.

6

Intellectual Property Rights in the Balance

INTRODUCTION

As seen in Chapter 5, the Court's expansive construction of Article 1 of the First Protocol (A1P1) to include intellectual property rights (IPRs) as a type of 'possession' secured supranational protection of companies IPRs as a fundamental *human* right in Europe. This chapter examines how the Court's construction of companies' IPRs as protected *human* rights in the European Convention on Human Rights (ECHR) in turn opened the way for a new 'dynamic' approach,[1] whereby IPRs stood to be weighed and balanced against other fundamental rights, notably freedom of expression in Article 10 ECHR. The analysis shows that the optimistic expectations were foreshadowed by developments in the Court's jurisprudence, whose significance was underestimated and which ultimately resulted in a strengthening of Intellectual Property (IP) owners' rights in the balance with Article 10 ECHR.

This chapter is divided into three sections. Section 6.1 sets out the arguments from European IP scholars who have welcomed the turn to human rights as counterweights to the seemingly unstoppable expansion of Intellectual property rights (IPRs).[2] Section 6.2 reviews the Court's case law

[1] For a general discussion of the dynamics of IP protection, see Gustavo Ghidini, *Rethinking Intellectual Property: Balancing Conflicts of Interest in the Constitutional Paradigm* (Cheltenham: Edward Elgar, 2018).

[2] Notably, the seminal article by P. Bernt Hugenholtz, 'Copyright and Freedom of Expression in Europe' in Rochelle Cooper Dreyfuss, Diane Leenheer Zimmerman and Harry First (eds.), *Expanding the Boundaries of Intellectual Property: Innovation Policy for the Knowledge Society* (Oxford: Oxford University Press, 2001), p. 343; Christophe Geiger, 'Fundamental Rights, a Safeguard for the Coherence of Intellectual Property Law?' (2004) 35 *Industrial Internet Consortium* 268 and 280; Alain Strowel and François Tulkens, 'Freedom of Expression and

on Article 10 ECHR which, it is suggested, is underpinned by two incongruent rationales: a moral rationale grounded on human, personal development and an economic rationale grounded on the commercial interests of corporations in free markets. The analysis reveals the emergence of a body of key decisions from the Court in the 1990s which blur the two rationales, conflating freedom of expression with unfair competition and granting Member States a wide margin of appreciation to protect commercial expression, deemed by the Court to lack a public interest or political dimension. The discussion shows how the Court's deferential approach, combined with the elevation of IPRs to fundamental rights in A1P1, has resulted in the strengthening of IP owners' rights in the balancing exercise between Article 10 ECHR and IPRs. Section 6.3 examines why the Court's judgments have confounded expectations in order to draw some lessons for the future. It identifies three aspects of the Court's methodology which, it is argued, stand in the way of Convention rights acting as breaks on IPRs.

6.1 HUMAN RIGHTS AS COUNTERWEIGHTS TO IPRS

In the last two decades, an important body of IP scholarship in Europe has turned attention to human rights as possible counterweights to the expanding scope of protection of IPRs, spurred by a seminal article by Hugenholtz on the potential for Article 10 ECHR to limit overbroad protection of IPRs. The expectation was that the external balancing of IPRs against fundamental rights, and Article 10 in particular, would be more effective in constraining the expanding scope of protection of IPRs than the established internal, built-in limitations on IPRs, such as the distinction between expression and ideas, list of exceptions and three-step rule in copyright. This section outlines Hugenholtz's arguments before considering whether his optimistic expectations have been met.

Hugenholtz's article starts from the premise that copyright and freedom of expression stand potentially in conflict because every copyright work contains, in part, 'information and ideas' whilst Article 10 protects freedom to receive and impart ideas. Hugenholtz argues that the potential conflict had long been ignored in European law, with a paucity of legal scholarship and dearth of decisions. Reviewing the case law of national courts and the Council of Europe Commission at the turn of the millennium, Hugenholtz points to a

Copyright under Civil Law: Of Balance, Adaptation, and Access' (2005) *Copyright and Free Speech, Comparative and International Analyses* 287–313; Duncan Matthews, 'Intellectual Property Rights, Human Rights and the Right to Health' in W. Grosheide (ed.), *Edward Elgar Intellectual Property Rights and Human Rights: A Paradox*, Queen Mary School of Law Legal Studies Research Paper No. 24/2009 (2009).

nascent jurisprudence in the 1990s which suggests that Article 10 could act as a 'lifebuoy for bona fide users drowning in a sea of intellectual property'[3] to inform the delineation and scope of protection of IPRs.[4]

For instance, German courts had begun to acknowledge, in a series of cases dating back to the 1960s, that the unauthorized rebroadcasting or publication of books without permission could be justified on the grounds that the statutory limitations in German copyright law were to be interpreted in the light of the constitutional protection of freedom of expression in Article 5[5] and/or provided an extra statutory layer of protection.[6] On the other hand, Hugenholtz acknowledges that the Federal Constitutional Court of Germany adopted a more cautious approach in 1987 by reasoning that Article 5 did not provide a defence to copyright infringement because freedom of the press was already incorporated in the German Copyright Act.[7] A decade later, in CB Bank, the Federal Constitutional Court of Germany further held that the public interest in accessing information did not justify a departure from the narrow construction of statutory limitations on copyright whilst underlying that copyright does not protect information as such.[8] Dutch courts' long resistance to applying Article 10 had also begun to change in the 1990s. The Supreme Court acknowledged in *Dior* v. *Evora* (1996) that, in principle, the use of (trademarks (TMs) and) copyrights may conflict with Article 10 ECHR, although on the facts of the case it was not necessary to invoke Article 10.[9] Three years later, in *Anne Frank Fonds* v. *Het Parool*,[10] the

3 Hugenholtz, 'Copyright and Freedom of Expression in Europe'.

4 Ibid. The context for the turn to Article 10 was a draft EU copyright at 343. Directive which critics feared would unduly expand the scope of copyright.

5 Ibid. Hugenholtz points to the constitutional basis of IPR protection in Germany in Article 1 (dignity) – which protects moral rights – whilst rights of exploitation are founded on Article 14 – property rights, subject to limits due to 'social function' of property – in a series of landmark cases initiated by IPR owners.

6 *Maifeiern*, Landgericht Berlin, [1962] GRUR 1962.

7 Hugenholtz, 'Copyright and Freedom of Expression in Europe', citing *Lili Marleen*, German Federal Supreme Court 7 March 1985, [1987] GRUR 34 and *CB-Infobank I*, German Federal Supreme Court 16 January 1997, [1997] GRUR 459, at 463; and *CB-Infobank II*, German Federal Supreme Court 16 January 1997, [1997] GRUR 464, at 466.

8 Thus, a commercial company remained free to provide information services including facts, data and bibliographical information.

9 *Dior* v. *Evora*, Dutch Supreme Court (Hoge Raad) 20 October 1995, [1996] Informatierecht/AMI 51. Infringement claim against a daily newspaper's use of a photograph including prominent artwork, held not to be necessary for the purpose of the news reported in *De Volkskrant*. Note that Dutch law had no defence of *fair use* – and that in the Netherlands, Article 10 has precedence over national law.

10 *Anne Frank Fonds* v. *Het Parool*, Court of Appeal Amsterdam 8 July 1999, [1999] Informatierecht/AMI 116.

Amsterdam's Court of Appeal acknowledged the public interest in publication of 'missing pages' of Anne Frank's diary but held that the freedom of expression and information guaranteed by Article 10 did not override the copyright restrictions.[11] French courts had also long been reluctant to apply Article 10 as a defence to infringement claims, unsurprisingly, Hugenholtz argues, in light of France's long tradition of strong support for authors' rights.[12] In a series of cases for breach of copyright for inclusion of artworks in TV broadcasts, not a single French court had mentioned Article 10 until the *Utrillo* case against France 2 in 1999[13] where the Paris Court recalled that Article 10 is superior to national law and that the right of the public to be informed of important cultural events should prevail over the interests of copyright users. Hugenholtz concludes that the emerging trend in the national courts' decisions and a couple of Commission cases shows a willingness to accept that freedom of expression may limit the scope of copyright protection, particularly in 'hard core' cases where freedom of the press is at stake.[14] However, Hugenholtz concedes that the courts' reasoning is still largely based on principle rather than with explicit reference to Article 10, and the decisions are hesitant and mixed. His optimistic conclusion in 2002 was that Article 10 defences to infringement claims were

> likely to succeed against copyright claims aimed at preventing political discourse, curtailing journalistic or artistic freedoms, suppressing publication of government-produced information or impeding other forms of 'public speech'. In practice, this might imply that the Court would be willing to find infringement of Article 10 where national courts fail to broadly interpret or 'stretch' existing copyright limitations to permit quotation, news reporting, artistic use or re-utilization of government information. The Court might also be willing to find national copyright laws in direct contravention with Article 10 if they fail to provide exceptions for uses such as parody.[15]

Have these optimistic expectations been borne out in the subsequent case law? Fast-forward two decades and the jurisprudence of the European Court of Human Rights (ECtHR) on the balance between freedom of expression

[11] Ibid.

[12] Cited at note 79.

[13] Court of First Instance Paris 23 February 1999, Case 98/7053 (unpublished).

[14] Hugenholtz, 'Copyright and Freedom of Expression in Europe', citing M. Löffler, 'Das Grundrecht auf Informationsfreiheit als Schranke des Urheberrechts' (1980) *Neue Juristische Wochenschrift* 201; Herman Cohen Jehoram, 'The Freedom of Expression in Copyright and Media Law' (1983) (6/7) *GRUR International* 385–389.

[15] Except for France and Belgium, copyright laws in Europe do not provide for express parody exemptions.

and IPRs has significantly increased in terms of landmark cases. The analysis of the case law below suggests that the judicial shift to external balancing of IPRs with Article 10, contrary to expectations, has not generally been effective at containing the expansion of IPRs and, in some cases, has even resulted in strengthening the rights of IPR owners. Why?

In the early 2000s, the balance between Article 10 and IPRs might have looked like a promising avenue to strengthen public users' rights, perhaps in part because the Court had not yet confirmed that all IPRs enjoy protection as a fundamental right under A1P1.[16] Until then, the conflict between freedom of expression and IPRs in the ECHR did not strictly concern the balance between two conflicting rights as such.[17]

The call for balancing Article 10 ECHR against IPRs predated the Court's unequivocal affirmation that IPRs are fundamental rights enjoying protection in the ECHR. As discussed below, the Grand Chamber's (GC) elevation of IPRs to fundamental rights in the ECHR in the landmark judgement of *Anheuser-Busch* in 2007[18] enabled the reconceptualization of IPRs as fundamental rights of equal status with freedom of expression and a shift to external balancing of IPRs with freedom of expression.[19] By then, as detailed below the Court had separately established that companies' commercial speech enjoyed Article 10 protection in the ECHR putting the Convention 'at the forefront of fundamental rights regimes in promoting the interests of for-profit entities'.[20] Once Article 10 protection was extended to corporate commercial speech, the extent to which Article 10 ECHR could act as a counterweight to IPRs would depend on the rationale for Article 10. The next subsection reviews the rationale for Article 10 before analysing its application to companies' IPRs by the Court.

16 See Chapter 5.

17 For a typology of balancing mechanisms, see Christina Angelopoulos, 'European Copyright and Human Rights in the Digital Sphere' in M. Susi (ed.), *Human Rights, Digital Society and the Law: A Research Companion* (London: Routledge, 2019).

18 Application no. 73049/01, *Anheuser-Busch* v. *Portugal* (Grand Chamber), decision 11 January 2007.

19 On balancing of rights of equal status see, for instance, Application no. 931/13, *Satakunnan Markkinaporssi Oy and Satamedia Oy* v. *Finland* (Grand Chamber), decision 27 June 2017: The Court said that Article 8 and Article 10 rights were of equal status: 123. Bearing in mind the need to protect the values underlying the Convention and considering that the rights under Articles 10 and 8 of the Convention deserve equal respect, it is important to remember that the balance to be struck by national authorities between those two rights must seek to retain the essence of both.

20 Marius Emberland, *The Human Rights of Companies: Exploring the Structure of ECHR Protection* (Oxford: Oxford University Press, 2006).

6.1.1 *The Rationale for Article 10: Human Freedom or Corporate Freedom?*

Article 10 – Freedom of expression:

1. Everyone has the right to freedom of expression. This right shall include freedom to hold opinions and to receive and impart information and ideas without interference by public authority and regardless of frontiers. This article shall not prevent States from requiring the licensing of broadcasting, television or cinema enterprises.
2. The exercise of these freedoms, since it carries with it duties and responsibilities, may be subject to such formalities, conditions, restrictions or penalties as are prescribed by law and are necessary in a democratic society, in the interests of national security, territorial integrity or public safety, for the prevention of disorder or crime, for the protection of health or morals, for the protection of the reputation or rights of others, for preventing the disclosure of information received in confidence, or for maintaining the authority and impartiality of the judiciary.

As seen in Chapter 1, the drafters' rationale for protection of everyone's 'enjoyment of possessions' in A1P1 was the moral ideal that a minimum of personal belongings and home are necessary to facilitate the full development of each human being's personality. Similarly, freedom of expression was thought to be essential to enable each human person to access a plurality of information and ideas to facilitate public debate and participation in a democratic society.[21] The moral ideal grounding freedom of expression and (a minimum of personal) property rights in the ECHR was identical, namely to secure the protection of the rights which are necessary for the full development of each human being's personality. The underlying, overarching universal value in each case is belief in the intrinsic worth and dignity of each individual human being and each human person's capacity for autonomy and self-determination.[22]

[21] This moral ideal was articulated by Lauterpacht in his International Bill of the Rights of Man: Hersch Lauterpacht and Philippe Sands, *An International Bill of the Rights of Man* (Oxford: Oxford University Press, 2013). As explained by Morsink, the ideal found expression in the Universal Declaration of the Rights of Man (1948): Johannes Morsink, *The Universal Declaration of Human Rights: Origins, Drafting, and Intent* (Philadelphia: University of Pennsylvania Press, 1999). In relation to Article 10 ECHR see Eric Barendt, *Freedom of Speech*, 2nd ed. (Oxford: Oxford University Press, 2009).

[22] Morsink, *The Universal Declaration of Human Rights* and Barendt, *Freedom of Speech*.

Some of the landmark judgments of the Court on Article 10 reflect this moral rationale. For instance, in *Handyside* v. *UK*, the Court stated that freedom of expression was 'one of the basic conditions . . . for the development of every man'.[23] The Court linked freedom of expression to democracy as 'one of the essential foundations of [democratic] society' and made it clear that the freedom relates not only to the imparting of information and ideas but also to the public's right to receive information.[24] The content of the views expressed, whether they are well received or not, whether they 'offend, shock or disturb the State or any sector of the population'[25] is immaterial as the expression of a plurality of ideas is essential to a functioning democracy.[26] The press have a 'pre-eminent' role in a State governed by the Rule of Law.[27] Without freedom of expression, the press cannot play the vital role of acting as a 'public watchdog'. Its task is to impart information and ideas, and the public has a right to receive them.[28]

However, as discussed in Chapter 1, the inclusion of legal persons in A1P1 points to a different rationale from the moral rationale that relates to

[23] In Application no. 5493/72, *Handyside* v. *the United Kingdom*, decision 7 December 1976, the Court noted that 'freedom of expression constitutes one of the essential foundations of a democratic society; subject to paragraph 2 of Article 10 (Article 10(2)), it is applicable not only to information or ideas that are favourably received or regarded as inoffensive or as a matter of indifference, but also to those that offend, shock or disturb the State or any sector of the population' (p. 23, para. 49).

[24] Furthermore, the Court has said that whilst the mass media must not overstep the bounds imposed in the interests of the proper administration of justice, it is incumbent on them to impart information and ideas concerning matters that come before the courts just as in other areas of public interest. Not only do the media have the task of imparting such information and ideas: the public also has a right to receive them'. Application no. 13585/88, *Observer and Guardian* v. *the United Kingdom*, decision 26 November 1991, para. 59(b).

[25] Application no. 5493/72, *Handyside* v. *the United Kingdom*, para. 49.

[26] Application nos. 3002/03 and 23676/03, *Times Newspapers Ltd.* v. *the United Kingdom*, decision 10 March 2009, para. 27 and Application no. 36769/08, *Ashby Donald and Others* v. *France*, decision 10 January 2013. Other cases reiterating the rationale for freedom of expression are Application no. 39401/04, *MGN Ltd* v. *the United Kingdom*, decision 18 January 2011, citing Application nos. 21279/02 and 36448/02, *Lindon, Otchakovsky-Laurens and July* v. *France* (Grand Chamber), decision 22 October 2007.

[27] Application no. 39401/04, *MGN Ltd* v. *the United Kingdom*, para. 141.

[28] Ibid., 'Not only does it have the task of imparting such information and ideas: the public also has a right to receive them. Were it otherwise, the press would be unable to play its vital role of "public watchdog"' (Case No. 13585/88, *Observer and Guardian* v. *the United Kingdom*, para. 59; Application no. 13778/88, *Thorgeir Thorgeirson* v. *Iceland*, decision 26 June 1992, para. 63; Application no. 21980/93, *Bladet Tromsø and Stensaas* v. *Norway* (Grand Chamber), decision 30 May 1999 and Application no. 16023/07, *Gutiérrez Suárez* v. *Spain*, decision 1 June 2010).

individual, personal freedoms rather than economic freedoms.[29] Economic freedoms are also potentially implicated in Article 10(1) which specifically refers to TV, broadcasting and cinema enterprises:

> This article shall not prevent States from requiring the licensing of broadcasting, television or cinema enterprises.

The moral and economic perspectives on fundamental rights are conceptually distinct and carry different, potentially conflicting, normative implications on the construction of Convention rights. On the moral reading of the Convention, the balance and contours of property-based limitations on freedom of expression would be drawn by reference to the individual human interests at stake in participation in democratic societies. By contrast, an economic reading of fundamental rights would put the market freedoms of corporate actors in the balance. There is no conceptual or normative alignment between these two rationales as recognized by Emberland in his defence of the human rights of companies in the ECHR. As pointed out by Emberland, the moral reading of Article 10, grounded on human dignity, does not 'fit' with the liberal, market-oriented perspective.[30] In the event of a conflict between Article 10 and A1P1, between either protection of pharmaceutical corporations' IPRs and human health, or public access to books/the internet and publishing companies/multimedia corporations' IPRs, a balancing exercise may thus pull in different, potentially diametrically opposed, directions depending on the lens through which each Article is construed. The next subsection examines how the Commission and Court have resolved the conceptual and normative tensions.

6.1.2 *Corporate Commercial Speech: The Court's Case Law*

The Commission's and Court's tilt towards the human developmental moral rationale for Article 10 is discernible in the early case law which centres on the content of the speech and enhanced protection for speech which contributes to public and political debate, irrespective of whether the source was a private, for-profit organization or not.[31] However, in the 1990s, the Court's approach

[29] On the historical background to the conflation of economic freedoms with personal freedoms in the ECHR see A. W. Brian Simpson, *Human Rights and the End of Empire: Britain and the Genesis of the European Convention* (Oxford: Oxford University Press, 2004).

[30] Emberland, *The Human Rights of Companies*, p. 119.

[31] Application no. 6538/74, *The Sunday Times* v. *the United Kingdom*, decision 26 April 1979; Application no. 10572/83, *Markt Intern Verlag GmbH and Klaus Beermann* v. *Germany*, decision November 20,1989 and Application no. 10890/84, *Groppera Radio and Others* v. *Switzerland*, 10 March 1990.

took a different direction, with a trio of landmark judgments that put the Convention 'at the forefront of fundamental rights regimes in promoting the interests of for-profit entities'.[32] As detailed below, the Court unequivocally affirmed that Article 10 protects the speech of corporate commercial actors where the content of the speech is content-neutral and a matter of complete indifference. In addition, the Court merged the attributes of 'natural persons' and 'legal persons' in a decision to award non-pecuniary damages to a company which claimed to have suffered anxiety and inconvenience as a result of the excessive delays in Portugal's judicial processes.

The first decision affirming that commercial speech is protected by Article 10 when the content of the speech contributes to public debate was in the *Sunday Times* case (1979).[33] The applicant, the privately owned Times newspaper, had challenged a UK Court's injunction which prevented the paper from publishing an article on a company (Distillers) that had marketed the Thalidomide drug which had caused 'appalling personal tragedy to hundreds of individuals'.[34] The Strasbourg Court noted the 'undisputed public interest' in whether a powerful company should bear moral and legal responsibility for the tragedy and whether existing laws were adequate to secure compensation for personal injuries. The UK Court's injunction preventing the *Times* from publishing the article was held by a majority of the Court to be a violation of Article 10. In reaching this conclusion, the Court contrasted its own approach to that of the UK House of Lords, stating that

> The Court is faced not with a choice between two conflicting principles but with a principle of freedom of expression that is subject to a number of exceptions which must be narrowly interpreted.[35]

In the majority's view, UK courts had erred in failing to give primacy to freedom of expression in circumstances where the commercial speech had a significant public dimension and had given undue weight to conflicting interests beyond what was strictly necessary.

However, the Court's subsequent case law on commercial speech widened the scope of application of Article 10 in two important ways. Firstly, in *Groppera Radio and Others* v. *Switzerland*, the Court extended the scope of application of Article 10 to commercial speech which did not have a public

[32] Emberland, *The Human Rights of Companies*, p. 134.
[33] Application no. 6538/74, *The Sunday Times* v. *the United Kingdom*.
[34] Ibid.
[35] Ibid., para. 65.

interest dimension.[36] The applicant, an Italian radio station, had been refused a licence to operate cross-borders by the Swiss authorities. The Swiss government sought to have the Article 10 complaint to the ECtHR dismissed on the grounds that the applicant broadcaster was not imparting 'information and ideas' but mainly 'light music and commercials'. The Court disagreed, without committing to a definition of 'information and ideas', and concurred with the Commission that broadcasting of programs and cable transmissions are covered by Article 10(1):

> without there being any need to make distinctions according to the content of the programmes.[37]

The Court held, by sixteen votes to three, that there had been no violation of Article 10. Secondly, the underpinning rationale for the Court's reading of Article 10, in this case, was not the human personal development of listeners, since the content of the programmes was deemed irrelevant. Instead, the rationale related to the State's use of licensing powers to regulate market monopolies in broadcasting. In the subsequent case of *Informationsverein Lentia* v. *Austria*,[38] the Court rejected the Austrian government's argument that licensing of private broadcasters would lead to the creation of private monopolies, holding that market liberalization of the media is consistent with Article 10 in promoting media pluralism, and stating that 'a public monopoly is the one which imposes the greatest restrictions on the freedom of expression'.[39]

The liberal economic reading of Article 10 in *Groppera* was also further affirmed by the Court in *Hertel* v. *Switzerland* in 1998.[40] The Court held that Switzerland was in breach of Article 10 for imposing an injunction and criminal sanction on Hertel, a scientist who had published in a journal his research warning against the health risks posed by microwaves. The *Hertel* decision is standardly cited as evidence that the margin of appreciation enjoyed by States in the application of Article 10 is narrow when 'what is at

36 Application no. 10890/84, *Groppera Radio and Others* v. *Switzerland*. Contrast concurring and dissenting opinions at paras. 2 and 3.

37 Ibid., para. 55.

38 Application nos. 13914/88, 15041/89, 15717/89, 15779/89 and 17207/90, *Informationsverein Lentia* v. *Austria*, decision 24 November 1993, para. 39.

39 See Alastair Mowbray's commentary in Alastair R. Mowbray, *Cases, Materials, and Commentary on the European Convention on Human Rights*, 3rd ed. (Oxford: Oxford University Press, 2012), p. 686. As noted by Mowbray, the Court's analysis made it 'virtually impossible for States to defend a state monopoly of audio-visual broadcasting'.

40 Application no. 25181/94, *Hertel* v. *Switzerland*, decision 25 August 1998.

stake is not a given individual's purely commercial statements, but his participation in a debate affecting the general interest'[41] or the when content of the speech has a public interest and political dimension.[42] Whilst this is true, less attention is drawn to other aspects of the decision which potentially run counter to the individual, human developmental rationale for Article 10. Notably, the Court asserted that a 'margin of appreciation is particularly essential in commercial matters, especially in an area as complex and fluctuating as that of unfair competition'.[43] In addition, the Court sided with the Swiss government in rejecting the applicant's submission that he was not a competitor or supplier of microwaves and could not have foreseen that, in sending a research article to a journal, he could be committing an act of 'unfair competition' within the meaning the UCL Act of 1989.[44]

One possible route, not taken by the Court, would have been to accept the argument that the legal definitions of 'unfair competition' in the Swiss Competition Law Act were unclear. On this alternative line of reasoning, the ECtHR could have found Switzerland in breach of Article 10(2) on the grounds that the restrictions on freedom of expression entailed by the UCL Act did not meet the requirement of being 'prescribed by law' because the wording of the Act was not sufficiently precise to enable a citizen to reasonably foresee the consequences of her action.[45] A decision on these grounds would have left open the question of the possible extension of Article 10 to the context of economic and competition law. Instead, the Court accepted the Swiss government's submission that breach of the UCL Act was foreseeable. Moreover, the Court went further than *Groppera* in expressly stating that the regulation of unfair competition was a legitimate aim to secure protection of the rights of others under Article 10(2), although on the facts, the restrictions on publication imposed on Hertel were held to be disproportionate by the majority. The two judges in the minority also accepted that competition law and unfair competition, which they acknowledged had a technical and economic orientation, fell within the range of legitimate interferences in

[41] Ibid., para. 47.

[42] See Mowbray, *Cases, Materials, and Commentary on the European Convention on Human Rights*, p. 659.

[43] Application no. 25181/94, *Hertel* v. *Switzerland*, para. 47.

[44] Section 2 UCL Act 1989 defines as unfair and illegal 'any conduct or commercial practice ... if it is deceptive or in any other way offends the principle of good faith and if it affects relations between competitors or between suppliers and customers'. Section 3(a) provides that a person acts unfairly if, in particular, he denigrates others or the goods, work, services, prices or business of others by making inaccurate, misleading or unnecessarily wounding statements.

[45] On the meaning of 'prescribed by law' see Mowbray, *Cases, Materials, and Commentary on the European Convention on Human Rights*, pp. 662 ff.

Article 10(2). They dissented from the majority only on the related width of the margin of appreciation. Judge Matscher thought that 'in unfair competition cases States should be afforded a wider margin of appreciation than in other spheres of freedom of expression. Otherwise, the system for preventing unfair competition, one that is beneficial to the business world, will be destroyed'. Judge Bernardht noted that 'the judgment accepts that it is indispensable for national authorities to enjoy a considerable margin of appreciation in determining what restrictions on the freedom of expression which may be necessary in economic matters and especially in the field of unfair competition'. Both dissenting judges disagreed with the majority that Switzerland had exceeded its margin of appreciation in the instant case and would have upheld the Federal Court's judgment against the applicant.

The decision in *Hertel* arguably has elusive, complex dimensions which point in conflicting directions. The real competing interests at stake here were the Association of Microwave Manufacturers' potential loss of sales caused by harm to reputation (for which no evidence was submitted in court) and the scientist's freedom to publish his research.[46] Faced with this conflict of interests, the Court adopted an equivocal approach. On the one hand, the Court affirmed that scientists' freedom of expression to publish their research is protected under Article 10. On the other hand, the Court also accepted the legitimacy of restricting publication of scientific research under Article 10(2) to protect 'the right of others', namely the commercial interests of companies in regulated free markets. Moreover, the divided opinions at the ECtHR were not on whether corporate commercial interests may legitimately limit scientists' freedom of expression but on the circumstances under which they may do so. Hertel thus opens the way for two contradictory approaches to Article 10: one whereby Article 10 may act as a break on the expansion of companies' IPRs, and another where companies' IPRs may prevail over freedom of speech (see further discussion below).

Amongst other cases ringing alarm bells on Article 10 is the ECtHR's judgment in *Autronic* AG v. *Switzerland*[47] described by Emberland as a

[46] Judgment of the Swiss Federal Court stated that 'The smooth operation of competition and economic freedom, freedom of expression, scientific freedom and freedom of the press must be guaranteed as well as possible, but at the same time limited so that the various constitutional objectives may be reconciled in practice.. . . Anyone claiming scientific freedom is therefore wholly free to expound his knowledge in the academic sphere but, where competition is concerned, he may not claim to have the truth on his side where the opinion he is putting forward is disputed.' Cited in Application no. 25181/94, *Hertel* v. *Switzerland*, p. 23.

[47] Application no. 12726/87, *Autronic* AG v. *Switzerland*, decision 22 May 1990.

'watershed' decision.[48] The company Autronic, had been barred by the Swiss government from taking part in a trades fair to demonstrate a novel type of satellite dish enabling transmission of programmes in Russia. Autronic complained that the ban was in breach of its Article 10 right to impart information. In response, the government claimed that

> the right to freedom of expression was not relevant to the applicant company's complaint in the present case. In the first place, the company had not attached any importance to the content of the transmission (programmes in Russian), since it was pursuing purely economic and technical interests. The company was a corporate body whose activities were commercial and its sole object had been to give a demonstration at a fair of the capabilities of a dish aerial in order to promote sales of it. Freedom of expression that was exercised, as in the present case, exclusively for pecuniary gain came under the head of economic freedom, which was outside the scope of the Convention. The 'information' in question was therefore not protected by Article 10. (Article 10)[49]

The Court disagreed, stating that

> neither Autronic AG's legal status as a limited company nor the fact that its activities were commercial nor the intrinsic nature of freedom of expression can deprive Autronic AG of the protection of Article 10 (art. 10). The Article (art. 10) applies to 'everyone', whether natural or legal persons ... Furthermore, Article 10 (art. 10) applies not only to the content of information but also to the means of transmission or reception since any restriction imposed on the means necessarily interferes with the right to receive and impart information. Indeed, the Article (art. 10) expressly mentions in the last sentence of its first paragraph (art. 10-1) certain enterprises essentially concerned with the means of transmission.[50]

The decision is of particular significance because, as noted by the two dissenting judges and by contrast with the Court's earlier decisions on

[48] Emberland, *The Human Rights of Companies*, p. 129.

[49] Application no. 12726/87, *Autronic AG* v. *Switzerland*, para. 44.

[50] Ibid., para. 47. Like the Commission, the Court also found that the right to receive TV programmes fell within the first two sentences of Article 10 without it being necessary to ascertain the reason and purpose for which the right is to be exercised. In *Groppera* v. *Switzerland*, the government had argued that the content of the radio station broadcasts was light music and commercial did not constitute 'information or ideas'. The Court said that it did not need to give a precise definition of information and ideas but, like the Commission, it considered that 'both broadcasting of programmes over the air and cable retransmission of such programmes are covered by the right enshrined in the first two sentences of Article 10 § 1 (art. 10-1), without there being any need to make distinctions according to the content of the programmes' at para. 55.

Article 10, the content of the information was a matter of complete indifference to the applicants. There was no significant (public) dimension to the content of the information which the applicants sought to disseminate by the dish aerials. Moreover, the applicants had not been restricted from selling the dish aerials. For this reason, Judges Bindschedler-Robert and Matscher dissenting, thought, arguably correctly, that it was not possible 'to derive a restriction of freedom of information from an alleged restriction of trade in technical equipment for radio-communication'.[51]

The final assimilation by the Court of the commercial interests of corporate entities in free markets with the fundamental rights of individual, human persons to freedom of expression is in the remarkable judgment of the Grand Chamber in *Comingersoll* SA v. *Portugal* (2000).[52] Comingersoll, the applicant company, claimed, inter alia, non-pecuniary damages under Article 41[53] for the feelings of anxiety regarding loss of reputation, uncertainty in decision-planning and disruption of management due to excessive delays in Portugal's judicial processes, which the Court had found were a violation of Article 6 ECHR. In reply, the Portuguese government had submitted that the purpose of awarding non-pecuniary damages was to compensate the claimant for mental stress and anxiety. Such feelings, the government said, 'were peculiar to natural persons and could under no circumstances entitle a juristic person to compensation'.[54] The majority of the Grand Chamber disagreed. Non-pecuniary damages, the Grand Chamber held, could include the effect of the breach on 'the company's reputation, uncertainty in decision-planning, disruption in the management of the company (for which there is no precise method of calculating the consequences)'.

In addition, the majority included in the list (albeit to a lesser degree):

> the anxiety and inconvenience caused to the members of the management team.[55]

This is a remarkable decision that has, rightly, attracted criticism from legal scholars.[56] The decision is problematic in conflating legal persons with

[51] Dissenting Opinion of Judges Bindschedler-Robert and Matscher, p. 25, paras. 1 and 2.

[52] Application no. 35382/97, *Comingersoll* SA v. *Portugal*, decision 6 May 2000.

[53] Article 41 of the Convention provides: 'If the Court finds that there has been a violation of the Convention or the Protocols thereto, and if the internal law of the High Contracting Party concerned allows only partial reparation to be made, the Court shall, if necessary, afford just satisfaction to the injured party.'

[54] Application no. 35382/97, *Comingersoll* SA v. *Portugal*, para. 28.

[55] Ibid., para. 35.

[56] See for instance Turkeler Isiksel, 'Corporate Human Rights Claims under the ECHR' (2019) 17 *Georgetown Journal of Law & Public Policy* 979 and Karol Karski and Bartosz Ziemblicki,

natural persons from a conceptual and normative perspective. Conceptually, as argued by Isiksel, only individual human beings are uniquely capable of feelings of anxiety, frustration, stress, mental and physical pain, sadness, trauma, depression, shame, anguish or humiliation.[57] Companies are legal constructs; they do not have feelings and they cannot suffer anxiety. Their interests are, by definition, economic.[58] Moreover, the majority's approach is at odds with domestic laws and international norms which assume that damages for mental distress can only be awarded to human beings.[59] The blurring of the two legal categories of natural and legal persons is also problematic in cutting across established legal distinctions between a company and its members, directors or shareholders which the Court itself has acknowledged in other cases.[60]

In short, the European Commission and the ECtHR have, in the main, concurred that political speech or commercial speech with a significant public dimension enjoy a higher level of protection than commercial speech, triggering a stricter level of review of national restrictions from the Court, in recognition of the significance of freedom of expression in enabling individual human participation in the political process of democratic societies.[61] On the

'Commercial Companies as Applicants before the European Court of Human Rights' (2021) 23(5) *International Community Law Review* 503–525.

57 Isiksel, 'Corporate Human Rights Claims under the ECHR'.

58 Isiksel, 'Corporate Human Rights Claims under the ECHR', citing Ernst Freund, *The Legal Nature of Corporations* (Chicago: University of Chicago Press, 1897), note 63.

59 Royston Miles Goode, Herbert Kronke and Ewan McKendrick, eds., *Transnational Commercial Law: Text, Cases and Materials*, 2nd ed. (Oxford: Oxford University Press, 2015). See also the dissenting opinion of Judges Rozakis, joined by Judges Sir Nocolas Bratza, Caflisch and Vajic who concurred that the basis for awarding non-pecuniary damages to companies is not feelings of anxiety felt by the humans but because attributes of legal persons such as reputation may be impaired by acts or omissions of the State. The dissenting judges also disagreed with the analogy of the Turkey precedent which concerned a political party, by its nature a loose association, in circumstances where the issue at stake was freedom of association.

60 As note by Isiksel, 'Corporate Human Rights Claims under the ECHR' '... in earlier case law, the ECtHR had followed the International Court of Justice's finding in the Barcelona Traction decision that 'even if a company is no more than a means for its shareholders to achieve their economic purpose, so long as it is in esse it enjoys an independent existence. Therefore, the interests of the shareholders are both separable and indeed separated from those of the company' (para. 65). See also Surya Deva et al. (eds.), 'Beyond Human Rights due Diligence: What Else Do We Need?' (2023) 8(2: Special Issue) *Choudhury Business and Human Rights Journal* 180–196.

61 Christopher McCrudden, 'The Impact on Freedom of Speech' in Basil Markesinis (ed.), *The Impact of the Human Rights Bill on English Law* (Oxford: Oxford University Press, 1998), p. 90. On artistic freedom see Dirk Voorhoof, *Critical Perspectives on the Scope and Interpretation of Article 10 of the European Convention on Human Rights* (Mass media files, No. 10) (Strasbourg: Council of Europe Press, 1995).

other hand, there is also a line of decisions from the Commission and Court confirming that commercial speech enjoys ECHR protection under Article 10, irrespective of content, whether political or not, and irrespective of public interest dimensions (as defined by the Court). In such cases, States are left a wide margin of appreciation to regulate the speech with the Court adopting a lenient, light touch approach to review of national laws. Yet, the implications of the Court's deferential approach to State regulation of commercial speech are unclear where companies' rights in domestic laws extend to exclusive rights of control over the use of content. In particular, there is a risk that the wide margin of appreciation granted to States might enable national IPR laws to evade scrutiny and reinforce rather than contain IPRs. As will be seen in Section 6.2, this is indeed what has happened in the case law of the Court on IPRs.

In short, the above discussion has shown that there are different, indeed colliding rationales underpinning the decisions of the Commission and the Court and some uncertainty on the application of the relevant principles by domestic Courts. In this light, the potential for Article 10 to act as a safeguard against the expansion of companies' IPRs could be highly dependent on judicial attitudes/cultures and might turn out to be considerably less effective than originally anticipated. Section 6.2 shows how the high expectations for Article 10 to act as a counterweight balance to IPRs have not been met.

6.2 ARTICLE 10 V. IPRS

6.2.1 *The Commission's Decisions*

The first two decisions of the Commission take Article 10 as their starting point in claims alleging that statutory rights of exclusivity in national IP laws are inconsistent with Article 10. The first decision was in 1976. The complaint had been filed by a private company *De Geillustreerde Pers* N.V. (a publisher of magazines of 'general interest') in respect of rights of exclusivity granted to members of the Dutch Broadcasters Foundation (a private entity) over publication of the list of TV programmes produced by the members.[62] The applicant alleged that the Dutch broadcasting statutes of 1967 and 1969, which created these rights of exclusivity, constituted an interference with

[62] Commission's report of Case No. 5178/71, *De Geillustreerde Pers* N.V. v. *the Netherlands*, decision 6 July 1976.

the right of the public to receive information, contrary to Article 10(2), because the information was only available to subscribers of the specialized publication (para. 16).[63] The claimant further complained that the legislation was also an interference with the freedom of the press to communicate information to the public (para. 17), a freedom recognized as essential in any democracy by the Parliament. The Commission disagreed in a decision whose laconic rationale has been highlighted by commentators.[64] The Commission's approach was to construe Article 10(2) as directed at State controls preventing the holder of information from communicating it to the public. This was not the case on the facts. Accordingly, in the absence of State censure or unjustified restrictions on diffusion of the information or interference with the public's right to receive information, albeit subject to payment, the Commission concluded that there was no violation of Article 10. Whilst conceding that the claimant's inability to publish the list of programmes might cause the applicant commercial losses, the Commission's view was that 'the wording of Article 10 did not indicate that the purpose was to protect the commercial interests of newspapers or magazines of general interest, as such'.[65] As noted above, by 1990 the Court had clarified that commercial speech is protected under Article 10, even when its content has no public interest dimension.

The Commission construction of Article 10 in *FRANCE 2* v. *France* (1997) reflects this change.[66] The applicant was an IP collecting society (SPADEM) acting on behalf of the estate of a visual artist whose painting was shown in full for a total of 49 seconds during a TV programme on a theatre production. In 1995, the French Court de Cassation had upheld the judgment of the courts below, ordering FRANCE 2 to pay FF 12,000 damages for infringement. The applicant's defence that the reproduction was a brief citation was rejected on the grounds that the reproduction of a work of art in its entirety, whatever the form

63 Article 22 of the 1967 Broadcasting Statute states that all reproductions and publications without the authorization of the Foundation are a breach of copyright (droit d'auteur). A decision of the Dutch Supreme Court (5 June 1965) that the author is the NOS foundation, a legal and not a natural person and that notwithstanding the absence of a 'personal' link to the information, an infringement will consist not only in respect of literal reproduction of a text, but translations or edited copies too.

64 See for instance Christophe Geiger and Elena Izyumenko, 'Shaping Intellectual Property Rights through Human Rights Adjudication: The Example of the European Court of Human Rights' (2020) 46(3) *Mitchell Hamline Law Review* 527 and Hugenholtz, 'Copyright and Freedom of Expression in Europe'.

65 Moreover, the Commission also noted the issues raised by the claimant in respect of discrimination under Article 14 related to unfair competition (para. 88).

66 Case No. 30262/96, *Société Nationale de Programmes FRANCE 2* v. *France*, decision 15 January 1997.

and duration, cannot be considered a brief citation under the French Copyright law of 11 March 1957 and Intellectual Property Code.[67] Ten years had passed since the filing of the infringement claim against FRANCE 2 in the French courts in 1988 when the Commission issued its report. On appeal to the ECtHR, FRANCE 2 had alleged that the French Courts' judgments were in violation of the press's right to freely impact information under Article 10.[68] The Commission accepted that authors' rights of exclusivity to exploit, reproduce and communicate to the public their artistic or literary creations in the French Copyright law constituted an interference with the press's right to communicate information freely under Article 10. However, the Commission found that the interference was justified under Article 10(2) because it was prescribed by law, necessary (to protect the rights of others) and proportionate. It was not for the Commission to review the application of this law by the national courts. Nor was it for the Commission or Court to settle the conflicts likely to emerge between authors' rights and rights of communication to the public, but to determine whether the limitations on freedom of expression found in the copyright laws were justified as necessary and proportionate. Accordingly, there was no violation of Article 10.

As noted by commentators, the decision's laconic reasoning is disappointing.[69] It is true that the Commission and Court are not intended to function as a first instance court of appeal on the application of domestic law to the facts of the case, as is consistently reiterated in the judgments. On the other hand, the Commission did not consider why it was necessary to protect the rights of authors through copyright laws which fix the term of protection to the life of the author plus fifty years, nor how this was proportionate. It is worth noting that the infringement claim against FRANCE 2 had been filed by the artist's estate almost fifty years after his death.[70] Moreover, as argued by FRANCE 2 in the domestic courts, the artist's painting was on display in the foyer of the Theatre des Champs Elysees, a public space freely accessible to the public.[71] The effect of the Commission's decision was therefore to add an international layer of judicial legitimacy to the artist's estate extraction of the vast sum of FF 12,000 from the

67 Article 41, 3°, de la loi du 11 mars 1957 (article L. 122-5-3°, a du Code de la propriété intellectuelle).

68 Case No. 30262/96, *Société Nationale de Programmes FRANCE 2* v. *France*.

69 Hugenholtz, 'Copyright and Freedom of Expression in Europe'; Geiger and Izyumenko, 'Shaping Intellectual Property Rights through Human Rights Adjudication' and Strowel and Tulkens, 'Freedom of Expression and Copyright under Civil Law'.

70 Edouard Vuillard (1968–1940). See '10 things to know about Édouard Vuillard', Christie's (christies.com).

71 Vuillard had been commissioned by the Theatre des Champs Elysees to paint the panels.

broadcaster in questionable circumstances. The painting had been commissioned in 1912 by the Theatre des Champs Elysees and was readily accessible to the public in a space owned since 1970 by the Caisse des Depots, a public sector financial institution. The case thus illustrates how the weight attached to the rights of others in Article 10(2), errs on the side of IPR holders in affirming the extended term of protection of copyright holders and disproportionately curtails the rights of the media and the public relating to an author's/artist's work.

The next subsection shows how IPR holders' rights against the public users' rights were further reinforced by the Court. By the time the next set of IPR cases reached the Court in 2013, the Grand Chamber had unequivocally affirmed that companies' IPRs were one of the fundamental human rights protected in A1P1 enabling the conflict to be expressly recast as an external balancing exercise between two Convention rights.

6.2.2 *The Court's Case Law*

The two leading cases decided by the Court after the Grand Chamber's decision in *Anheuser-Busch* v. *Portugal* (2007)[72] are *Ashby Donald and Others* v. *France* (2013)[73] followed three months later by the 'Pirate Bay case' (2013).[74] As noted by IP scholars,[75] both cases acknowledge the conflict between the freedom to impart and receive information under Article 10 and the IPR owners' rights to 'enjoyment of their possessions' in the A1P1, triggering a balancing exercise. As detailed below, the Court follows a formulaic approach to the balancing exercise whereby IPRs are construed as an interference with freedom of expression under Article 10(2), raising the question of whether the interference is lawful, necessary and proportionate. In each case, the Court is seen to take the view that the defendant State has a wide margin of appreciation to define the contours of IPR-based limitations on freedom of expression, with the end point of the balancing exercise resulting in a strengthening of IPR owners' rights.

6.2.2.1 *Ashby Donald and Others* v. *France*

The decision was an appeal to the ECtHR from three photographers who had been convicted and sentenced to imprisonment, under the French Code de la

[72] Application no. 73049/01, *Anheuser-Busch* v. *Portugal*.

[73] Application no. 36769/08, *Ashby Donald and Others* v. *France* (available only in French).

[74] Application no. 40397/12, *Neij and Sunde Kolmisoppi* v. *Sweden* ('The Pirate Bay case'), decision 19 February 2013.

[75] Notably Geiger and Izyumenko, 'Shaping Intellectual Property Rights through Human Rights Adjudication'.

Propriété Intellectuelle, for publishing on their internet website, without consent, photographs of a fashion show that the organizers had invited them to attend in Paris. On appeal, the French criminal court had accepted that the accused could rely on an exception in the Code and quashed the sentence on the grounds that the requisite mental intent for a criminal conviction under L. 335-2 et L. 335-3 was absent.[76] The decision was reversed by the Court of Appeal and Cour de Cassation. The defendants then challenged the domestic courts' judgment at the ECtHR, alleging violations of Article 10 and Article 7 which prohibit the retroactive application of a criminal law to the detriment of the accused. The ECtHR declared the Article 7 claim inadmissible on the grounds that the applicants were effectively calling into question the national courts' interpretation of the application of a list of exceptions to infringement, which the claimants alleged retrospectively expanded the scope of copyright protection in the Code. Having dismissed the Article 7 claim, stating that such a review was outside the remit of the Court, the Court declared that the Article 10 claim was admissible.

The claimants alleged that they had a right to impart information under Article 10 which extended to the publication of photographs of an event which was of general interest to the public who in turn had a right to receive the information in a timely manner. In the claimants' view, the imposition of a criminal sanction and the penalty of FF 30,000 for copyright infringement, whilst in accordance with law, constituted a disproportionate interference which was not necessary to protect the rights of others under Article 10(2). The Court disagreed in a unanimous judgment which found that there was no violation of Article 10.

The Court adopted a well-established approach to the balancing of Article 10 with other Convention rights citing previous decisions which confirmed that the publication of photographs[77] on the internet,[78] whether for profit or not[79]

[76] Article L. 122-5 Lorsque l'œuvre a été divulguée, l'auteur ne peut interdire : . . . [inséré par la loi no 2006-961 du 1er août 2006] 90 La reproduction ou la représentation, intégrale ou partielle, d'une œuvre d'art graphique, plastique ou architecturale, par voie de presse écrite, audiovisuelle ou en ligne, dans un but exclusif d'information immédiate et en relation directe avec cette dernière, sous réserve d'indiquer clairement le nom de l'auteur. Le premier alinéa du présent 90 ne s'applique pas aux œuvres, notamment photographiques ou d'illustration, qui visent elles-mêmes à rendre compte de l'information.

[77] Application nos. 40660/08 and 60641/08, *Von Hannover* v. *Germany (no 2)*, decision 7 February 2012.

[78] Application nos. 3002/03 and 23676/03, *Times Newspapers Ltd* v. *the United Kingdom (nos. 1 and 2)*.

[79] Application no. 12726/87, *Autronic AG* v. *Switzerland*.

and irrespective of the content,[80] fell within the right to impart and receive ideas under Article 10. From this, the Court inferred that the publication of photographs of a fashion show was covered by Article 10. Next, the Court recalled that limitations on freedom of expression had to be in accordance with law, pursue a legitimate aim, be 'necessary in a democratic society' and proportionate to the aims. Since the claimants' complaint related to the compatibility of the provisions on infringement in Articles L. 335-2 and L. 335-3 of the Code with Article 10, the Court inferred that the limitations were in accordance with law. The Court also accepted that the purpose of the law was to protect the rights of others, namely the (copy)rights of fashion companies whose creations formed the content of the infringing photographs.[81] The next question was whether the restrictions were necessary in a democratic society. The Court noted that the applicable principles had been well established in several decisions.[82] The preeminent role of freedom of expression in a democratic society was reiterated, as was the importance of pluralism and the expression of different ideas in the development of the human personality.[83] Nonetheless, the Court noted that Article 10 contains some exceptions which must be narrowly interpreted and sufficiently justified. The Court recalled its own definition of 'necessary' as addressing a 'pressing social need' and reiterated that States enjoy a variable margin of appreciation in this respect. One particularly important consideration was the nature and content of the information, ideas or speech. The Court reiterated that there was very little scope for States to restrict freedom of expression in political matters. By contrast, States enjoy a wide margin of appreciation with respect to commercial speech, unless the content of the speech contributes to a debate of general interest. In this instance, there were two conflicting Convention values. The Court cited *MGN Ltd* v. *the United Kingdom* (2011) on how the balance between two conflicting values was to be conducted:[84]

> The balancing of individual interests, which may well be contradictory, is a difficult matter and Contracting States must have a broad margin of appreciation in this respect since the national authorities are in principle better placed than this Court to assess whether or not there is a 'pressing social need' capable of justifying an interference with one of the rights guaranteed by the Convention.[85]

80 Application no. 10890/84, *Groppera Radio and Others* v. *Switzerland*.
81 Application no. 36769/08, *Ashby Donald and Others* v. *France*. Ibid., para. 36.
82 Ibid., Citing, inter alia, Application no. 15890/89, *Jersild* v. *Danemark*, decision 23 September 1994; Application no. 25181/94, *Hertel* v. *Switzerland*.
83 Ibid., at para. 38.1.
84 Application no. 39401/04, *MGN Ltd* v. *the United Kingdom*, decision 12 June 2004.
85 Citing Application nos. 25088/94, 28331/95 and 28443/95, *Chassagnou and Others* v. *France* (Grand Chamber), decision 29 April 1999.

In the Court's view, the publication of fashion show photographs, whilst appealing to the public, did not in itself contribute to a debate on a topic of general interest. Consequently, the defending State had a wide margin of appreciation. The French government had not exceeded the margin of appreciation in criminalizing copyright infringement. Protection of the fashion house's IPRs was a legitimate aim since the Grand Chamber had declared in *Anheuser-Busch* (2007) that IPRs were fundamental rights under A1P1.[86] Neither were the criminal sanctions disproportionate when the applicants, as was the case here, had knowingly published the photographs without the consent of the copyright holders and offered no evidence that damages exceeding FF 100,000 would 'strangle them financially'. Accordingly, there was no violation of Article 10.

6.2.2.2 The Pirate Bay Case

A similar line of reasoning was adopted by the Court three months later in the Pirate Bay case,[87] in a decision that further strengthened the rights of IP owners in recalling that States are under a positive obligation to take effective measures to secure protection of IP holders' rights, and that particular weight is attached to the fact that the rights of IP holders are protected under A1P1.[88]

The facts are well known: the two applicants had been convicted of complicity to commit crimes under Sweden's Copyright Act by running a website which enabled users to share copyright-protected digital movies, music and computer games. They were sentenced to ten and eight months' imprisonment respectively and held jointly liable for damages of approximately EUR 5 million. In rejecting the applicants' defence that they should be absolved of criminal liability, the domestic courts emphasized that the applicants had committed the offences intentionally, taken no precautionary measures to avert the sharing of copyrighted materials and had failed to remove the copyrighted materials despite warnings and requests to do so.

On appeal to the ECtHR, the applicants complained that the convictions interfered with their right to impart information under Article 10 and were

[86] Citing Application no. 73049/01, *Anheuser-Busch* v. *Portugal*, para. 40. 'Dès lors que l'article 1 du Protocole no 1 s'applique à la propriété intellectuelle, elle visait ainsi à la protection de droits garantis par la Convention ou ses Protocoles.'

[87] Application no. 40397/12, *Neij and Sunde Kolmisoppi* v. *Sweden*, decision 19 February 2013.

[88] See Chapter 5 for a discussion on how the Court has construed A1P1 as entailing not only negative obligations for States to abstain from interfering with the right to 'enjoyment of possessions' but also a positive obligation to ensure that IPRs are effectively protected in national laws.

neither necessary nor proportionate. The Court disagreed. It acknowledged that Article 10 guarantees the right to disseminate information on the internet and the right of the public to receive it, citing, inter alia, its recent decision in *Ashby Donald and Others*.[89] The Court also cited *Autronic*,[90] reiterating that Article 10 protects the right of 'everyone' and makes 'no distinction according to whether the aim pursued is profit-making or not'. The Court further noted that dissemination and receipt of information is protected, irrespective of content and means of transmission, since 'restriction on the means necessarily interferes with the right to receive and impart information'.[91]

Applying these principles, the Court then stressed that, in considering whether the restriction was necessary to protect the right of others under Article 10(2), weight had to be added to the protection of copyright holders since 'intellectual property benefits from the protection afforded by A1P1, citing *Anheuser-Busch Inc.*[92] The Court also recalled its own decision that States had a positive obligation to protect IP.[93] As in *Ashby Donald and Others*, the Court found that the type of information for which the applicants had been convicted did not enjoy the same level of protection as political expression and debate.[94] When these factors were weighed together in the instant case, the margin of appreciation was 'particularly wide' (*Ashby Donald and Others*, para. 41). Hence, the criminal convictions and penalties fell within the ambit of discretion enjoyed by Sweden. The sentences were not disproportionate in light of the national authorities' findings that the crimes were intentional. Thus, there was no violation of Article 10.

6.3 THE LIMITS OF BALANCING IPRS WITH CONVENTION RIGHTS

The review of the Court's case law on the balance between IPRs and freedom of expression has shown that, contrary to expectations, the balancing exercise has resulted in a strengthening of the rights of IP holders. The external

[89] Application no. 36769/08, *Ashby Donald and Others* v. *France*. As well as Application no. 13585/88, *Observer and Guardian* v. *the United Kingdom* and Application nos. 3002/03 and 23676/03, *Times Newspapers Ltd* v. *the United Kingdom (nos. 1 and 2)*.

[90] Application no. 12726/87, *Autronic AG* v. *Switzerland*.

[91] Citing Application no. 48939/99, *Öneryıldız* v. *Turkey* (Grand Chamber), decision 30 November 2004. But see Opinion of dissenting judges in Autronic (above) querying the analogy.

[92] Application no. 73049/01, *Anheuser-Busch* v. *Portugal*.

[93] On the Court's development of positive obligations see Alastair R. Mowbray, *The Development of Positive Obligations under the European Convention on Human Rights by the European Court of Human Rights* (Oxford: Hart, 2004).

[94] Application no. 36769/08, *Ashby Donald and Others* v. *France*.

balancing of IPRs against fundamental rights, and Article 10 in particular, has not proved more effective in constraining the expanding scope of protection of IPRs than the established internal, built-in limitations on IPRs such as the distinction between expression and ideas, list of exceptions and three-step rule in copyright.[95] The discussion below seeks to understand why the Court's judgments have confounded expectations in order to draw some lessons for the future. It identifies three aspects of the Court's methodology which, it is argued, stand in the way of Convention rights acting as breaks on IPRs: the Court's eschewal of a principled review of domestic IP laws, the margin of appreciation granted to States to regulate commercial speech and the Court's selective reference to EU and international human rights law.

6.3.1 *Judging Principles*

A grey area in the jurisprudence of the Court on Article 10 and IPRs is the distinction between principles and their application to the facts of a case. The distinction is at the heart of the Court's jurisdiction and its powers of review of domestic laws. However, according to Judge David Thór Björgvinsson, dissenting from the majority in *MGN* v. *the United Kingdom*: 'It has been the consistent approach of this court that it is not enough, in itself, that the domestic courts consider the relevant principles; they must also be applied correctly.'[96] In Judge Thór Björgvinsson's view, it is appropriate for the Court to substitute its own views for those of the domestic courts when making 'its own independent assessment of the facts involved and of the application of the relevant principles to those facts'.[97] The Court, we are told, has reversed the findings of domestic courts in numerous cases 'without suggesting that the domestic courts had considered irrelevant principles or applied improper criteria in the overall assessment made'.[98] The difficulty with this view, as repeatedly reiterated by the Court itself, is that the Court is not a first instance court of appeal. Its role is not to review the national courts' application of

95 On internal v. internal balancing of IPRs see Daniel J. Gervais, 'Making Copyright Whole: A Principled Approach to Copyright Exceptions and Limitations' (2008) 5 *University of Ottawa Law and Technology Journal* 1; Reto Hilty and Sylvie Nérisson (eds.), *Balancing Copyright – A Survey of National Approaches*, vol. 18 (New York: Springer, 2012); Christophe Geiger and Elena Izyumenko, 'From Internal to External Balancing, and Back? Copyright Limitations and Fundamental Rights in the Digital Environment' in Conception Saiz Garcia and Julian Lopez (eds.), *Digitalización, acceso a contenidos y propiedad intelectual* (Madrid: Dykinson, 2022).

96 Application no. 39401/04, *MGN Ltd* v. *the United Kingdom*, para. 232.

97 Ibid.

98 Ibid.

domestic laws to the facts of the case but to determine whether domestic laws are compliant with Convention rights. Moreover, substitution of the domestic courts' application of the law to the facts of the case is not equivalent to a principled review of the law and, at worst, can evade principled scrutiny of the domestic laws (see below).

In theory, the Court's balancing exercise would involve a review of domestic law(s) in the light of the relevant fundamental rights in the Convention (Article 10, Article 8 or Article 6, etc.). In practice, as seen above, the Court's decisions often look like a review of the national courts' application of domestic laws to the facts of the case. The decision in *Hertel* is a good example of how judges at the ECtHR may concur on national laws' compliance with Article 10 but come to a different conclusion from the domestic courts on the application of the law to the facts.[99] In *Hertel*, there was no disagreement on the applicable principles between the majority and minority judges at the Court, or between the Court and the domestic courts. It was accepted by all that Hertel had an Article 10 right to freedom of expression which included publication of his research highlighting the potential health risks of microwaves. Neither was there disagreement that the national authorities' control of the content of the publication constituted an interference with Hertel's Article 10 rights or whether the interference was legitimate. Instead, the disagreement between the Court's (majority) and the domestic courts was whether the interference was disproportionate. The majority disagreed with Switzerland's Supreme Court and held that the national restrictions on the publication of Hertel's research were in breach of Article 10(2). The minority disagreed with the majority that there had been a violation of Article 10(2). In the minority's view, the majority had substituted its own judgment to that of the domestic courts and engaged in a de facto review of the facts, contrary to the established parameters of the Court's jurisdiction. This sounds right. Moreover, neither the minority nor the majority undertook a scrutiny of the domestic courts' construction of Hertel's publication as an act of 'unfair competition' under Switzerland's UCL Act or the categorisation of Hertel as a competitor or supplier of microwaves, even though the proceedings in the national courts show that the legal definitions in the UCL Act were unclear. Nor did the majority or minority of the Court consider or question the potentially far-reaching implications for freedom of expression and chilling effect on scientific research of categorizing the publication of scientific research as an act of (unfair) competition. The Court's deference to the domestic courts on this point is all the more disquieting because the obvious legal route not taken by

[99] Application no. 25181/94, *Hertel* v. *Switzerland*.

the microwave manufacturers to challenge the content of the publication was defamation. One can only speculate as to the reasons why, although it is possible that this avenue was not pursued because no evidence was submitted at trial that the manufacturers had actually suffered a loss of sales. Thus, whilst at a practical level, the Court's review was an affirmation of Hertel's freedom of expression, a closer analysis reveals that, in reality, the Court did not engage with the issues of principle raised by the case. It accepted the questionable domestic courts' legal construction of Hertel's conduct as an act of unfair competition whilst failing to consider the potential chilling effect on freedom of expression.

If the Court's scrutiny of national laws' compliance with Article 10 tacitly assumes that Article 10 protects economic freedoms and the Court, instead, reviews the application of Convention law to the facts, it is unclear how Article 10 could act as a counterweight to intellectual property rights. A de facto review of domestic courts' application of Convention law to the facts of the case carries the risk of under-scrutinizing compliance of domestic laws with Convention principles. The decisions of the Court in *Ashby Donald* and the 'Pirate Bay' case are good illustrations.[100] In both cases, the issue of principle concerned compliance of domestic copyright legislation criminalizing infringement with Article 10. In neither case did the Court consider whether criminalizing infringement was, as a matter of principle, proportionate and consistent with Article 10. The question was avoided by the Court which, instead, engaged in a de facto review of whether, on the facts, the applicants had shown the requisite mental intent for criminal convictions under the respective national laws. In a similar vein, in FRANCE 2, the Commission did not question whether the term of protection for copyright of life of the author plus fifty years was necessary and proportionate to protect the rights of authors under Article 10(2).[101] Instead, the nature of the substantive rights and remedies in the domestic laws on copyright were tacitly accepted. Yet, a

[100] Application no. 36769/08, *Ashby Donald and Others* v. *France* and Application no. 40397/12, *Neij and Sunde Kolmisoppi* v. *Sweden* ('The Pirate Bay case').

[101] See Jerome H. Reichman, 'The Duration of Copyright and the Limits of Cultural Policy' (1996) 14 *Cardozo Arts & Entertainment Law Journal* 625; William M. Landes and Richard A. Posner, 'Indefinitely Renewable Copyright' (2003) 70 *The University of Chicago Law Review* 471; William M. Landes and Richard A. Posner, 'An Economic Analysis of Copyright Law' (1989) 18(2) *The Journal of Legal Studies* 325–363. Liu specifically proposes that courts should adjust length of protection in Joseph P. Liu, 'Copyright and Time: A Proposal' (2002) 101(2) *Michigan Law Review* 409–481; Kristelia A. García and Justin McCrary, 'A Reconsideration of Copyright's Term' (2019) 71 *Alabama Law Review* 351 and Scott M. Martin, 'The Mythology of the Public Domain: Exploring the Myths behind Attacks on the Duration of Copyright Protection' (2002) 36 *Loyola of Los Angeles Law Review* 253.

principled review would have been consistent with the Court's own approach in other cases where the award of damages for breach was considered disproportionate.[102] Arguably, in order for Article 10 to discharge the function of acting as a counterweight to IPRs, the Court would need to approach the balancing exercise with a clear focus on principle. The alternative de facto review in reality defers to Member States on the nature and scope of IPR protection, its limits and remedies.

6.3.2 *Margins of Appreciation*

The Court's decisions on Article 10 present the balancing exercise as a structured approach, with a checklist of factors to guide the Court's assessment of whether IPRs interference with freedom of expression has a legitimate aim, is lawful, necessary in a democratic society and proportionate.[103] A closer look reveals layers of complexity behind the Court's methodology. A critical dimension of the Court's approach is the margin of appreciation granted to States to determine the content and scope of national laws which limit freedom of expression.[104] A wide margin of appreciation entails light-touch review and deference to States whilst a narrow margin of appreciation requires strict scrutiny of domestic laws. The Court's classification of the content of a publication, broadcast or image and whether it relates to a matter of 'public interest' is decisive in determining the appropriate level of scrutiny. A decision by the Court to categorize the content of an image, publication or broadcast as lacking a public interest dimension triggers a light-touch review, leaving States a wide margin of appreciation to decide how far to limit the expression and (indirectly) ownership of the related information. In *Ashby Donald and Others*, the Court rejected the photographers' evidence of substantial public interest in photographs of catwalks as fulfilling the requirement that publication of the photographs was in the public interest.[105] The same is true of

[102] See for instance, Case No. 18139/91, *Tolstoy Miloslavsky* v. *the United Kingdom*, decision 13 July 1995. The author is grateful to Ian Cram for bringing this case to her attention.

[103] See also Council of Europe's Guidance on Article 10, updated 30 August 2022.

[104] On the margin of appreciation, see Steven C. Greer, 'The Margin of Appreciation: Interpretation and Discretion under the European Convention on Human Rights', vol. 17 (Council of Europe, 2000), www.lawyersnjurists.com/article/the-margin-of-appreciation-interpretation-and-discretion-under-the-european-convention-on-human-rights-part-3/; Dean Spielmann, 'Whither the Margin of Appreciation?' (2014) 67 *Current Legal Problems* 49 and Mikael Rask Madsen, 'The Challenging Authority of the European Court of Human Rights: From Cold War Legal Diplomacy to the Brighton Declaration and Backlash' (2016) 79 *Law and Contemporary Problems* 141.

[105] Application no. 36769/08, *Ashby Donald and Others* v. *France*.

Autronic where the Court dismissed listeners' interest in light music as meeting the 'public interest' criterion.[106] In both cases, and in the 'Pirate Bay' case, the subject matter of the information protected by Article 10 were images, broadcasts or publications which ordinarily fall within the rubric of 'popular culture' which, in the Court's view, do not contribute to public/political debate in democratic societies.[107] In addition, scientific or educational resources which, in contrast to Hertel's research, are judged by the Court not to contribute to category of 'public debate', also fall outside the scope of the Court's strict scrutiny. Unless the subject matter/content of the IPR, the text, publication, broadcast or image happens to fall within the Court's 'public interest' category, the Court will not undertake a strict scrutiny of compliance of IP laws with Article 10. Hence, once the subject matter/content of the IP is categorized as lacking a public interest dimension, States are effectively granted discretion to determine the nature and scope of IP owners' rights. The implication is that IP laws enabling appropriation and control of content-neutral cultural, scientific and educational resources and materials will avoid the Court's scrutiny of compliance with the right to impart and receive information under Article 10. Protection of IP owners' rights is further reinforced and consolidated by the Court's construction of IPRs as fundamental rights enjoying protection under A1P1. In this light, it is unclear how the 'external' balancing of freedom of expression with IPRs in the ECHR could halt the expanding scope of IPRs.

Neither is it clear whether and how the invocation of Article 10 ECHR adds anything of substance to the 'internal' restrictions in section 1(2) of the First Protocol which specifies that States may limit the right to enjoyment of possessions in the public interest. Thus, whilst balancing of Convention rights could in theory enable a fair(er) balance between IP owners' and public users' rights, in practice the Court's combined approach to the construction of Article 10 and A1P1 has hedged towards reinforcement and consolidation of corporate IPRs.

6.3.3 *International Law*

A final consideration bearing on the balancing of Convention rights is the background European and international legal context on IP and human rights. The ECHR is not an isolated legal island in an international sea. Formally, the legal obligations imposed on each Member State to comply

[106] Application no. 12726/87, *Autronic AG* v. *Switzerland.*

[107] Application no. 40397/12, *Neij and Sunde Kolmisoppi* v. *Sweden.*

with the ECHR derive from the State's accession to the ECHR treaty. The Court has no jurisdiction over Member States' compliance with other treaties, several of which contain extensive, detailed provisions on IP and human rights. This includes the voluminous body of EU directives and regulations on copyright, TMs and (to a lesser extent) patents, in EU treaties, the European Patent Convention (EPC), the Unified Patent Court, the World Trade Organization (WTO) Trade-Related Aspects of Intellectual Property Rights (TRIPS) agreement, World Intellectual Property Organization (WIPO) Treaties, bilateral and multilateral investment treaties and the International Covenant on Civil and Political Rights (ICCPR) and International Covenant on Economic, Social and Cultural Rights (ICESCR). The Court has clearly stated that it has no power of review over the European Patent Convention's (EPC) process for the grant of patents in cases alleging breach of Article 6 ECHR and reminded Member States of their separate obligations under the ECHR. At the same time, the Council of Europe has been mindful that factual situations could arise where Member States' obligations under the EU treaties, in particular, may conflict with their obligations in the ECHR. The accession of the EU to the ECHR was intended to avoid such conflicts but the process stalled after the Court of Justice of the European Union (CJEU) rejected the terms of accession as incompatible with the treaties. Nevertheless, whilst the Strasbourg court has formally developed its own, 'autonomous' interpretation of Convention rights, as shown in Chapter 5, some of the Court's landmark decisions on IPRs are aligned with the legal definitions of IP rights as a species of property right contained in EU law. The Grand Chamber's landmark decision on the scope of application of the A1P1 to IPRs in *Anheuser-Busch* is a notable example.[108]

As discussed (in Chapter 5), the modulation of Convention law by EU IP law is to some extent unavoidable as States are under (separate) obligations to comply with both EU law and Convention law. On the other hand, the Court's construction of Article 10 ECHR through an economic, free market lens appears to go beyond the (tacit) acknowledgement of the legal reality of Member States' potentially conflicting EU and ECHR obligations in the de facto importation of definitions of the nature and scope of IPRs in EU legislation. The Strasbourg court's construction of Article 10 could also be read as an implicit reflection and endorsement of the liberal, free market ideals embedded in the EU treaties whose express raison d'etre since 1957, by contrast to the Convention, has been the creation of a common market with free movement of goods, people, services and capital. The incorporation of

[108] Application no. 73049/01, *Anheuser-Busch* v. *Portugal*.

human rights in the EU treaties was a late addition when the Charter was adopted in 2000 and formally added in the Treaty of Lisbon in 2016. Until then, and to date, the EU treaties formally look to the ECHR as the standard setter on human rights as expressed in Article 51(3) of the Charter:

> In so far as this Charter contains rights which correspond to rights guaranteed by the Convention for the Protection of Human Rights and Fundamental Freedoms, the meaning and scope of those rights shall be the same as those laid down by the said Convention.

The last sentence of Article 51(3) adds that 'This provision shall not prevent Union law providing more extensive protection'. This is an ambiguous statement in light of the mix of economic freedoms, including the freedom to conduct a business (Article 16) with the personal, human freedoms to be found in international human rights texts UDHR, ICCPR and ICESCR, as noted by human rights scholars who are critical of the EU Charter's mix of so-called fundamental rights.[109] In orienting its reading of the ECHR towards the EU legal order, the ECtHR is arguably at risk of losing its own raison d'etre and purpose as a *human* rights court, duplicating the CJEU, without the counterpart textual mandate to the EU Treaties or the legal and institutional resources to navigate the political and social parameters of economic freedoms.

For Emberland, the Court's liberal, free market interpretive lens, whilst at odds with the moral rationale for Convention rights, is nevertheless justified on the grounds that the Court has adopted a teleological, pragmatic, approach centred on protection of the core values of a functional liberal market economy founded on democracy, equality and the rule of law.[110] However, as argued by Isiksel, the Court's generous interpretation of corporate commercial interests as a proxy for broader democratic values can come at the expense of the rights, interests and freedoms of other individuals and groups. Maximizing freedom of commercial expression, and indeed corporate ownership and control of information, 'can burden consumers by allowing monopolistic behavior to go unchecked and deceptive business practices to flourish'.[111] Unlike ordinary citizens, powerful corporations are able to leverage a wealth of resources to secure protection of their financial

[109] Philip Alston, 'Resisting the Merger and Acquisition of Human Rights by Trade Law: A Reply to Petersmann' (2002) 13(4) *European Journal of International Law* 815–844.

[110] Emberland, *The Human Rights of Companies*, pp. 135 ff.

[111] Turkuler Isiksel, 'The Rights of Man and the Rights of the Man-Made: Corporations and Human Rights' (2016) 38(2) *Human Rights Quarterly* 294.

interests and IPRs in national courts, in international courts, in investment tribunals and at WTO. Tobacco companies have aggressively pursued legal challenges in courts and tribunals around the world, seeking to overturn laws restricting the use of tobacco TMs adopted by States to protect their citizens' health, nearly bankrupting one of the defendant States.[112] Pharmaceutical companies own millions of patents worldwide standing in the way of equitable access to medicines.[113] World-leading academic publishers have filed infringement claims against colleges in developing countries which had made photocopies of textbooks available to students.[114] Scientists in developing countries have their research published in international journals which their own institutions cannot afford to subscribe to.[115] There is no shortage of courts and tribunals around the world to hear the complaints of corporations alleging violations of their property and infringement of their IPRs. The ECtHR is uniquely placed to allow the voice of the individual human person to be heard instead. The normative ideal consistent with the Convention is that protection of the interests of the individual natural person, individual human writers, authors, artists, students and the public's interest in access to 'information and ideas' should at the very least act as a counterweight to, if not necessarily prevail over, the economic interests of corporate entities. In developing its case law on the balance between IPRs and human rights, the Court could enrich its decisions by turning its attention to other international human rights treaties, specifically Article 27 UDHR and Article 15 ICESCR. In particular, the Court would do well to reflect on the guidance of the UN Rapporteur on Article 15 ICESCR which unequivocally states that intellectual property rights are not human

[112] Sergio Puig, 'Tobacco Litigation in International Courts' (2016) 57 *Harvard International Law Journal* 383; Alvaro Fernandez-Mora, 'Trade Marks and the Right to Health: A Growing Tension' in Himani Bhakuni and Lucas Miotto (eds.), *Justice in Global Health* (London: Routledge, 2023), pp. 111–130; Jonathan Griffiths, '"On the Back of a Cigarette Packet": Standardised Packaging Legislation and the Tobacco Industry's Fundamental Right to (Intellectual) Property' (2015) *Intellectual Property Quarterly* 343–369.

[113] Laurence R. Helfer, 'Pharmaceutical Patents and the Human Right to Health' in Terence C. Halliday and Gregory Shaffer (eds.), *Transnational Legal Orders* (Cambridge: University Press, 2015), pp. 311–339; Kenneth C. Shadlen, Bhaven N. Sampat and Amy Kapczynski, 'Patents, Trade and Medicines: Past, Present and Future' (2020) 27(1) *Review of International Political Economy* 75–97.

[114] Emmanuel Kolawole Oke, 'The Right-to-Education Responsibilities of Book Publishing Companies' (2018) 14 *Indian Journal of Law and Technology* 212.

[115] M. P. Ram Mohan and Aditya Gupta, 'Right to Research and Copyright Law: From Photocopying to Shadow Libraries' (2021) 11 *NYU Journal of Intellectual Property and Entertainment Law* 185.

rights. IPRs are time-limited legal rights which protect IP owners' financial interests. Whilst legal protection of IPRs may be justified, it also carries the risk of standing in the way of the fundamental human right of every individual human person to access the benefits of science and culture. The conclusion next examines the potential avenues open to the ECtHR to take develop its case law on IPRs in line with international human rights law.

Conclusion

The aim of this study was to investigate the history and rationale for the extension of human rights to companies in the European Convention on Human Rights (ECHR) and to examine the jurisprudence of the European Court of Human Rights (ECtHR) in light of the findings. The enquiry was prompted by the paradox that transnational corporations, which are typically perpetrators of global human rights violations, can file claims as victims of violations of their 'right to enjoyment of possessions' in Article 1 of the First Protocol (A1P1). The manifestations of the paradox have been particularly striking in the field of intellectual property (IP) where pharmaceutical, tobacco and biotech multinational giant corporations have sought to enforce their intellectual property rights (IPRs) through every possible national and international tribunal and court in the world. The defendants in many of these cases have been States that had adopted legislation limiting companies' use of their IPRs, often to protect their citizens' right to health. In one notorious instance, the defendant State had to rely on external financial support to defend the claim.[1] A fortiori, individual persons rarely have the resources, legal or economic, to assert their right to health, science, education or privacy against multinational corporations. Whilst private companies can legally challenge State policies in a myriad of courts and tribunals to protect their economic interests, NGOs seeking to defend human rights often face insuperable legal hurdles to establish standing.[2] Thus, in the last two decades, efforts to rebalance the international legal system to secure better protection of

[1] Eric Crosbie et al., 'Defending Strong Tobacco Packaging and Labelling Regulations in Uruguay: Transnational Tobacco Control Network versus Philip Morris International' (2018) 27 *Tobacco Control* 185–194.

[2] Heidi N. Haddad, *The Hidden Hands of Justice: NGOs, Human Rights, and International Courts* (Cambridge: Cambridge University Press, 2018).

human rights have been targeted at the definition and elaboration of the human rights obligations of corporations.[3] In a separate initiative, the UN Special Rapporteur on Cultural Rights has investigated the tension between the right to science and culture and IP, concluding that the rights of authors and inventors should not be conflated with positive, time-limited IPRs.[4] There is no human right to patent or copyright protection, nor is there a human right to exclusive control and exploitation of one's invention or work for twenty years, the life of the author plus fifty or seventy years after death. The only human right relating to IPRs is 'the right of every person to benefit from the protection of the moral and material interests resulting from anything scientific, literary or artistic production of which s/he is the author' in Article 15 of the International Covenant on Economic, Social and Cultural Rights (ICESCR).

Against this background, the extension of human rights to companies in the ECHR appears not only incongruous but also a potential threat to the enforcement of human rights. Unsurprisingly, there have been few scholarly attempts to develop a convincing normative framework to explain the incongruence. Emberland's *The Human Rights of Companies: Exploring the Structure of ECHR Protection* stands out as the most sustained defence to date of the grant of human rights to companies in the ECHR.[5] For Emberland, the ascription of human rights to companies is not only justified but also necessitated by what he describes as a sui generis European liberal vision of human rights that the Convention allegedly sought to express. It is fair to say that Emberland spends little time articulating a theoretical justification for his claim. Instead, the reader is offered an analysis of decisions from the Court which are aligned with his thesis. The spectrum of cases discussed by Emberland is very broad and his analysis detailed, but it is not specifically targeted at the Court's interpretation of A1P1 or indeed IP. The aim of this study was to fill the gap.

The first step was to elucidate the normative foundations of the ECHR. Chapter 1 argued that these are to be found in Lauterpacht's *International Bill of Rights* for three reasons. Firstly, Lauterpacht's defence of international human rights was published shortly before the adoption of the Universal

[3] Surya Deva and David Birchall (eds.), *Research Handbook on Human Rights and Business* (Cheltenham: Edward Elgar, 2020). Robert McCorquodale, *Business and Human Rights* (Oxford: Oxford University Press, 2024).

[4] United Nations General Assembly (UNGA) Report of the Special Rapporteur in the field of cultural rights, Copyright policy and the right to science and culture (2014) UN Doc A/HRC/28/57; United Nations General Assembly (UNGA) Report on patent policy and the right to science and culture (2015) UN Doc. A/70/279 (hereinafter Patents Report).

[5] Marius Emberland, *The Human Rights of Companies: Exploring the Structure of ECHR Protection* (Oxford: Oxford University Press, 2006).

Declaration of Human Rights (UDHR) in 1948 and the adoption of the ECHR in 1950. Secondly, Lauterpacht's work offers the most sophisticated intellectual defence of international human rights at the time. Finally, the ECHR drafters expressly sought to align the ECHR with the UDHR. The key point that emerges on the substantive, normative foundations of international human rights is that the subject thereof is the individual human person. Individual human personhood is central to the articulation of the normative framework of human rights because the enunciated rights are those required to achieve the full development of the human personality and to enable each individual human person to live a life with dignity. The UDHR set out the full spectrum of the substantive civil, political, social and economic rights whose protection is required to give effect to this moral ideal. By contrast, as shown in Chapter 2, the ECHR was deliberately designed to initially limit the rights protected to civil and political rights, although it was the same universal moral vision that animated the elaboration of the ECHR and the inclusion of property rights which was intended to be in line with Article 17 UDHR. The inclusion of property rights was highly controversial but those in favour argued that home and personal belongings were the natural, even sacred, right of each human person and were necessary to foster the development of the human person and the family. Chapters 3 and 4 show that the moral vision was lost and compromised in the final wording of the text of A1P1 in a disconnect between the ordinary and legal meanings of the terms 'legal person'/'personne morale' and 'possessions'/'biens'. The chapters show that in civil and common law jurisdictions, both terms are legal fictions created to enable ownership and transfer not only of homes and personal belongings but also of all types of tangible and intangible property, including IP. The analysis further highlights that the classification of 'intellectual' property as a fictitious type of intangible 'possession' was based on a conflation of the ill-defined objects of IPRs (the work or invention) with the rights themselves. The assimilation of IPRs with physical things set IP law on a path strewn with ambiguities and conceptual difficulties which continue to manifest themselves today in efforts by legislators and courts to adapt IP law categories to emerging technologies.

The conclusion of the historical and normative parts of the study is that the extension of human rights to companies in A1P1 ECHR was not necessitated by a sui genesis European liberal conception of human rights. Rather, it was the result of a political compromise manifested in a text that obscured the breadth of the legal, proprietary rights protected and the inclusion of private companies as subjects of the rights. Regrettably, the Court's jurisprudence in the following decades did not correct the text's hidden deviation from the moral foundations. Instead, Chapters 5 and 6 show that companies had no difficulty in establishing standing as 'legal persons' and indeed were amongst the first claimants to test the judicial construction of A1P1. On the other hand, the legal breadth of 'possessions' in A1P1 proved initially less clear. At first, doubts were expressed in the Commission and Court decisions as to whether or not 'possessions' included intangible property, but the doubts gave way to majority decisions in the 1980s and 1990s which effectively secured a complete disconnect between the now-forgotten moral foundations of A1P1 with the range of private corporate economic proprietary interests protected. Prophetically, the first IP claim was filed by a transnational pharmaceutical corporation seeking to invalidate a compulsory licence on a medicinal product.[6] The Commission found that the compulsory licence was justified so the claim was unsuccessful but the decision signalled that other IP claims could succeed, and they did. In the landmark decision *Anheuser-Busch* v. *Portugal* (2007),[7] a specially constituted Grand Chamber (GC) held that the trademarks (TMs) protecting a well-known beer brand were 'possessions' whose 'enjoyment' the applicant alleged he had been deprived of by the Portuguese courts in violation of A1P1. The applicant, the US multinational Anheuser-Busch, lost the action on the facts but the effect of the decision was seismic as for the first time the ECtHR unequivocally stated that A1P1 protects *all* types of IPR. The decision goes even further in extending the scope of protection of companies' IPRs to registrations for TMs in circumstances where the validity of the registered mark had not been exhausted in national law, contrary to the ECtHR's prior jurisprudence. In the same decade, the Court had also put an end to the expectations/hopes of IP scholars that the human right to freedom of expression in Article 10 ECHR could act as a counterweight against the ever-expanding reach of corporate IPRs. Instead, the Court adopted an expansive approach to the construction of companies' rights to freedom of expression. So, what does the future hold for the protection of IP and human rights at the ECtHR? The answer much depends on whether and how far the Court is prepared to follow the road not thus far taken. The discussion below canvasses three possible scenarios and identifies further research questions asked by the present study. The aim is not to engage in a detailed discussion of these questions but to highlight some of the issues which would benefit from further investigation. Scenario 1 considers and dismisses the likelihood of the Court reversing its decisions on IPRs.

6 Case No. 12633/87, *Smith Kline and French Laboratories Ltd* v. *the Netherlands*, decision 4 October 1990.

7 Application no. 73049/01, *Anheuser-Busch* v. *Portugal* (Grand Chamber), decision 11 January 2007.

Scenario 2 suggests that the Court may refrain from significant departures from its established case law and outlines some reasons justifying restraint, notably in connection with substantive definitions of the subject matter of IPRs. Scenario 3 outlines how the Court could develop the principles on limitations and exclusions relating to the balance of protection of IPRs in line with international human and in so doing go some way towards recovering the original moral intent of the ECHR.

SCENARIO 1

Formally, the Court is not legally bound to follow its own decisions.[8] Under this scenario, absent a doctrine of binding precedent, the Court could in theory depart from its past decisions on the application of A1P1 to IPRs and declare that, henceforth, 'possessions'/'biens' will no longer include intellectual property rights. This, however, would be a spectacular reversal which is not formally impossible but would require compelling reasons. In *Christine Goodwin* v. *UK* (2002),[9] the GC stated that whilst it is not formally bound to follow its own judgments, 'it is in the interests of legal certainty, foreseeability and equality before the law that it should not depart, without good reason, from precedents laid down in previous cases'. In one such instance, *Z and Others* v. *UK* (2001),[10] the GC declared that its decision on the UK's liability for breach of Article 6 in an important previous judgment was based on a (mis) understanding of UK law which had to be reviewed.[11] There is no such misunderstanding of national or international IP laws in the Court's case law. In another case, the Court cited as a good reason 'the emergence of a new European and international consensus'.[12] There is no emerging European or international consensus to deny legal protection to IPRs: quite the opposite. In this light, a reversal of *Anheuser-Busch* looks implausible and would inevitably add to the uncertainty already attached to the ambiguous text of A1P1, contrary to the Court's stated position on precedent.

8 See David J. Harris et al., *Law of the European Convention on Human Rights*, 5th ed. (Oxford: Oxford University Press, 2023).

9 Case No. 28957/95, *Christine Goodwin* v. *the United Kingdom* (Grand Chamber), decision 7 July 2002.

10 Case No. 29392/95, *Z and Others* v. *the United Kingdom* (Grand Chamber), decision 4 April 2001.

11 Case No. 23452/94, *Osman* v. *the United Kingdom* (Grand Chamber), decision 28 October 1998.

12 Case No. 28957/95, *Christine Goodwin* v. *the United Kingdom*.

SCENARIO 2: CONVENTION RIGHTS THROUGH THE LENS OF EU LAW

In this scenario, the Court would stand by its case law on the application of A1P1 to IPRs whilst refraining from adding substantive changes or extending further the scope of protection of IPRs in the ECHR. There are multiple benefits in the Court adopting a restrained approach. It is, after all, meant to be a *human rights* court. It is not an IP court, nor is it a commercial court or investment tribunal staffed by judges with the requisite knowledge and expertise of IP to develop principles on the substantive subject matter of national and international laws on patents, copyright or TMs. This deficit, of course, is also shared to some extent by senior judges in national supreme courts.[13] But, as an international court, the Court is facing additional constitutional difficulties regarding its competence. The Court's role is defined by a treaty, the ECHR, whose overriding purpose is the protection of fundamental human rights. In this respect, as discussed in Chapter 5, the ECtHR is quite different from the Court of Justice of the European Union (CJEU), the authoritative interpreter of EU treaties. By contrast to the Convention, the objectives of the EU treaties are primarily economic and directed at the creation of a European internal market founded on the free movement of goods. To this purpose, the EU has adopted a dedicated body of directives and regulations to regulate copyright, TMs and, to a lesser extent, patents. Together with Article 17(2) of the EU Charter of Fundamental Rights declaring 'Intellectual Property Shall be Protected', this body of EU law forms the building blocks that the CJEU can draw on to decide IP cases. As noted in Chapter 5, there is no such dedicated body of legislation on IPRs attached to the Convention on which the Court can lean to lend legitimacy to its construction of A1P1 and to provide a degree of certainty on IPRs. It is therefore not altogether surprising that by its own admission the Court has rarely had to decide claims on IPRs. The numbers run in the low hundreds rather than thousands. In the absence of empirical evidence to explain the low number of claims, one may speculate that there is too much legal uncertainty in the ECHR system for commercial actors. This could be because of the unclarity attached to the text of the ECHR, the paucity of IPR decisions on A1P1 and/or the limited expertise of ECtHR judges on IPRs. This too would explain why the Court in *Anheuser-Busch* largely drew on EU law to disambiguate the States' Convention obligations on IPRs under A1P1 ECHR. The GC relied on a definition of TM rights

[13] David Neuberger, 'Intellectual Property in the UK and Europe' (Burrell Lecture for the Competition Law Association, London, 1 April 2014).

in a EU directive and on the defendant State's incorporation of EU law on geographical indications to define the scope of application of the term 'possessions' to the applicants' TMs. The ECtHR thus effectively opted to construe the Convention claim through the lens of EU IP law. In so doing, the Court arguably signalled to corporate IP owners that the Convention cannot be relied upon to avoid or circumvent EU laws definition(s) of IPRs and their scope of protection. An additional reason for the Court to align its decisions on IPRs with EU law is that the EU has not acceded to the ECHR. The practical implication is that EU Member States would be put in an impossible position should the Court reach a decision (say, on the definition of a work, invention or TM) which happened to conflict with EU definitions in directives and regulations. If the Court stands by its own case law on IPRs in future IP challenges against EU Member States, there are no clear benefits for corporate applicants in pursuing appeals at the ECtHR rather than the EU Court. The practical effect of the decision in *Anheuser-Busch* could thus well be to keep the number of corporate IP disputes at the ECtHR to a minimum, as corporate applicants are disincentivized from looking to the ECtHR as the last court of appeal.

This still leaves potential defendant States which are not members of the EU. The most significant in terms of commercial IP activity is the UK. At the time of writing and following the UK's exit from the EU, UK Courts are no longer under an obligation to apply EU IP law. However, for the time being, there are no planned legislative changes to substantive UK IP laws and no significant departures from established decisions incorporating EU law are anticipated in the near foreseeable future.

Other members of the Council of Europe which, like the UK, are not EU members are nevertheless members of the World Trade Organization (WTO) which adopted the TRIPS Agreement. As noted in *Anheuser-Busch*, TRIPS sets minimum standards of IP protection which are legally binding on the WTO contracting States. Thus, States which are members of the Council of Europe but not the EU are still under an obligation in international law to secure protection of IP as provided in the TRIPS Agreement. Under A1P1, the Court's decisions relating to deprivation of property must be 'subject to conditions provided for by law and by the general principles of international law'. Thus, outside EU directives and regulations on IP, TRIPS (and indeed other relevant international agreements on intellectual property)[14] effectively impose substantive limits on the Court's application of A1P1 to IPRs which require the Court to exercise normative restraint.

[14] E.g. the European Patent Convention.

TRIPS

TRIPS incorporated the Paris Convention on Industrial Property (1883) and the Berne Convention for the Protection of Literary and Artistic Works (1886).[15] The former requires, inter alia, a minimum of twenty years' patent protection (Article 33) for inventions in all fields of technology (Article 27(1)). The term 'invention' was left undefined in the Paris Convention and remains undefined in TRIPS. The Court has hitherto refrained from giving further definition to the term 'invention'. It was accepted in 1982 by the now defunct European Commission of Human Rights that patents on pharmaceutical inventions were a type of 'possession' protected under A1P1.[16] At the time many countries, like India, known as the 'pharmacy of the world', excluded pharmaceuticals in national patent laws. A decade later, the TRIPS Agreement put an end to the exclusion whilst States retained flexibility to define the term 'invention'. As seen in Chapter 4, there has been a long-standing controversy over the definition of an invention, specifically in connection with the distinction between (inventive) ideas (not patentable) and the physical embodiment of an idea (patentable) other constitutive elements of an original work. For this reason, it is arguably appropriate for the Court to continue to exercise restraint in this area and refrain from contributing substantive definitions of the subject matter of IPRs as 'possessions'.

Artificial Intelligence (AI)

As noted in Chapter 4, some of the most pressing challenges faced by legislatures and Courts today concern the adaptation of existing IP law requirements to AI.[17] The key questions raised by AI are manifold. One set of questions relates to the subject matter of IPRs. Are the algorithmic outputs of computer programs, the visual images, the texts of ChatGPT, the isolated molecules or genes the type of subject matter protected by patents or copyright, and by implication 'possessions' under A1P1? Do AI-generated outputs fall within existing legal definitions of a work or an invention? Are they intangible ideas (not protected) or an expression, fixation or embodiment of ideas (protected)? Do the algorithmic codes and the data used to 'train' AI systems satisfy the

[15] Except for moral rights.

[16] Case No. 12633/87, *Smith Kline and French Laboratories Ltd* v. *the Netherlands*.

[17] See, for instance, Johanna Gibson, 'People or Patents, Inventors or Owners: Why the Supreme Court Decision on Artificial Intelligence and Invention in Thaler Is Significant for All Intellectual Property' (2024) 14(1) *Queen Mary Journal of Intellectual Property* 1–6.

requirements of originality or novelty/inventive step? Do songs generated by AI in the style of a well-known artist infringe the artist's copyright? Are AI programs or computer programs the (real) authors or inventors of the outputs? These questions are new to the extent that they relate to the fit of a novel technology within the existing legal definitions and criteria for IP protection. Yet whilst the questions may seem novel, the roots of today's puzzles can be traced back to a long-standing conflation of intangibles/ideas (not protected by IP) with their physical expression or embodiment (protected by copyright and patents). As argued in Chapter 4, the problems of identifying the subject matter and boundaries of IPRs are conceptual and obscured by the assimilation of the inventions/works with physical, tangible things. Given the limited expertise of the Court and the human rights orientation of the ECHR, it is not clear how the Court could be justified in adding substance or definition to AI generative outputs as 'possessions'.

On the other hand, current questions about the social and economic impact of AI on human actors, performers, writers and singers are of a different nature altogether but pressing and extremely serious. As argued by Bracha (2023),[18] these questions are not about the subject matter or substantive requirements for IPRs; they are about the attribution, just remuneration and livelihood of human beings in creative fields. On these questions, the Court could arguably contribute to the delineation of the balance between protection of IP owners' rights case law and users by developing its case law along a new path more closely aligned with the moral, human rights ideals of the Convention.

SCENARIO 3: ARTICLE 15 ICESCR AND EXCLUSION, EXCEPTIONS AND LIMITATIONS

Under this scenario, the Court would build on its existing body of case law to develop the principles relating to the application of A1P1 to IPRs in line with the moral aspirations of the European Convention to facilitate the realization of the human rights ideals originally enunciated in the UDHR. The legal basis for the Court taking the case law forward in a new direction on IPRs may be found in the text of A1P1 and its own case law on 'fair balance' as discussed in Chapter 6. The second sentence of the first paragraph of A1P1 permits deprivations of property 'in the public interest' 'subject to the conditions provided by for by law and by the general principles of international law'.

[18] Oren Bracha, 'The Work of Copyright in the Age of Machine Production' (24 September 2023), Legal Studies Research Paper, University of Texas Law (2023).

The second paragraph of A1P1 states that the use of property may be limited or controlled if necessary 'in accordance with the general interest'.

The international law sources relevant to the interpretation of these provisions include not only the exclusions, limitations and flexibilities in the TRIPS Agreement, but also Article 27 UDHR which is the predecessor of the legally binding Article 15 ICESCR. In particular, Article 15(1) states that the States Parties to the present Covenant recognize the right of everyone:

(a) To take part in cultural life;
(b) To enjoy the benefits of scientific progress and its applications;
(c) To benefit from the protection of the moral and material interests resulting from any scientific, literary or artistic production of which he is the author.

As of February 2024, the ICESCR has 174 signatories, making it a persuasive source of considerable weight, not least in European countries like France with a monist system, to assist in delineating the scope of IP protection under A1P1. Arguably, Article 15(1) could be an important point of reference in guiding the Court's interpretation of the scope of exclusions and limitations to rights of exclusivity in patents and copyright. The Court could draw on Article 15 ICESCR, together with the normative guidance elaborated by the UN Special Rapporteur in the field of cultural rights, to align its application of A1P1 to IPRs with the international human rights legal order's understanding of the rights of authors, inventors and the public.[19] In particular, the UN Rapporteur has emphasized the importance of exclusions, exceptions and flexibilities being fully used in the implementation of multilateral IP treaties because they are essential to secure an appropriate balance between private and public interests to ensure respect for a wide range of human rights.

There is a growing body of scholarship on the relevance of Article 15 ICESCR to protection of IPRs,[20] but hitherto no systematic analysis of how Article 15 could specifically guide the scope of protection, exclusions and limitations to IPRs in the ECHR system. It is beyond the scope of this study to

[19] United Nations General Assembly (UNGA) Report of the Special Rapporteur in the field of cultural rights, Copyright policy and the right to science and culture (2014) UN Doc A/HRC/28/57; United Nations General Assembly (UNGA) Report on patent policy and the right to science and culture (2015) UN Doc. A/70/279 (hereinafter Patents Report).

[20] Rochelle Cooper Dreyfuss, 'Human Rights in a Technological Age: The Right to Participate in Science' (2023) 55 *New York University Journal of International Law and Politics*, NYU School of Law, Public Law Research Paper No. 23-35, NYU Law and Economics Research Paper No. 23-31; Helle Porsdam (eds), *The Right to Science: Then and Now* (Cambridge: Cambridge University Press, 2022); Aurora Plomer, *Patents, Human Rights and Access to Science* (Cheltenham: Edward Elgar, 2015).

conduct such an analysis but the lines of enquiry could, for instance, involve a deeper understanding of what protection of the moral and material interests of authors may entail if A1P1 were to be interpreted in line with the UN's Rapporteur normative guidance on Article 15 ICESCR. As detailed in Chapter 5, the Court has left open the possibility that authors, as distinct from IP collecting agencies, could file claims for violation of their moral rights.[21] IP scholars have suggested that the claims could fall under the remit of the right to privacy in Article 8 ECHR.[22] The Court has also recently reviewed the national courts' interpretation of an exclusion clause on publication of a book without the author's consent in Azerbaijan's copyright laws and found a violation of the author's A1P1 rights.[23] In *Balan* v. *Moldova*, the Court awarded pecuniary and non-pecuniary damages for Moldova's use of a photograph taken by the applicant, holding that the national courts had failed to strike a fair balance between the applicant and the community in their interpretation of exclusions in the national copyright laws.[24] In short, the principles established by the Court could potentially be further developed in line with Article 15 ICESCR as the battles between corporate digital giants and users intensify. However, whilst transnational global corporations have legal standing to file claims which allege violation of the human right to property at the ECtHR, it is essential for NGOs and public interest groups to be granted standing to file or defend IPR-related claims at the ECtHR. The individual 'natural' person, human author or inventor rarely has the resources to challenge a company at the ECtHR, and, in reality, the interests and rights impacted may affect a wide class of users.

A more radical move would involve the Court calling into question the compatibility of the terms of protection for copyright consisting of a minimum of the life of the author plus fifty years under the Berne Convention and TRIPS. Since the adoption of the first international IP treaties in the nineteenth century, the tendency has been towards a never-ending expansion of

[21] Application no. 48679/99, *Aepi S.A.* v. *Greece*, decision 11 April 2002. See also Application no. 19247/03, *Balan* v. *Moldova*, decision 29 January 2008.

[22] Josef Drexl, 'Constitutional Protection of Authors' Moral Rights in the European Union – Between Privacy, Property and the Regulation of the Economy' in K. S. Ziegler (ed.), *Human Rights and Private Law: Privacy as Autonomy* (Oxford: Hart, 2007), pp. 173–174. See also Christophe Geiger and Elena Izyumenko, 'Shaping Intellectual Property Rights through Human Rights Adjudication: The Example of the European Court of Human Rights' (2020) 46(3) *Mitchell Hamline Law Review* 11 citing the Court's decision on photographs and trademarks in Application no. 66801/01, *Vorsina and Vogralik* v. *Russia*, decision 5 February 2004.

[23] Application no. 885/12, *Safarov* v. *Azerbaijan*, decision 1 September 2022.

[24] Application no. 19247/03, *Balan* v. *Moldova*.

the scope and terms of IP protection whilst limiting the range of exceptions, limitations and defences. In the field of copyright, the term of protection in EU law now stands at the life of the author plus seventy years. From a human rights perspective, it is simply indefensible for the estate of an author, often a global publishing empire, to monetize the work at the expense of the public, pupils, students, researchers and everyone whose work involves 'building on the shoulders of giants'. As a human rights court armed with the UN's reports on Article 15 ICESCR, the ECtHR could boldly face up to the World Intellectual Property Organization (WIPO), WTO and the EU in declaring that the existing terms of protection for copyright in international treaties are inconsistent with human rights. Of course, the Court does not have the power to alter the Berne Convention. But in an appropriate factual situation, the Court could signal the need to recall the international human rights obligations of States and the need for international IP standards to lend greater weight to human rights.

Overall, the story emerging from this research is that the high moral ideals and promises which gave birth to the Convention have not been fulfilled and have been compromised in translation by the Court. The Court's room of manoeuvre to recover these universal, moral ideals is severely limited by its own jurisprudence and the extensive legal protection enjoyed by IP owners in national and international laws. But the Court is also in a unique position to light a beacon on IPRs by developing its case law in alignment with the international human rights obligations of States.

Bibliography

Allen, Tom, *Property and the Human Rights Act 1998* (Oxford: Hart, 2005).

Alston, Philip, 'Resisting the Merger and Acquisition of Human Rights by Trade Law: A Reply to Petersmann' (2002) 13(4) *European Journal of International Law* 815–844.

Angelopoulos, Christina, 'European Copyright and Human Rights in the Digital Sphere' in M. Susi (ed.), *Human Rights, Digital Society and the Law: A Research Companion* (London: Routledge, 2019).

Barendt, Eric, *Freedom of Speech* (Oxford: Oxford University Press, 2nd ed., 2009).

Barron, Anne, 'Kant, Copyright and Communicative Freedom' (2012) 31(1) *Law and Philosophy* 1–48.

Baty, Thomas, 'The Rights of Ideas: And of Corporations' (1920) 33(3) *Harvard Law Review* 358–375.

Bentham, Jeremy, 'Anarchical Fallacies' in Jeremy Waldron (ed.), *Nonsense upon Stilts: Bentham, Burke and Marx on the Rights of Man* (London: Methuen, 1987).

Bently, Lionel et al., *Privilege and Property: Essays on the History of Copyright* (Cambridge: Open Book Publishers, 2010).

Benvenisti, Eyal, and George W. Downs, *Between Fragmentation and Democracy: The Role of National and International Courts* (Cambridge: Cambridge University Press, 2017).

Blackstone, William, *Commentaries on the Laws of England*, edited by D. Gallanis (Oxford: Oxford University Press, 2016).

Blackstone, William, and Thomas P. Gallanis, *The Oxford Edition of Blackstone's: Book II: Of Private Wrongs* (Oxford: Oxford University Press, 2016).

Borgwardt, Elizabeth, *A New Deal for the World: America's Vision for Human Rights*, 1st Harvard University Press pbk. ed. (Cambridge, MA: Harvard University Press, 2007).

Bouscaren, Anthony Trawick, 'The European Christian Democrats' (1949) 2(1) *Western Political Quarterly* 59–73.

'The MRP in French Governments, 1948–1951' (1952) 14(1) *The Journal of Politics* 104–131.

Bracha, Oren, 'The Commodification of Patents 1600–1836: How Patents Became Rights and Why We Should Care' (2004) 38 *Loyola of Los Angeles Law Review* 177–244.

The History of Intellectual Property Law (Cheltenham: Edward Elgar, 2018).
'The Work of Copyright in the Age of Machine Production' (September 24, 2023) Legal Studies Research Paper, University of Texas Law.

Braudel, Fernand, *The Structures of Everyday Life: The Limits of the Possible. Civilisation and Capitalism. 15th–18th Century, Volume 1* (London: Collins, 1981).

Bridge, Michael et al., *The Law of Personal Property* (London: Sweet & Maxwell, 2021).

Broadhurst, Spencer, 'Is Copyright a Chose in Action?' (1895) 11 *Law Quarterly Review* 64–75.

Broadie, Sarah, and Christopher Rowe (eds.), *Aristotle Nicomachean Ethics: Translation, Introduction, and Commentary* (Oxford: Oxford University Press, 2002).

Buckland, William Warwick, *A Text-Book of Roman Law from Augustus to Justinian* (Cambridge: Cambridge University Press, 2nd ed., 1932).

Cohen Jehoram, Herman, 'Freedom of Expression in Copyright and Media Law' (1983) (6/7) *GRUR International* 385–389.

Coulter, Moureen, *Property in Ideas: The Patent Question in Mid-Victorian Britain* (Philadelphia: Thomas Jefferson University Press, 1991).

Council of Europe, *Collected Edition of the 'Travaux Préparatoires' of the European Convention on Human Rights*, 8 vols. (The Hague: Martinus Nijhoff, 1975).

Crosbie, Eric et al., 'Defending Strong Tobacco Packaging and Labelling Regulations in Uruguay: Transnational Tobacco Control Network versus Philip Morris International' (2018) 27 *Tobacco Control* 185–194.

De Villiers, Jean Etienne Reenen, *The History of the Legislation Concerning Real and Personal Property in England during the Reign of Queen Victoria* (London: C. J. Clay and Sons, 1901).

de Zulueta, Francis, *The Institutes of Gaius: Commentary* (Oxford: Clarendon Press, 1946).

Deva, Surya et al. (eds.), 'Beyond Human Rights Due Diligence: What Else Do We Need?' (2023) 8(2: Special Issue) *Choudhury Business and Human Rights Journal* 180–196.

Deva, Surya, and David Birchall (eds.), *Research Handbook on Human Rights and Business* (Cheltenham: Edward Elgar, 2020).

Dewey, John, 'The Historic Background of Corporate Legal Personality' (1926) 35(6) *The Yale Law Journal* 655–673.

Diderot, Denis, *Lettre sur le commerce de la librairie* (Paris: Librairies Fontaine, 1984).

Dinwoodie, Graeme B., *A Neofederalist Vision of TRIPS: The Resilience of the International Intellectual Property Regime* (Oxford: Oxford University Press, 2012).

Drahos, Peter, *A Philosophy of Intellectual Property* (London: Routledge, 2016).

Drassinower, Abraham, *What's Wrong with Copying?* (Cambridge, MA: Harvard University Press, 2015).

Drexl, Josef, 'Constitutional Protection of Authors' Moral Rights in the European Union: Between Privacy, Property and the Regulation of the Economy' in Katja S. Ziegler (ed.), *Human Rights and Private Law: Privacy as Autonomy* (Oxford: Hart, 2007).

Dreyfuss, Rochelle Cooper, 'Human Rights in a Technological Age: The Right to Participate in Science' (2023) 55 *New York University Journal of International Law and Politics* 581–626, NYU School of Law, Public Law Research Paper No. 23-35, NYU Law and Economics Research Paper No. 23-31.

Duranti, Marco, *The Conservative Human Rights Revolution: European Identity, Transnational Politics, and the Origins of the European Convention* (Oxford: Oxford University Press, 2017).

Dworkin, Ronald, *Taking Rights Seriously* (London: Duckworth, 1977).

Elphinstone, Howard, 'What Is a Chose in Action?' (1893) 9 *Law Quarterly Review* 314.

Emberland, Marius, *The Human Rights of Companies: Exploring the Structure of ECHR Protection* (Oxford: Oxford University Press, 2006).

Fawcett, James E. S., 'Legal Aspects of State Trading' (1948) 25 *British Yearbook of International Law* 34–51.

Feldman, Robin, 'Regulatory Property: The New IP' (2016) 40 *Columbia Journal of Law & the Arts* 53–103.

Fernandez-Mora, Alvaro, 'Trade Marks and the Right to Health: A Growing Tension' in Himani Bhakuni and Lucas Miotto (eds.), *Justice in Global Health* (London: Routledge, 2023).

Freund, Ernst, *The Legal Nature of Corporations* (Chicago: University of Chicago Press, 1897).

Standards of American Legislation (Chicago: University of Chicago Press, 1917).

Friedman, Milton, *Capitalism and Freedom* (Chicago: University of Chicago Press, 1962).

Galvez-Behar, Gabriel, 'The 1883 Paris Convention and the Impossible Unification of Industrial Property' in Graeme Gooday and Steven Wilf (eds.), *Patent Cultures: Diversity and Harmonization in Historical Perspective* (Cambridge: Cambridge University Press, 2020), pp. 38–68.

García, Kristelia A., and Justin McCrary, 'A Reconsideration of Copyright's Term' (2019) 71 *Alabama Law Review* 351.

Geiger, Christophe, 'Fundamental Rights, a Safeguard for the Coherence of Intellectual Property Law?' (2004) 35 *Industrial Internet Consortium* 268–280.

(ed.), *Research Handbook on Intellectual Property and Investment Law* (Cheltenham: Edward Elgar, 2020).

Geiger, Christophe, and Elena Izyumenko, 'From Internal to External Balancing, and Back? Copyright Limitations and Fundamental Rights in the Digital Environment' in Conception Saiz Garcia and Julian Lopez (eds.), *Digitalización, acceso a contenidos y propiedad intelectual* (Madrid: Dykinson, 2022).

'Shaping Intellectual Property Rights through Human Rights Adjudication: The Example of the European Court of Human Rights' (2020) 46(3) *Mitchell Hamline Law Review* 527–612.

Gervais, Daniel J., 'Making Copyright Whole: A Principled Approach to Copyright Exceptions and Limitations' (2008) 5 *University of Ottawa Law and Technology Journal* 1–41.

Ghidini, Gustavo, *Rethinking Intellectual Property: Balancing Conflicts of Interest in the Constitutional Paradigm* (Cheltenham: Edward Elgar, 2018).

Gibson, Johanna, 'People or Patents, Inventors or Owners: Why the Supreme Court Decision on Artificial Intelligence and Invention in Thaler Is Significant for All Intellectual Property' (2024) 14(1) *Queen Mary Journal of Intellectual Property* 1–6.

Gierke, Otto, 'Persons: Fictitious and Real' in George Heiman (ed. and trans.), *Associations and Law: The Classical and Early Christian Stages* (Toronto: University of Toronto Press, 1977).

Gill, Stephen, and A. Claire Cutler (eds.), *New Constitutionalism and World Order* (Cambridge: Cambridge University Press, 2014).

Ginsberg, Jane C., 'A Tale of Two Copyrights: Literary Property in Revolutionary France and America' (1990) 64 *Tulane Law Review* 991–1031.

Goode, Royston Miles, Herbert Kronke and Ewan McKendrick (eds.), *Transnational Commercial Law: Text, Cases and Materials* (Oxford: Oxford University Press, 2nd ed., 2015).

Grear, Anna, 'Challenging Corporate "Humanity": Legal Disembodiment, Embodiment and Human Rights' (2007) 7(3) *Human Rights Law Review* 511–543.

Greer, Steven C., 'The Margin of Appreciation: Interpretation and Discretion under the European Convention on Human Rights', vol. 17 (Council of Europe, 2000), www.lawyersnjurists.com/article/the-margin-of-appreciation-interpretation-and-discretion-under-the-european-convention-on-human-rights-part-3/.

Griffiths, Jonathan, '"On the Back of a Cigarette Packet": Standardised Packaging Legislation and the Tobacco Industry's Fundamental Right to (Intellectual) Property' (2015) 4 *Intellectual Property Quarterly* 343–369.

Griffiths, Jonathan, and Tuomas Mylly (eds.), *Global Intellectual Property Protection and New Constitutionalism: Hedging Exclusive Rights*, 1st ed. (Oxford: Oxford University Press, 2021).

Haddad, Heidi N., *The Hidden Hands of Justice: NGOs, Human Rights, and International Courts* (Cambridge: Cambridge University Press, 2018).

Hager, Mark M., 'Bodies Politic: The Progressive History of Organizational Real Entity Theory' (1988) 50 *University of Pittsburgh Law Review* 575.

Hall, Karl, 'The Struggle over the Social Function of Intellectual Work in the Economy of Nations' in Graeme Gooday and Steven Wilf (eds.), *Patent Cultures: Diversity and Harmonization in Historical Perspective*, vol. 52 (Cambridge: Cambridge University Press, 2020).

Hallis, Frederick, *Corporate Personality, a Study in Jurisprudence* (London: Oxford University Press, 1930).

Hamburger, Philip A., 'Natural Rights, Natural Law, and American Constitutions' (1993) 102 *Yale Law Journal* 907–960.

Harno, Albert J., 'Privileges and Powers of a Corporation and the Doctrine of Ultra Vires' (1925) 35(1) *The Yale Law Journal* 13–28.

Harris, David J. et al., *Law of the European Convention on Human Rights*, 5th ed. (Oxford: Oxford University Press, 2023).

Harris, Ron, 'The Transplantation of the Legal Discourse on Corporate Personality Theories: From German Codification to British Political Pluralism and American Big Business' (2006) 63(4) *Washington and Lee Law Review* 1421–1478.

Hartmann, Stephanie, 'When Two International Regimes Collide: An Analysis of the Tobacco Plain Packaging Disputes and Why Overlapping Jurisdiction of the

WTO and Investment Tribunals Does Not Result in Convergence of Norms' (2017) 21(2) UCLA *Journal of International Law and Foreign Affairs* 204–245.

Helfer, Laurence R., 'The New Innovation Frontier-Intellectual Property and the European Court of Human Rights' (2008) 49 *Harvard International Law Journal* 1.

'Pharmaceutical Patents and the Human Right to Health' in Terence C. Halliday and Gregory Shaffer (eds.), *Transnational Legal Orders* (Cambridge: University Press, 2015).

'Regime Shifting: The TRIPs Agreement and New Dynamics of International Intellectual Property Lawmaking' (2004) 29(1) *Yale Journal of International Law* 1–83.

Hilty, Reto, and Sylvie Nérisson (eds.), *Balancing Copyright – A Survey of National Approaches*, vol. 18 (New York: Springer, 2012).

Hindmarch, William Mathewson, *Observations on the Defects of the Patent Laws of This Country: With Suggestions for the Reform of Them* (London: Wm. Benning, 1851).

Hohfeld, Wesley Newcomb, 'Some Fundamental Legal Conceptions as Applied in Judicial Reasoning' (1913) 23(1) *The Yale Law Journal* 16–59.

Horwitz, Morton J., 'Santa Clara Revisited: The Development of Corporate Theory' (1985) 88 *West Virginia Law Review* 173.

Houlgate, Stephen, *An Introduction to Hegel: Freedom, Truth, and History*, 2nd ed. (Malden, MA: Blackwell, 2005).

Hugenholtz, P. Bernt, 'Copyright and Freedom of Expression in Europe' in Rochelle Cooper Dreyfuss, Diane Leenheer Zimmerman and Harry First (eds.), *Expanding the Boundaries of Intellectual Property: Innovation Policy for the Knowledge Society* (Oxford: Oxford University Press, 2001).

Hulme, E. Wyndham, 'The History of the Patent System under the Prerogative and at Common Law' (1896) 12 *Law Quarterly Review* 141–154.

Hume, David, *A Treatise of Human Nature: Being an Attempt to Introduce the Experimental Method of Reasoning into Moral Subjects* (Cambridge: Cambridge University Press, 2009).

Ireland, Paddy, 'Capitalism without the Capitalist: The Joint Stock Company Share and the Emergence of the Modern Doctrine of Separate Corporate Personality' (1996) 17(1) *Journal of Legal History* 41–73.

'Property and Contract in Contemporary Corporate Theory' (2003) 23(3) *Legal Studies* 453–509.

Isiksel, Turkeler, 'Corporate Human Rights Claims under the ECHR' (2019) 17 *The Georgetown Journal of Law & Public Policy* 979.

'The Rights of Man and the Rights of the Man-Made: Corporations and Human Rights' (2016) 38(2) *Human Rights Quarterly* 294–349.

Isoré, Jacques, 'De l'existence des brevets d'invention en droit français avant 1791' (1937) 16 *Revue historique de droit français et étranger (1922–)* 94–130.

Izyumenko, Elena, 'Ineffective Investigation into Making a Book Available for Illegal Download Breaches Copyright Holder's Right to Property, Rules the European Court of Human Rights' (2023) 18(4) *Journal of Intellectual Property Law & Practice* 269–271.

Johnson, Phillip, *Parliament, Inventions and Patents: A Research Guide and Bibliography* (London: Routledge, 2018).

Privatised Law Reform: A History of Patent Law through Private Legislation, 1620–1907 (London: Routledge, 2017).

Johnston, David (ed.), *The Cambridge Companion to Roman Law* (Cambridge: Cambridge University Press, 2015).

Karski, Karol, and Bartosz Ziemblicki, 'Commercial Companies as Applicants before the European Court of Human Rights' (2021) 23(5) *International Community Law Review* 503–525.

Khoury, Stefanie, and David Whyte, *Corporate Human Rights Violations: Global Prospects for Legal Action* (London: Routledge, 2016).

Kilmuir, David Patrick Maxwell Fyfe, *Political Adventure: The Memoirs of the Earl of Kilmuir* (London: Weidenfeld and Nicolson, 1964).

Kjeldgaard-Pedersen, Astrid, *The International Legal Personality of the Individual* (Oxford: Oxford University Press, 2018).

Klabbers, Jan, 'The Concept of Legal Personality' in Fleur Johns (ed.), *International Legal Personality* (London: Routledge, 2017).

Klitzke, Ramon A., 'Historical Background of the English Patent Law' (1959) 41 *Journal of the Patent Office Society* 615.

Koessler, Maximilian, 'The Person in Imagination or Persona Ficta of the Corporation' (1948) 9 *Louisiana Law Review* 435.

Kohler, Josef, 'Aus der Praxis' (1875) 41 *Annalen der badischen Gerichte* 100–104.

Koskenniemi, Martti, *The Gentle Civilizer of Nations: The Rise and Fall of International Law, 1870–1960* (Cambridge: Cambridge University Press, 2002).

Kyd, Stewart, A *Treatise on the Law of Corporations*, vol. I (London: J. Butterworth, 1793).

Landes, William M., and Richard A. Posner, 'An Economic Analysis of Copyright Law' (1989) 18(2) *The Journal of Legal Studies* 325–363.

'Indefinitely Renewable Copyright' (2003) 70 *The University of Chicago Law Review* 471.

Laski, Harold J., 'The Personality of Associations' (1916) 29 *Harvard Law Review* 404–426.

Lauterpacht, Hersch, 'The Grotian Tradition in International Law' (1946) 23 *British Yearbook of International Law* 1–53.

'The Law of Nations, the Law of Nature and the Rights of Man' (1943) 29 *Transactions of the Grotius Society* 1–33.

'The Subjects of the Law of Nations' (1948) 64(1) *Law Quarterly Review* 97–119.

Lauterpacht, Hersch, and Philippe Sands, *An International Bill of the Rights of Man* (Oxford: Oxford University Press, 2013).

Lipgens, Walter, and Wilfried Loth, *Vol 4 Transnational Organizations of Political Parties and Pressure Groups in the Struggle for European Union, 1945–1950: (Including 129 Documents in their Original Languages on 3 Microfiches)* (Berlin, Boston: De Gruyter, 1991).

Long, Pamela O., 'Invention, Authorship, "Intellectual Property", and the Origin of Patents: Notes toward a Conceptual History' (1991) 32(4) *Technology and Culture* 846–884.

Liu, Joseph P., 'Copyright and Time: A Proposal' (2002) 101(2) *Michigan Law Review* 409–481.
Machlup, Fritz, and Edith Penrose, 'The patent controversy in the nineteenth century'. *The Journal of Economic History* 10.1 (1950): 1–29.
MacLeod, Christine, *Inventing the Industrial Revolution: The English Patent System, 1660–1800* (Cambridge: Cambridge University Press, 2002).
Madsen, Mikael Rask, 'The Challenging Authority of the European Court of Human Rights: from Cold War Legal Diplomacy to the Brighton Declaration and Backlash' (2016) 79 *Law and Contemporary Problems* 141.
Maine, Henry Sumner, *Ancient Law: In Connection with the Early History of Society, and Its Relation to Modern Ideas* (Kitchener, ON: Batoche, 1999).
Maitland, Frederic William, 'Moral Personality and Legal Personality' (1905) 6(2) *Journal of the Society of Comparative Legislation* 192–200.
Marc, Alexandre 'Une lettre et un bref rappel du 'Programme' de l'U.E.F.,' HAEU, European Union of Federalists Papers 91, 5.
Martin, Scott M., 'The Mythology of the Public Domain: Exploring the Myths Behind Attacks on the Duration of Copyright Protection' (2002) 36 *Loyola of Los Angeles Law Review* 253.
Matthews, Duncan, 'Intellectual Property Rights, Human Rights and the Right to Health' in W. Grosheide (ed.), *Edward Elgar Intellectual Property Rights and Human Rights: A Paradox*, Queen Mary School of Law Legal Studies Research Paper No. 24/2009.
May, Christopher, 'The Hypocrisy of Forgetfulness: The Contemporary Significance of Early Innovations in Intellectual Property' (2007) 14(1) *Review of International Political Economy* 1–25.
Mayer, Carl J. 'Personalizing the Impersonal: Corporations and the Bill of Rights' (1989) 41 *Hastings Law Journal* 577.
McCorquodale, Robert, *Business and Human Rights* (Oxford: Oxford University Press, 2024).
McCrudden, Christopher, 'The Impact on Freedom of Speech', in Basil Markesinis (ed.), in *The Impact of the Human Rights Bill on English Law* (Oxford: Oxford University Press, 1998).
Morsink, Johannes, *Inherent Human Rights: Philosophical Roots of the Universal Declaration* (Philadelphia: University of Pennsylvania Press, 2009).
The Universal Declaration of Human Rights: Origins, Drafting, and Intent (Philadelphia: University of Pennsylvania Press, 1999).
Moser, Petra, 'Innovation without Patents: Evidence from World Fairs' (2012) 55(1) *Journal of Law and Economics* 43–74.
Mowbray, Alastair R., *Cases, Materials, and Commentary on the European Convention on Human Rights*, 3rd ed. (Oxford: Oxford University Press, 2012).
Mowbray, Alastair, *The Development of Positive Obligations under the European Convention on Human Rights by the European Court of Human Rights* (Oxford: Hart, 2004).
Neuberger, David, 'Intellectual Property in the UK and Europe' (Burrell Lecture for the Competition Law Association, London, 1 April 2014).
Nicholas, Barry, and Ernest Metzger, *An Introduction to Roman Law* (Oxford: Oxford University Press, 2008).
Nicol, Danny, *The Constitutional Protection of Capitalism* (London: Bloomsbury, 2010).

Nozick, Robert, *Anarchy, State, and Utopia* (New York: Basic Books, 1974).
Oke, Emmanuel Kolawole, 'The Right-to-Education Responsibilities of Book Publishing Companies' (2018) 14 *Indian Journal of Law and Technology* 212.
Oliver, Peter, 'Companies and Their Fundamental Rights: A Comparative Perspective' (2015) 64(3) *International and Comparative Law Quarterly* 662.
Penner, James E., *The Idea of Property in Law* (Oxford: Oxford University Press, 2003).
Peukert, Alexander, *A Critique of the Ontology of Intellectual Property Law* (Cambridge: Cambridge University Press, 2021).
Plant, Raymond, *Equality, Markets, and the State* (London: Fabian Society, 1984).
Plomer, Aurora, *Patents, Human Rights and Access to Science* (Cheltenham: Edward Elgar, 2015).
'Trading Intellectual Property Rights in Europe: From IP Nationalism to International IP', *LSE Legal Studies Working Paper No. 12/2022* (June 16, 2022).
Pollock, Frederick, and Frederic William Maitland. *The History of English Law before the Time of Edward I*, vol. II (London: Cambridge University Press, 1898).
The History of English Law before the Time of Edward I, reprint 2nd ed. (Indianapolis: Liberty Fund, 2010).
Porsdam, Helle (eds.), *The Right to Science: Then and Now* (Cambridge: Cambridge University Press, 2022).
Pound, Roscoe, *Jurisprudence* (St. Paul, MN: West Publishing, 1959).
Pretto-Sakmann, Arianna, *Boundaries of Personal Property Law: Shares and Sub-Shares* (Oxford: Hart, 2005).
Puig, Sergio, 'Tobacco Litigation in International Courts' (2016) 57 *Harvard International Law Journal* 383.
Ram Mohan, M. P., and Aditya Gupta, 'Right to Research and Copyright Law: From Photocopying to Shadow Libraries' (2021) 11 *NYU Journal of Intellectual Property & Entertainment Law* 185.
Rawls, John, *A Theory of Justice*, rev. ed. (Oxford: Oxford University Press, 1999).
Reichman, Jerome H., 'The Duration of Copyright and the Limits of Cultural Policy' (1996) 14 *Cardozo Arts and Entertainment Law Journal* 625.
Renner, Karl, *The Institutions of Private Law and Their Social Functions* (London: Routledge & Kegan Paul, 1949).
Rognstad, Ole-Andreas, *Property Aspects of Intellectual Property. Cambridge Intellectual Property and Information Law* (Cambridge: Cambridge University Press, 2018).
Rolin, Henri, 'Controle International des Juridictions Nationales' (1967) 3(1) *Le Revue Belge de Droit International (Belgian Review of International Law)* 1–23.
Ruggie, John G., 'Business and Human Rights: The Evolving International Agenda' (2007) 101(4) *American Journal of International Law* 819–840.
Just Business: Multinational Corporations and Human Rights (London: WW Norton & Company, 2013).
Ruggie, John G., et al., 'Ten Years After: From UN Guiding Principles to Multi-fiduciary Obligations' (2021) 6(2) *Business and Human Rights Journal* 179–197.
Ryan, Alan, *Property and Political Theory* (New York: Blackwell, 1986).
Sands, Philippe, *East West Street: On the Origins of Genocide and Crimes against Humanity* (London: Weidenfeld & Nicolson, 2016).

Schabas, William A., 'The Omission of the Right to Property in the International Covenants' (1991) 4 *Hague Yearbook of International Law* 135–170.

Sell, Susan K., *Private Power, Public Law: The Globalization of Intellectual Property Rights* (Cambridge: Cambridge University Press, 2003).

Sell, Susan K., and Christopher May, 'Moments in Law: Contestation and Settlement in the History of Intellectual Property' (2001) 8(3) *Review of International Political Economy* 467–500.

Sen, Amartya, *Development as Freedom* (Oxford: Oxford University Press, 2001).

Shadlen, Kenneth C., Bhaven N. Sampat and Amy Kapczynski, 'Patents, Trade and Medicines: Past, Present and Future' (2020) 27(1) *Review of International Political Economy* 75–97.

Shelton, Dinah, *Remedies in International Human Rights Law*, 3rd ed. (Oxford: Oxford University Press, 2015).

Simonds, William, E., 'Natural Right of Property in Intellectual Production' (1891) 1(1) *The Yale Law Journal* 19.

Simpson, A. W. Brian, *Human Rights and the End of Empire: Britain and the Genesis of the European Convention* (Oxford: Oxford University Press, 2004).

Slobodian, Quinn, *Globalists: The End of Empire and the Birth of Neoliberalism* (Cambridge, MA: Harvard University Press, 2018).

Smit, Lise et al., *Study on Due Diligence Requirements through the Supply Chain* (Luxembourg: Publications Office of the European Union, 2020).

Spielmann, Dean, 'Companies in the Strasbourg Courtroom' (2016) 5(3) *Cambridge International Law Journal* 405.

'La contribution des juges belges au rayonnement de la Convention europeenne des droits de l'hommes' (2015) 101 *Revue trimestrielle des droits de l'homme* 25–38.

'Whither the Margin of Appreciation?' (2014) 67 *Current Legal Problems* 49.

Stein, Peter, *Roman Law in European History* (Cambridge: Cambridge University Press, 1999).

Steininger, Silvia. 'What's Human Rights Got to Do with It? An Empirical Analysis of Human Rights References in Investment Arbitration' (2018) 31(1) *Leiden Journal of International Law* 33–58.

Steininger, Silvia, and Jochen Von Bernstorff. 'Who Turned Multinational Corporations into Bearers of Human Rights? On the Creation of Corporate 'Human' Rights in International Law', *On the Creation of Corporate 'Human' Rights in International Law (September 25, 2018). Max Planck Institute for Comparative Public Law & International Law (MPIL) Research Paper* 2018-25 (2018).

Strowel, Alain, and François Tulkens, Freedom of Expression and Copyright under Civil Law: Of Balance, Adaptation, and Access' (2005) *Copyright and Free Speech, Comparative and International Analyses* 287–313.

Sweet, C., 'Choses in Action' (1895) 11 *Law Quarterly Review* 238.

Talbot, Lorraine, *Critical Company Law* (London: Routledge, 2015).

Teitgen, Pierre-Henri, *Faites entrer le témoin suivant: 1940–1958: de la Résistance à la Ve République* (Rennes: Ouest France, 1988).

Thayer, Albert S., 'Possession' (1905) 18(3) *Harvard Law Review* 196–213.

Tulkens, Françoise, 'A Propos de le Controle International des Juridictions Nationales de Henri Rolin' (2015) 48 *Revue Belge de Droit International (Belgian Review of International Law)* 465–471.

'Twenty-Eighth Conference of the Inter-Parliamentary Union at Geneva, July 20–26, 1932: Resolutions Adopted' (1932) 95(2) *World Affairs* 124–128. www.jstor.org/stable/20662142.

United Nations General Assembly (UNGA), Report of the Special Rapporteur in the Field of Cultural Rights, Copyright Policy and the Right to Science and Culture (2014) UN Doc A/HRC/28/57.

United Nations General Assembly (UNGA), Report on Patent Policy and the Right to Science and Culture (2015) UN Doc A/70/279.

VerSteeg, Russ 'The Roman Law Roots of Copyright' (2000) 59 *Maryland Law Review* 522.

Vojáček, Jan, A *Survey of the Principal National Patent Systems* (New York: Prentice-Hall, 1936).

von Hayek, Friedrich A., *The Road to Serfdom* (London: Routledge, 2001).

Voorhoof, Dirk, *Critical Perspectives on the Scope and Interpretation of Article 10 of the European Convention on Human Right* (Mass media files, No. 10) (Strasbourg: Council of Europe Press 1995).

Waldron, Jeremy, *The Right to Private Property* (Oxford: Clarendon Press, 1988).

Walterscheid, Edward C., 'Defining the Patent and Copyright Term: Term Limits and the Intellectual Property Clause' (2000) 7 *Journal of Intellectual Property Law & Practice* 315.

White, E. Wyndham, 'Report by the Committee of the International Chamber of Commerce on the Legal Treatment of Foreign Companies' (1939) 3(1) *The Modern Law Review* 54–58.

Williams, Joshua, *Principles of the Law of Personal Property: Intended for the Use of Students in Conveyancing*, 4th ed. (London: H. Sweet, 1860).

Rights of Common and Other Prescriptive Rights: Being Twenty-four Lectures Delivered in Gray's Inn Hall in the Year 1877 (London: H. Sweet, 1880).

Williams, T. Cyprian, 'Property Things in Action and Copyright' (1895) 11 *Law Quarterly Review* 223–237.

Woodward, Susan E., 'Limited Liability in the Theory of the Firm' (1985) 141(4) *Zeitschrift Für Die Gesamte Staatswissenschaft (Journal of Institutional and Theoretical Economics)* 601–611.

Wright, Quincy, 'International Law and Commercial Relations' (1941), *Proceedings of the American Society of International Law* 30–40.

Yu, Peter K., 'The Investment-Related Aspects of Intellectual Property Rights' (2016) 66 *American University Law Review* 829.

Index

For EU product safety concerns, contact us at Calle de José Abascal, 56–1°,
28003 Madrid, Spain or eugpsr@cambridge.org.

www.ingramcontent.com/pod-product-compliance
Lightning Source LLC
LaVergne TN
LVHW011814200926
848484LV00005B/1191
9781108841771